THE ORGANIZATION OF
RESEARCH ESTABLISHMENTS

THE
ORGANIZATION OF
RESEARCH
ESTABLISHMENTS

EDITED BY

SIR JOHN COCKCROFT

Master of Churchill College, Cambridge

CAMBRIDGE
AT THE UNIVERSITY PRESS
1965

PUBLISHED BY
THE SYNDICS OF THE CAMBRIDGE UNIVERSITY PRESS

Bentley House, 200 Euston Road, London, N.W. 1
American Branch: 32 East 57th Street, New York, N.Y. 10022
West African Office: P.O. Box 33, Ibadan, Nigeria

©

CAMBRIDGE UNIVERSITY PRESS

1965

Printed in Great Britain by
THE STELLAR PRESS LTD.
UNION STREET, BARNET, HERTS.
Library of Congress Catalogue
Card Number: 65-14353

CONTENTS

1

INTRODUCTION

by S I R J O H N C O C K C R O F T, O.M., K.C.B., Sc.D., F.R.S.

Basic and applied research are today amongst the most creative elements in our civilization. Basic research in the biological and physical sciences continues to produce exciting and important results adding to the store of knowledge on which applied research draws. Investment in applied research by industry is one of the principal factors in economic growth, as can be seen by the development of new industries based on solid state physics, nuclear physics, electronics, the chemistry of polymers, pharmaceuticals, insecticides, selective weed killers. This kind of applied research has to be justified by the new products it creates.

We are today spending very large sums on basic and applied research. In Britain we spend about £65 million a year on basic research and £320 million on applied research and development, and £245 million on defence research. The United States expenditure is an order of magnitude more—about 15 billion dollars a year for all purposes, of which only about 25 per cent. is spent by industry for civilian purposes. Expenditure in France and Germany is at present about half that in Britain but growing fast.

It is therefore important from time to time to determine the factors which make for creativity in research establishments, since creativity in the scientists of an establishment determines whether or not the large sums invested in research will produce important new results in basic research and yield adequate returns in the form of increased productivity and new products from applied research.

Organization of Research Establishments

I was fortunate in being a member of the Cavendish Laboratory during one of its most creative periods—from 1924 to 1939. This creativity was due to a number of important factors. First of all, because we had a great Director in Rutherford, a Director who was passionately devoted to getting new results in nuclear physics, with little interest in sidelines. He encouraged his young people to put forward ideas for new lines of research, selected those which were most promising and thereafter left them to get on with the work uninterrupted, apart from his occasional tours to survey progress and to apply a little or a lot of stimulus when required. This kind of treatment was good for morale.

Rutherford devoted great care to the selection of research students and his staff. The only point which counted in selecting staff was their promise for research, though when they were appointed they were required to do their share of teaching or laboratory administration.

A third important factor in the work of the laboratory was the general intellectual environment. Our lives were enriched by the presence of great seniors—Aston, Eddington, R. H. Fowler, J. J. Thomson, C. T. R. Wilson; and by the frequent visits of the great physicists of the day—Bohr, Einstein, Heisenberg, Millikan, Schrodinger and others—to discuss their latest work whilst it was still fresh and exciting. We were also fortunate in the lively group of our contemporaries from many countries attracted by Rutherford.

These circumstances enabled us to discuss in frequent meetings and colloquia the rapid development of physics; so that we were well informed and able to take rapid advantage of new discoveries elsewhere.

The general organization of the Cavendish Laboratory was very simple. There were no committees, but responsibility for different parts of the laboratory work was delegated; Chadwick being responsible for seeing that research equipment was provided, whilst I was responsible for buildings and services, and others for teaching and finance.

2

Introduction

Rutherford had a system of 'polling the jury', consulting senior staff members individually on important new issues. Decisions were not therefore taken over their heads.

These factors, a good director, clear objectives, good selection of staff, a good intellectual environment and an efficient but minimal organization, are important in the work of present day research laboratories. The problems of applied research organizations are, however, more complex because of their larger size and because of the need, in industrial organizations, to choose lines of work which are likely to be profitable for their companies. They have, therefore, to be so organized that the new developments in basic science are quickly appreciated, and the most promising of those which could be applied with profit to the objectives of the company are followed up. It is necessary also that this second stage of research should, when fruitful, be carried through to a stage when a large part of the practical problems, often unforeseen in the first place, will have been encountered and solved. After this comes the development stage when prototypes are built and the necessary technological development carried out.

One of the main problems of organization of the Harwell Atomic Energy Research Establishment, of which I was Director, was to focus the work of the scientists from several different disciplines on to the major projects with which the establishment or its sister establishments were concerned. The main tool for this was the design committee or building committee or research committee, held at regular intervals, monthly or two monthly. Some of these committees were large, but all the members represented groups working on the project, and they were able to have their say, though the final decision had inevitably to be taken by the chairman, who carried the final responsibility for the project.

In addition to seeing to the functioning of the project organization, the director has an important role to play in large establishments by promoting the cross fertilization

3

between divisions and preventing the growth of human potential barriers between divisions. He must also see that the establishment has a first class information system which can produce information on relevant papers and activities in other organizations within hours or at most days.

He must also ensure that human relations in his research establishment are good. Young scientists are likely to provide most of the creative ideas in the establishment during their early years, and their ideas should flow upwards and be quickly considered. On the material side they should be provided with the facilities which enable good ideas to bear fruit. The procedures for selection and promotion of staff should be recognized to be fair and should be operated by the staff themselves. It is equally important that the other varieties of staff who contribute to the work of the establishment, whether they are technicians, clerical staff, draughtsmen, craftsmen, process workers or unskilled workers should be recognized as making an essential contribution to the work.

Good relations between scientists and administrators are important in making a healthy research establishment. The administrator's task is to facilitate the work of the scientist by providing the services he requires and by applying the essential minimal financial control. Every establishment has, of course, to produce an annual budget and to work within it when approved. The director has the annual job of trimming the estimates of his senior staff to a total which is likely to be approved by his management board. After this annual examination it is important that as much as possible of the responsibility for expenditure within their budgets should be delegated to divisions or groups and that they should be assisted by administrative staff to keep within their budgets.

There is a not inconsiderable danger that as establishments grow they may be over-administered. A great deal of valuable time of scientists can be wasted, for example, by detailed costing of basic research projects when the information is not, in fact, used.

All of these are necessary conditions for a creative and healthy research establishment, though they are not perhaps sufficient conditions. The most important problem of a director is to decide, amongst many competing ideas coming from below, which projects to work on, to decide on the scale of support and to decide when to drop unfruitful lines. The last decision is the hardest of all, for those working on projects usually believe in them and are nearly always loath to see them dropped.

Within the last few years new types of research establishments have appeared. International research establishments founded corporatively by a group of countries have appeared: C.E.R.N., the E.N.E.A. Dragon Reactor project at Winfrith, the E.N.E.A. Heavy Water Reactor project in Norway, the Eurochemie Laboratory at Mol, the Dubna Nuclear Physics Laboratory in the U.S.S.R. are examples.

We have also seen the foundation of laboratories which serve a group of universities—such as the Brookhaven National Laboratory and the National Institute for Nuclear Research at Harwell. These laboratories have their own characteristics and problems which are discussed in later chapters.

The objective of this book is to discuss the factors which make for creativity and productivity in a wide variety of research establishments. We hope that the varying experiences and ideas put forward will be of value to all those who have the responsibility for research.

2

THE NATIONAL PHYSICAL LABORATORY

by Sir Gordon Sutherland, Sc.D., Ll.D., F.R.S.

INTRODUCTION

The decision to create a National Physical Laboratory was taken in 1896 as a result of considerable agitation by the British Association for the Advancement of Science and the Royal Society, that Britain should have a national laboratory comparable to the Physikalisch-Technische Reichsanstalt, which had been established in Germany (under the direction of Helmholtz) in 1887. The Royal Society was 'invited to control the proposed institution and to nominate a governing body on which commercial interests should be represented'. This governing body held its first meeting in 1899 and Sir Richard Glazebrook took office as the first director on 1 January 1900.

The laboratory was initially defined as 'a public institution for standardizing and verifying instruments, for testing materials and for the determination of physical constants'. These rather bleak terms of reference should be contrasted with the conception of a National Physical Laboratory put forward by Sir Oliver Lodge, who played a leading part in its creation. In an address to the British Association in 1891 Lodge had said:

But what I want to see is a much larger establishment (than the Board of Trade Laboratory) erected in the most suitable site, limited by no speciality of aim, nor by the demands of the commercial world, furnished with all the appropriate appliances, to

6

be amended and added to as time goes on and experience grows, invested with all the dignity and permanence of a national institution, a physical laboratory aiming at the highest quantitative work in all branches of physical science.

Under the guidance of the Royal Society, the National Physical Laboratory developed along the broad lines indicated by Lodge, while in no way neglecting its original function as a standards and testing laboratory. Starting with two divisions devoted to physics and engineering, by 1910 it had branched into metallurgy, aerodynamics and ship hydrodynamics. By 1950, new divisions had also been created in radio, electronics and mathematics. While the corresponding laboratories in Germany, Russia (Mendeléef Institute) and the United States (Bureau of Standards) remained essentially devoted to work on standards and accurate measurement, the National Physical Laboratory undertook basic and applied research on a wide variety of problems in physics and engineering. It thus fulfilled a double function by not only maintaining standards and improving methods of measurement of all physical quantities but also by pioneering and assisting in the application of physics to industrial problems.

When the Department of Scientific and Industrial Research* was created in 1917, the National Physical Laboratory became one of the research stations of that organization. In due course, some of the divisions of the National Physical Laboratory were hived off to become separate research stations of DSIR. For instance, in 1952 the Radio Division became the Radio Research Station and the Engineering Division became the National Engineering Laboratory. Much of the initial work of some of the other fifteen research stations of DSIR was started at NPL, for example the Hydraulics Research Station, the Road Research Laboratory and the Building Research Station. Thus the National Physical Laboratory has a long tradition

* Referred to in future as DSIR.

7

of pioneering research in various fields but when further development would be more advantageously undertaken by the creation of an independent institution (or by industry), that line of work is dropped, freeing space, effort and facilities for the encouragement of some completely new line of research.

At the present time, the work of the National Physical Laboratory is organized in ten divisions:

Standards
Applied Physics
Light
Basic Physics
Mathematics
Autonomics
Metallurgy
Aerodynamics
Ship Hydrodynamics
Administration and Central Services.

One might have expected the divisional structure of the laboratory to have reflected the various branches into which pure and applied physics are conventionally subdivided. The reason that this is not so, is that the divisional structure is based on the functions of the laboratory. This explains why Standards Division comes first as our primary responsibility and is followed by the Applied Physics and Light Divisions, each of which have certain responsibilities for work on standards. None of the other divisions devotes any effort to standards. Basic Physics and Mathematics Divisions have been put next in the list because most of the work in these two divisions is of a rather basic nature but with potential applications in many industries. The remaining four scientific divisions have a much closer relationship with specific sections of industry.

The total staff of the laboratory is now close to 1,350, of

8

whom about 230 are Scientific Officers (200), or Research Fellows (30), who either have a Ph.D. degree or (especially in the case of the older men) could have acquired it if circumstances had permitted. These are backed by over 300 Experimental Officers and some 200 Scientific Assistants. The former have had a sound training in science and the senior members are capable of taking charge of important projects in applied or experimental work. The divisions are not all of equal size, the largest being Applied Physics, Aerodynamics and Standards while the smallest are Light and Mathematics. Naturally the total staff of a division depends partly on the experimental facilities which must be manned and partly on its role in the national pattern of research. It turns out, however, that the smallest division (Mathematics) has in fact more Scientific Officers than the largest division (Applied Physics). The largest number of Research Fellows (ten) are in the Basic Physics Division.

It will be helpful at this stage to give in outline the main lines of work in each of the nine scientific divisions. Administration and central services will be discussed in the section on Internal Administration.

Standards

Every major industrial country must have a national standards laboratory. Although each industry has to maintain its own standards, it must be provided with expert help and guidance in verifying and continually improving them. The degree of precision required varies from one industry to another and even from one firm to another, depending on the nature of the manufactured article. Clearly it makes economic sense to centralize research on standards of physical measurement, incidentally providing an impartial authority on all ultimate questions in this field. Moreover there has to be international agreement on all primary standards and this can only be achieved between national standards laboratories, each under Government control.

9

Organization of Research Establishments

The instruments used to measure physical quantities by each industry are normally calibrated against secondary standards which in turn can be calibrated against the primary standards of the national standards laboratory. Since the demand for increased precision is continuous, it is necessary for the Standards Division to strive to be ahead of current industrial requirement by a factor of ten. In turn this leads to a search for new ways of defining the primary standards. Whereas length standards until 1960 were referred to the distance between two very fine lines on a bar of platinum iridium kept at Sèvres, they are now referred to the wavelength of a certain line in the spectrum of Krypton gas. This change increased the precision of the measurement of length in terms of the primary standard by a factor of 40. Time and frequency, which used to be referred to the motions of the astronomical bodies, are now in the process of being referred to a certain frequency associated with an energy change in the caesium atom—the so-called atomic clock.

This trend for the old primary standards based on the concepts of classical nineteenth-century physics to be replaced by new primary standards based on the more sophisticated concepts of modern atomic and nuclear physics will continue.

Applied Physics

The name of this division is rather misleading since it only covers a few branches of physics, mainly acoustics, radiological standards, electrotechnics and the testing of a variety of instruments. This odd mixture is a historical accident. As the laboratory grew, the original Physics Division became so large that new divisions were gradually formed from several of its sections and the Applied Physics Division contains those units which are not large enough to be recognized as separate divisions, together with Test House.

The National Physical Laboratory

Light

The province of this division is the infra-red, visible and ultra-violet regions of the spectrum. It has two responsibilities: (*a*) radiation, photometric and colorimetric standards, and (*b*) the development of new optical techniques and devices.

Basic Physics

This division was created in 1958 with the object of pioneering research in a few chosen fields which are of potential industrial importance. At present the emphasis is on molecular physics, for example, physics of high polymers, nuclear and electron spin resonance, spectroscopy and ultra high pressures.

Mathematics

The Mathematics Division has two main functions. The first is to exploit the use of electronic digital computers in the solution of a wide variety of problems in pure and applied mathematics. The second is to conduct research in certain branches of theoretical physics, usually (but not always) related to the experimental work going on in the other divisions of the laboratory.

Autonomics

Taking its name from the autonomic nervous system (which controls the action of the heart and lungs without reference to the brain) the Autonomics Division aims at relieving man's brain of some of the tedious tasks which are demanded of it in an increasingly technological civilization, for example, the recognition of printed characters, finding by trial and error the optimum conditions under which to operate certain industrial processes, the retrieval of information and the translation of languages.

Metallurgy

The Metallurgy Division was founded in 1906. Equipped

with a full range of physical and chemical techniques for the study of metals, its effort is at present largely concentrated on iron and its alloys together with a limited number of the non-ferrous metals, for example niobium and chromium.

Aerodynamics

Basic research on the aerodynamics of flight at all speeds up to Mach 20 is the main function of the Aerodynamics Division. This work is carried out in close collaboration with the corresponding establishments of the Ministry of Aviation at Farnborough and Bedford. A secondary function of increasing importance is basic and applied research in industrial aerodynamics, for example stability in strong winds of bridges, high towers and buildings.

Ship Hydrodynamics

The traditional function of this division has been to provide the optimum shapes for the hulls and propellers of merchant ships from the standpoint of hydrodynamic efficiency. The correlation of the results obtained from the behaviour of models in tanks and water tunnels with those obtained from the full-scale versions is an extremely complex business, especially since we want to predict behaviour in rough seas of a defined character. Now that unconventional craft such as hovercraft and hydrofoil ships are coming into use, entirely new problems are being encountered.

The foregoing brief summaries of divisional responsibilities give some idea of the immense variety of the work carried out by the National Physical Laboratory. There are about 100 major projects under way at any one time and roughly twice that number of minor ones. The NPL is really a complex of nine laboratories, all interacting with each other to a greater or lesser extent. The scientific policy and programme of the whole institution is determined by bodies representative of science, government and industry.

The National Physical Laboratory

When the NPL was founded, the Royal Society was solely responsible for its management and finance. An annual allocation was made by the Treasury to the Society, which controlled the laboratory through a General Board and an Executive Committee. After the NPL was incorporated into DSIR in 1917, all responsibility for financial matters was transferred to DSIR but the Royal Society retained responsibility for the scientific programme of work and for the appointment, promotion and dismissal of the scientific staff of the laboratory, subject to the approval of the Committee of the Privy Council for Scientific and Industrial Research. When DSIR was reorganized in 1956, the Council for Scientific and Industrial Research, a body appointed by the Minister for Science, replaced the Committee of the Privy Council in the relationship between the Royal Society and the government on the management of the National Physical Laboratory.

The General Board of the National Physical Laboratory is a very large body chosen to be representative of British science and industry. The President of the Royal Society is the Chairman of the Board and certain of the officers of the Royal Society are *ex-officio* members. There are 48 ordinary members, of whom eighteen are nominated by the following institutions, each institution being represented by two members: British Standards Institution; Institute of Metals; Institution of Civil Engineers; Institution of Electrical Engineers; Institution of Mechanical Engineers; Royal Institution of Naval Architects; Iron and Steel Institute; Royal Aeronautical Society; Society of Chemical Industry. The other 30 members are outstanding scientists appointed by the Royal Society, roughly half of them being chosen from universities and the rest from industry.

The Executive Committee of the General Board has the President, Treasurer and the Physical Secretary of the

Royal Society as *ex-officio* members. The Chairman and the twelve ordinary members are appointed by the President and Council of the Royal Society from the members of the General Board, care being taken to provide equal represen-tation for science and industry. In addition, there are three assessors on the Executive Committee representing the interests of the Admiralty, the Ministry of Aviation and the War Office, while the DSIR is represented by the Director of its Stations Division.

The General Board meets once a year during Open Week when the work of the laboratory is on display to industry and university scientists. It receives a report on the work of the laboratory for the preceding year and a statement of the programme of research for the following year. This provides an opportunity for a widely representative group of scientists in universities and industry to review and inspect the work of the laboratory. The President of the Royal Society always takes the chair at this meeting, the Annual Report being presented by the Chairman of the Executive Committee and the Research Programme by the Director of the Laboratory. Comments of the General Board and any recommendations are considered at the next meeting of the Executive Com-mittee.

The Executive Committee is the body which effectively determines the scientific programme of the laboratory. It meets about six times a year to review the programmes of work put forward by the superintendents of the nine divi-sions. Changes in these programmes may be suggested by the Director of the Laboratory and by individual members. After approval by the Executive Committee, minor changes in programmes are put into effect by the director but major changes (especially where these involve increased expendi-ture) are the subject of recommendations to the Research Council of DSIR. Once a year the director puts before the Research Council his proposals for the research programme, staff requirements, new buildings and expenditure on equipment and apparatus. These must be approved by the Executive Committee before being presented to the Research Council.

Occasionally (for example in 1957 and 1960) a special *ad hoc* joint committee of the Research Council and the Executive Committee meets under the chairmanship of the Secretary of DSIR to consider whether any major changes are desirable in the organization or work of the laboratory (for example the removal of a division or the creation of a new one), and also to review the long-term growth pattern.

It is obvious that a committee of twelve is too small to provide the necessary technical knowledge required to scrutinize the programmes of work over the wide range of science and technology covered by the NPL. To meet this need, a small panel of experts is set up for each division under the chairmanship of a member of the Executive Committee. This panel spends one day at the laboratory examining the work and plans of the division in some detail. It makes a report to the Executive Committee which is considered along with a report by the superintendent in which he is free to put forward his own views about the future of his division. The meetings of these nine panels are spread out in such a way that the programme of the whole laboratory is reviewed in considerable detail every two years.

In the case of the Ship Division, however, there has been for many years a special committee (known as the Froude Committee) which meets three times a year to discuss the affairs of that division. The Froude Committee contains representatives from the following bodies: British Ship Research Association; The Liverpool Steam Ship Owners Association; Institution of Engineers and Shipbuilders in Scotland; North-East Coast Institution of Engineers and Shipbuilders; Lloyd's Register of Shipping; Admiralty; Royal Institution of Naval Architects; Chamber of Shipping of the United Kingdom.

The work of the Ship Division affects such a compact part

of British industry that it is possible to have this special arrangement for it. Moreover the Ship Division has the only large scale and fully equipped facilities in the United Kingdom available to all shipbuilders for test and research work on hull and propeller design of merchant ships. For the shipbuilding industry to be in close and continuous contact with the work of the Ship Division is vital to both parties.

The preceding description of the organization by which the work of the National Physical Laboratory is controlled does not indicate what factors determine the choice of projects in the various divisions. In a large establishment with such wide responsibilities, it is necessary to have some guiding principles. The subject of standards has already been discussed and presents no serious problems. It is the wider responsibility to industry as a whole which raises problems of selection. The application of physics to industry must be done, by and large, by industry itself, either through its own research laboratories or through those of the relevant research associations. However, many of the more speculative or expensive lines of research would be neglected entirely if the whole responsibility were left to industry. It is the function of the Executive Committee to identify these gaps in the research effort of the country and to apportion the limited effort of the NPL among a selection of them. In making these choices, certain considerations are always kept in mind which it will be best to illustrate by examples taken from recent work in the laboratory.

About eighteen years ago, the possibility of constructing a high speed automatic computer using electronic components had been established by Von Neumann at Princeton University. It was clear that if such a machine could be realized in practice it would have wide applications in the solution of important problems in mathematical physics and might also have some useful applications to the mechanization of clerical work in commerce and industry. However, no commercial firm in Britain could be expected to put capital into such a speculative venture. The NPL at that time had a very brilliant mathematician (the late Dr A. M. Turing, F.R.S.) on its staff who had made independent contributions to the logical design of such a machine. It also had a number of able mathematicians and electronics engineers so it was in a very favourable position to enter this new field. By 1950 a pilot model of a large electronic digital computer was working, and by the spring of 1952 it was necessary to operate it in the evenings and occasionally all night in order to cope with the demands on its services by outside bodies. The English Electric Company had been brought in to help with the construction of this computer and they produced an engineered version of it (known as DEUCE) for commercial use by 1955. The NPL continued with the construction of the larger version (ACE) which is at present our main computer for the solution of a bewildering variety of problems. However, ACE will be replaced by a much more powerful computer (KDF.9) in the near future. The laboratory has played no part whatever in the design or construction of this last computer which the firm concerned has built as a normal part of its business.

This example illustrates three considerations which govern the choice of an NPL project. A new field of research has to be opened up which has commercial possibilities but also requires more money and more high grade scientific effort than any firm can be expected to provide from its own resources because there is too much uncertainty about the eventual success and profitability of the venture. Secondly, the NPL has the high grade staff and in particular some leaders who have special expertise and an enthusiastic scientific interest in the problems which require to be solved. In the third place, NPL brings industry in to collaborate with it, so that eventually industry can take over entirely and free the NPL staff to move on to the solution of new problems. Some of the electronics engineers who pioneered digital computers are now engaged on pioneering research in the mechanical translation of Russian into English, in the mechanization of adaptive control and on other projects in the Autonomics Division. The mathematicians are fully engaged on the exploitation of digital computers in the solution of a wide variety of mathematical problems; some of them are still at NPL; others have moved into industry or to universities which have set up computing laboratories.

One of the most important tools in optical research on the properties of matter is the grating spectrometer. The performance of such an instrument depends largely on the quality and size of the diffraction grating. Several years ago, the Light Division undertook the development of a novel method of producing diffraction gratings suggested by Sir Thomas Merton. Basically, this was an original idea for the production of a perfect screw from which diffraction gratings might be made by taking plastic casts from the screw and mounting them on a plane glass surface. Various experimental difficulties were overcome and diffraction gratings of high quality and large area can now be manufactured quite cheaply, so long as the grating is not too fine. This has limited their applications in spectroscopy to the infra-red region of the spectrum, but an unexpected dividend was their use in metrological work and in the control of machine tools By combining two identical gratings to produce moiré fringes, it is possible to measure and control automatically the movement of a machine tool with quite remarkable precision. The industrial development of this application was pioneered by Ferranti Ltd but the moiré fringe method has found a number of other applications, for example the scanning of photographic plates used to detect high energy particles in nuclear physics. Although the original objective of the project was only achieved partially, the unforeseen applications of cheap coarse gratings have amply justified the cost of this research. The stage has now been reached where further developments can largely be left to industry and to the National Engineering Laboratory, allowing some of the staff to be transferred to the development of optical masers.

The NPL work on diffraction gratings is an example of basic research on the techniques of a branch of physics which is of interest to physicists and chemists having an unforeseen impact on engineering. The same may well prove to be true of the current work on optical masers.

When the Basic Physics Division was created, the choice of its new fields of research required careful consideration. There is a growing tendency to replace metals, wood and natural fibres by synthetic materials provided the latter possess the requisite physical properties. Unfortunately it is not possible to predict the physical properties of synthetic polymers and this is largely due to our ignorance of the relation between molecular structure and macroscopic properties. In comparison with metals, relatively little research is being done in industry or in the universities on the physics of high polymers. It was decided therefore to make molecular physics one of the main fields of research of the new division. A natural extension of this general plan was to enter the field of high pressure physics which was being completely neglected in Britain, although synthetic diamonds had been successfully produced in the U.S.A. and Sweden.

Occasionally the choice of a field of research is determined by the fact that the special facilities and expertise required are available at the National Physical Laboratory. A good example is the application of computers to problems in ship-building in which pioneer work has been done by collaboration between the Mathematics and Ship Divisions. The control of the noise of jet aircraft can be tackled by joint efforts on the part of Aerodynamics Division and the acoustics section of the Applied Physics Division. The Metallurgy Division has recently undertaken research on high field superconductors because the metallurgical properties of these alloys will be an important factor in their industrial exploitation.

Organization of Research Establishments

Figure 1 shows the internal organization of the laboratory. Once the programme of a division has been approved by the Executive Committee, the superintendent is given full responsibility for its implementation. However, because the Civil Estimates procedure is such that the annual programme has to be proposed and approved nearly one year in advance, it is inevitable that adjustments have to be made in the course of its execution. Superintendents are free to make minor changes, keeping the director informed; any important change is referred to the director, who decides whether it should be referred to the Executive Committee for decision or merely reported to them.

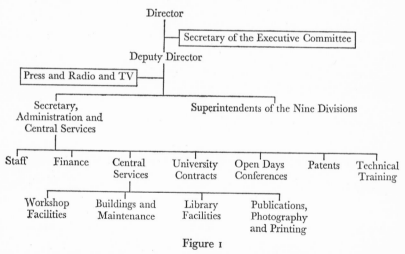

Figure 1

Administration Division, under the Secretary of the Laboratory, is responsible for the efficient operation of the laboratory in all matters concerning staff and finance, and for the provision of a multitude of common services. Allocations of staff and finance to the separate divisions are made by the director and the deputy director once a year. Since it is very rare indeed that the requests for staff and finance made through the Executive Committee to the Research Council are met in full, the optimum distribution of what is available is not an easy matter. In order to maintain maximum flexibility, divisions may be allowed to recruit staff over their allotted complement if other divisions have been unable to fill their vacancies. This is particularly true of scientific officer staff, where divisions may find five suitable candidates in one year or as few as one in a period of two years. Similarly, on the financial side, a large item of capital equipment which has been in the budget of one division may have its delivery delayed by several months. In such a case, other divisions may be able to bring forward the purchase of several smaller items of equipment, the delivery of which would otherwise have had to be postponed to the next financial year.

In order to keep such matters under continuous survey and to allow discussion of problems common to all the scientific divisions in their relations with Administration Division, the director and deputy director have regular monthly meetings with the secretary and all the superintendents. It is the custom at such meetings for one of the superintendents to give a short talk on the work of his division. In such a large laboratory, this not only promotes better co-operation, but not infrequently reveals instances where the scientific work in one division can benefit from that being carried out in some other division.

To Administration Division also falls the responsibility of providing central services where it is more economical to have a certain service centralized than to operate small units in each division. The most obvious example is, of course, workshop facilities. The Aerodynamics and Ship Divisions have such large requirements that they each have their own workshops. There are two other large workshops; one is operated by Standards Division on behalf of the Standards, Metallurgy and Light Divisions, the other is operated by Autonomics Division on behalf of the Autonomics, Basic Physics and Applied Physics Divisions. In addition, Light

Division has a small workshop of its own, largely for optical work. There is therefore no central workshop serving the whole of the laboratory. Very careful consideration was given to this point and co-operative workshops between three divisions was considered to be the best solution. The function of Administration is therefore confined to the staffing and equipping of these workshops and to seeing that expensive equipment is not duplicated without good reason.

The Ministry of Public Building and Works is responsible for the maintenance and furnishing of all existing buildings and for all new construction. Divisional requests for minor alterations and repairs are referred to Central Services which in conjunction with the Ministry draws up a priority list of minor works and watches progress on them by means of a monthly meeting. Decisions about major new buildings are taken by the Research Council following recommendations by the Director and the Executive Committee. Once Treasury approval has been granted, the detailed planning of the building is carried out co-operatively between the division concerned, Central Services and the Ministry, which is then solely responsible for the construction and furnishing of the new building.

There is a central library, but with the growth of the various divisions and the increase in the number of specialized journals, separate libraries have become essential in all divisions. The function of the central library is to provide books and journals which are not so frequently consulted that their duplication in nine divisional libraries can be justified. The central library has the general responsibility of ensuring that the library facilities of the laboratory are adequate as a whole. In this connexion, there is a Library Committee on which each division is represented.

The NPL is responsible for a large number of publications each year in addition to the papers which appear in scientific and technical journals. Although the Annual Report, the

Proceedings of Conferences, booklets on Applied Science and the Brief Guide to the NPL are published by HM Stationery Office, each division produces several reports per annum on items of current work which are circulated to interested parties and are not for sale or general release. About 100 copies of each of these reports are produced by the publications section, which also has to turn out about 1,500 copies of a recruiting booklet ('Opportunities for Research at the NPL') and 800 copies per month of a house magazine for the staff ('NPL News'). The advantages of having our own facilities for the production of such publications are considerable.

Finally, the laboratory has a training scheme for apprentices in the workshops and for the further education of junior technical staff who are allowed time off to attend courses in local technical colleges. Further education and training are encouraged at all levels and where university regulations allow it, staff may obtain a Ph.D. degree for research carried out at the NPL.

FORWARD PLANNING AND FUTURE DEVELOPMENTS

For over 50 years the laboratory was operated on a system of annual budgets and planning, but in 1954, the Treasury and the Department of Scientific and Industrial Research introduced quinquennial planning, similar to that which had been used for many years for the universities by the University Grants Committee. Under such a fixed quinquennial plan, a five-year budget was agreed and unexpended balances at the end of one year could be carried forward. In this way it was hoped that greater flexibility and stability would be provided by insulating the financing of scientific research to some degree from the annual variations in the state of the country's economy. However, in practice, the quinquennial plan had to be drawn up about eighteen months before it came into operation. It is, of course, impossible to look ahead nearly seven years in scientific research and draw up a plan which will be realistic financially when permission is not given to make any allowance for unforeseeable developments. Shortly after the second quinquennium began, it became clear that a fixed quinquennial plan was unworkable and in 1961 the concept of a 'rolling' five-year plan or a 'five-year forward look' was introduced between Treasury and DSIR. Under this scheme, the NPL reviews its five-year plan annually. It is understood that the plan agreed for the first year of the quinquennium is quite realistic in terms of staff complement and expenditure on equipment and services. For the succeeding two years, the plan is regarded as less firm and the provisional allocations for its fulfilment are understood to be subject to some revision in the light of unforeseen major changes in the financial or scientific situation. The plans for the last two years are accepted by both sides to be tentative estimates which will become progressively firmer year by year. Each rolling five-year plan assumes a constant value for money and any adjustment for increased costs is made when the following year's plan is agreed.

This method of forward planning has very obvious advantages over annual planning and fixed quinquennial plans. Annual plans and programmes are still essential, not only because of annual parliamentary estimates and accounting, but because one year is a suitable interval in which to make fairly detailed plans on which realistic estimates of expenditure can be based. On the other hand, the Treasury must have as much notice as possible of unusually large items of expenditure which those responsible for the future of the NPL regard as essential. The most obvious of these items are new buildings and new capital equipment. A large new building at NPL takes about one year to plan and over two years to build. Since there may be an interval of at least six months between the completion of the final plans and approval to start construction, the provision of adequate laboratory accommodation makes continuous forward planning of programmes, staff and capital equipment absolutely essential. With a fixed quinquennial plan, the director is liable to find himself in the position of being asked his plans for buildings in a quinquennium for which no firm commitments exist concerning programme or staff. This can lead to an undesirable concentration of building into the final two years of the quinquennium. Indeed it can become impossible to spend all the money allocated for building in the quinquennial period. Purchases of large items of equipment have also to be planned several years in advance so that the delivery of the equipment can be arranged to take place at the correct time with regard to the scientific programme of the laboratory and to the capacity of the departmental budget at that period. For instance, a modern computer with accessories can cost up to £500,000; it has to be ordered nearly two years in advance and the delivery of the accessory equipment may have to be spread over two to three years.

Having dealt with some of the more mundane aspects of forward planning, I shall now speculate a little on the possible long-term development of the National Physical Laboratory. The growth of applied science and technology which is vital to Britain's industrial future must be backed by a corresponding growth in the laboratory and a continual modification of its interests. The acoustics and radiology sections of the Applied Physics Division will possibly develop into full divisions and the same might be true of the theoretical physics section of the Mathematics Division. In the Autonomics Division, there is already some research being done on the biological systems which we are trying to imitate in our work on self-adaptive control. This could prove to be the nucleus of a Biophysics Division. As the Basic Physics Division widens its interests, it may become necessary to split it into two divisions, since restriction to molecular physics could seriously limit its usefulness to science and industry. The work of the Light Division will tend to become a combination of optics, electronics and atomic physics. These are some of the potential internal developments.

It is most important that relations with industry and with the universities and technical colleges become closer and more co-operative. We have had considerable success in accelerating the industrial exploitation of NPL work by persuading firms to second staff to the laboratory for periods of several months. This practice could be greatly extended with considerable profit to both sides.

In cases where the development of a new idea or technique is best carried out by industry, DSIR has recently begun to apply the stimulus of a development contract. The NPL is already playing a leading part in the managing of such a project for the computer industry; the same may happen for high field superconductors in the electrical industry. If these experiments are successful, closer relations between the laboratory and industry over a wide range of technology can be foreseen.

There is a great deal of unused teaching potential in the National Physical Laboratory. Although many of the staff give occasional lectures at universities and technical colleges, arrangements for some joint staff appointments with universities would be very beneficial in fields where the laboratory has unique research facilities which cannot be provided at the universities for economic reasons. It is frequently said that universities will fail in their teaching function unless their staff are actively engaged on research. Equally, there is a tendency for the staff of an institution wholly engaged on research to become rather narrow in their outlook if they are not forced by the discipline of lecturing to investigate new developments in fields related to their line of research. The National Physical Laboratory might even become the nucleus of a postgraduate technological university with associated research institutes. As has happened in the past, some of the present divisions may become independent research stations of DSIR, in order to allow for

The National Physical Laboratory

the inevitable extension of existing activities and the initiation of new fields of research. To predict the future of a laboratory with such wide interests and responsibilities is a little like trying to predict the future of science and technology. The only certainty is that the work of the National Physical Laboratory will increase and diversify in ways which will be as interesting and stimulating for the scientist, as they will be unexpected and profitable for the industrialist.*

* *Note added in proof.* Since the above was written, the Department of Scientific and Industrial Research has been dissolved. The National Physical Laboratory, along with the majority of other D.S.I.R. stations, has now become a research station under the new Ministry of Technology.

3

THE ROYAL AIRCRAFT ESTABLISHMENT

by Dr M. J. Lighthill, F.R.S., F.R.Ae.S.

I. HISTORICAL, FUNCTIONAL AND GEOGRAPHICAL SKETCH

The Royal Aircraft Establishment began to grow (under another name) on its Farnborough site in 1905, first as part of the War Office, and, later, of the Air Ministry (1918–40), Ministry of Aircraft Production (1940–46), Ministry of Supply (1946–59), and Ministry of Aviation (since 1959). Throughout these 57 years the science and technology of aircraft and, later, of missiles, have developed so fast that governments, mainly to meet defence needs, but also to stimulate civil aviation development, have thought it important to maintain RAE as a central reservoir of scientific and technological knowledge and skill on which all British producers and users of aircraft and missiles are able to call when they need. From the start, the work has included both extensive advanced research, leading to new ideas such as have been imperatively required to make aeronautical progress possible, and voluminous practical work of development and testing in flight and in ground facilities; the closeness of juxtaposition of these two types of activity has continuously caused each to fructify the other.

Design, and construction of prototypes, have also played important parts at Farnborough, although ceasing in 1916 as far as airframes were concerned, owing to a Government decision to transfer this work to industry. Similar transfers of design and construction responsibility to industry have occurred at later dates for successive categories of aircraft equipment and of missiles, being in every case preceded by deliberate building-up in industry of design teams with the necessary technical background, and supported thereafter from RAE with component development and testing, and with research aimed at identifying in advance the major design difficulties in a class of projects and obtaining solutions to them. In the meantime, RAE has taken up design and construction work in the new advanced technologies as they have come into being (for example, in that of satellites).

Another constantly important role of the establishment has been to assist the Services in the evolution of their aircraft and missile requirements in the light of the possibilities thrown up by research, as a preliminary to assessment of methods of meeting those requirements; similar functions are fulfilled with respect to projects for the airlines. At the other end of a project's history, the diagnosis and remedy of faults occurring in service, including the extreme case of accident diagnosis, has, whenever the main problems were technological, been a major task of the establishment. Yet another has been the maintenance of technical liaison with similar bodies overseas in support of international military and civil schemes of collaboration.

Within the aircraft and missile field, separate establishments have been set up, with some assistance from RAE, to deal with radar and propulsion problems: these are the Royal Radar Establishment (Malvern), the National Gas Turbine Establishment (Pyestock) and the Rocket Propulsion Establishment (Westcott). The testing and acceptance for the Services of prototype and production aircraft is carried out at the Aeroplane and Armament Experimental Establishment (Boscombe Down). Those mentioned form, with the Signals Research and Development Establishment (Christchurch), and the Explosives Research and Development Establishment (Waltham Abbey), the major experimental units assisting the recently formed Ministry of

Aviation to carry out its responsibilities. These, in brief, are for the continued development and procurement of aircraft and guided weapons for the three Services, and electronic equipment for the Army and the R.A.F., together with supervision of the associated industries, and of British civil aviation.

Outside radar and propulsion, almost all scientific and technological disciplines which contribute to aircraft and missile technology must be represented at RAE, in respect both of advanced research work and of practical testing and development. Some of these disciplines are listed in Fig. 2 under the names of the main research departments. The larger facilities maintained by RAE for research, development and testing of airframes, equipment and missiles, in flight and on the ground, are also listed, together with necessary supporting services such as workshops, drawing offices and the administrative organization.*

The wide range of these required disciplines and facilities demands a large, geographically dispersed establishment. For example, the Farnborough site was found unsuitable for the biggest wind-tunnel and experimental-flying facilities, which accordingly have been developed on two sites just north of Bedford, as part of RAE (although the 1945 plan to move more than half of the RAE to Bedford has been relinquished). Sites on the coast (Aberporth, West Freugh) and on Salisbury Plain (Larkhill) have been found suitable for the RAE ranges which, together with the Woomera range of the Australian Department of Supply, constitute the main governmental facilities for research, development and testing of missiles; important parachute and supply-dropping work is also undertaken. Furthermore, various smaller RAE stations with specialized functions exist (see Fig. 3), but a good air and road transport service ensures excellent and constant liaison between all the stations. The

* All facts and figures, in Fig. 2 and elsewhere in this chapter, refer to the position on 1 July 1962.

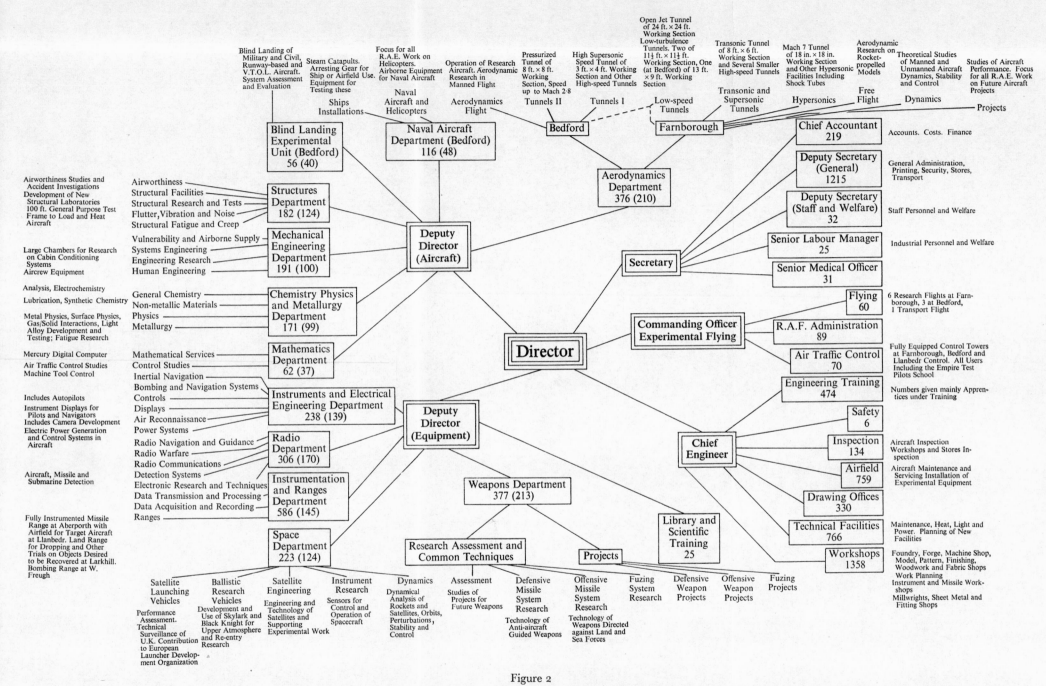

Figure 2

Unbracketed figures indicate total numbers of employees. Under Research Departments, bracketed figures indicate numbers of Q.S.E. Under other headings, figures are for R.A.E. as a whole, including parallel figures for outstations. Note, however, that this over-simplifies the organizational pyramid, since those providing parallel services at one of the outstations are under the control of the officer commanding, at least in day-to-day matters.

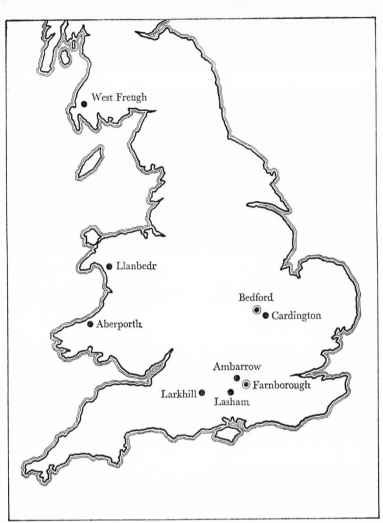

Location	Total numbers	(Q.S.E.)
Farnborough	5993	1198
Bedford	1332	190
Aberporth	627	42
West Freugh	218	7
Larkhill	129	4
Ambarrow	109	52
Cardington	50	2
Llanbedr	22	10
Lasham	16	10

Figure 3

scale of each part of RAE is indicated in Fig. 2 by quoting total numbers employed, together with numbers of Q.S.E. ('qualified scientists and engineers', including members of the Scientific, Experimental, and Engineer Classes of the Civil Service, and technical Serving Officers, but excluding laboratory assistants and technicians).

2. DEVOLUTION OF RESPONSIBILITY AT RAE

The total size of the Royal Aircraft Establishment (8,500 employees including 1,500 Q.S.E.) may give a misleading impression of unwieldiness. RAE has been described as 'big and concise at the same time, like an encyclopaedia'. Indeed, any one of the technological fields noted in Fig. 2, for example, flutter and vibration, is dealt with by a balanced, compact team, which carries out all the Establishment's theoretical and experimental research, development and testing work in that particular field. A very large degree of local autonomy, within a financial and manpower budget, is accorded to this team, which maintains direct links with industrial teams, university research workers or international bodies with interest in the field. Similar remarks apply in other fields, for example bombing and navigation systems.

The most important function of the RAE management in relation to such teams, which, by tradition, are usually called Divisions, is to ensure the closest possible collaboration and mutual understanding between them all. This is necessary not only because of the strong influence of technical developments in one field on those in another, but also because of the Establishment's closely homogeneous aim: to achieve any aeronautical advance, discoveries in many different fields have to be sought out, combined, or reconciled with one another. Another important management function is to ensure that scientists and engineers broaden their experience by properly timed moves to neighbouring fields of study, aimed at giving them effective and satisfying careers—which should in due course assist the management in a third function, the acquisition of good staff, by making the Establishment attractive to new recruits.

The management has also major financial responsibilities: to compare and adjust demands over the whole field in view of the needs of projects and of the advancement of knowledge, to prepare budgets and long-term estimates of expenditure for the Establishment as a whole, and to allocate current and capital expenditure between the different areas. Of great assistance in this is a proper cost accounting and estimating scheme, though, as we shall see, the appropriate techniques are different from those suitable to production and sales organization.

Now, in all these management functions—that is, in the effective planning of the scientific and technical work, of individual careers, and of finance—the most vital need in a large research and development establishment is a carefully-thought-out organizational structure, by means of which as many of the functions as possible can be delegated to heads of departments, fulfilling an 'intermediate management' function in departments, each consisting of several divisions, responsible for broad areas of the Establishment's work. It is desirable, as at RAE, for each of these departments to be so constituted that the knowledge represented within it forms a closely interrelated whole, of which a first-class research scientist or engineer may hope to attain detailed mastery in the course of his career. A well-chosen head of department can then exercise true scientific supervision and leadership throughout the department's work, and can enable staff, by means of decisions taken entirely within his own sphere of responsibility, to make over the years most of the changes of work that can usefully broaden their experience and maintain their freshness of approach. He also needs to forge particularly strong links with international bodies, industrial development teams, academic research workers, Ministry of Aviation Headquarters and the military and civil users of aircraft and missiles, while, financially, he acts as a vital intermediary in the comparison and adjustment of demands, and allocation of expenditure, between different fields of work.

3. THE MAIN ORGANIZATIONAL STRUCTURE

The appropriate definition of departmental boundaries at RAE varies with time, as new technologies grow up and as responsibility for work in the older technologies shifts gradually towards industry. At present, Fig. 2 shows that there are twelve research departments, of which seven are specified in terms of recognized branches of scientific or engineering knowledge: Aerodynamics; Structures; Mechanical Engineering; Chemistry, Physics and Metallurgy; Mathematics; Radio; Instruments and Electrical Engineering. This approach to departmental structure has sometimes been called 'organization by techniques'. The alternative, 'organization by end-products', would be inappropriate in the main airframe and equipment fields, where responsibility for detailed design and development is now carried by industry, and RAE's essential support, in the form of aimed research, testing and the technological monitoring of projects, is given principally in different specialized branches of knowledge, such as those just listed, although with Projects Division of Aerodynamics Department acting as a focus for RAE's whole contribution in the early stages of an aircraft project, and Airworthiness Division of Structures Department in the later stages.

By contrast, four of the research departments, concerned with matters where greater project development and/or design responsibility still remains with the Establishment, are defined by means of the class of project concerned: Weapons; Space; Blind Landing; Naval Aircraft. Each of these 'end-product' departments carries out extensive advanced research in technologies peculiar to its category of end-product (for example, fuze research in Weapons Department, orbital theory in Space Department, methods of energy absorption for arresting gear in Naval Aircraft Department); however, a 'technique' department, in close consultation with an 'end-product' department, maintains the necessary level of research and development in problems which stem from the application of its technique to the relevant category of end-product (for example, radio guidance components for blind landing systems).

The twelfth research department, Instrumentation and Ranges, is concerned with research, development and provision of scientific instrumentation for data handling (that is, for the acquisition, transmission, reduction and recording of data, particularly in large-scale testing), and with the operation of the Establishment's ranges.

Seven of the research departments (Aerodynamics, Structures, Mechanical Engineering, Chemistry, Physics and Metallurgy, Mathematics, Blind Landing, Naval Aircraft) are co-ordinated by the Deputy Director (Aircraft), who represents them on the Board of Management, leads the planning of work at RAE on problems of airframes, and exercises general supervision over the flying programme. The co-ordinator and representative on the Board of the other five research departments (Weapons, Radio, Instrumentation and Ranges, Instruments and Electrical Engineering, Space) is the Deputy Director (Equipment), who leads the planning of work at RAE on problems of aircraft equipment and of missiles, and co-ordinates the Establishment's activities with major electronic content.

The area of responsibility of a deputy director of RAE is greater than can be technically comprehended in depth by any one man, but his task is not impossible provided that he combines comprehension in depth of some major parts of it with wide interests and with the ability to evaluate and understand people in general, and scientists and technologists in particular. He must proceed, in the areas where his technical grasp is only partial, by a constant collation and assessment of the judgements of different experts, checked by clear recognition of the general characteristics of high-quality research and development work which experience in his own field has given him, and move gradually towards the formation of a sound overall judgement.

Three more members of the Board of Management represent departments concerned with matters other than research. The Chief Engineer's responsibility includes workshops, inspection, drawing offices, aircraft maintenance, the planning of new technical facilities and buildings, building maintenance, heat, light and power, the safety of installations and apprentice training. The Commanding Officer, Experimental Flying Department, commands the test pilots, is responsible for flying safety and air traffic control and, as Senior R.A.F. Officer, exercises general supervision over all Serving Officers in the Establishment (including technical Serving Officers in the research departments), and gives valuable representation of the ultimate users of much of RAE's work on its Board of Management.

The member of the Board responsible for finance (including pay and costing), personnel (including welfare and labour management), and general administration (including printing, security, police, stores and transport) is the Secretary, who also, as a member of the administrative class of the Civil Service, performs important jobs of interpretation, on the one hand, of the Establishment's problems, through his administrative colleagues at Ministry of Aviation Headquarters, to the Treasury, and on the other, of Treasury doctrine to scientists.

Meetings of the Board of Management, that is, of these five board members under the chairmanship of the Director, occur at least every fortnight, and, where necessary, more often. Each member represents the views of the departments for which he is responsible, as well as his own, at these meetings, which, supplemented by frequent informal discussions between members, cause a consistent policy for the Establishment on all matters of importance to be hammered out, and necessary decisions to be taken. Periodically, to help in the formulation of broad policy, a 'Heads of Departments Meeting' discusses a major issue, and, by this and other means, the board expects, over a period of years, to complete a review of the working of every significant area of the RAE organization.

The Director of the Royal Aircraft Establishment, besides being Chairman of the Board of Management, is personally responsible to the Ministry of Aviation's Research and Development Board, and, in particular to three of its members, the Chief Scientist, the Controller of Aircraft, and the Controller of Guided Weapons and Electronics, for every aspect of the Establishment's work, including, of course, the work of the administrative, flying and engineering departments as well as of the research departments. Evidently, he cannot be expert in all these areas; in practice, because science and technology (and their immediate fruits in design, testing and development) constitute RAE's main output, and lie at the heart of all its most difficult problems, he is chosen as a scientist or technologist. Certainly, it is necessary for him, by methods like those discussed above in connection with the Deputy Directors, to form a sound overall judgement of every technical issue on which important decisions affecting the Establishment will be required. Indeed, the stronger, clearer, and wider his scientific and technological abilities and interests are, the greater must be the confidence felt by staff who are needed to make creative contributions in those fields.

On the other hand, he must also pay close attention to aspects of the Establishment's work where science and technology are not necessarily dominant, such as finance, labour management, flying, maintenance, safety, etc. In matters such as these, just as in the sciences, it is important that he respects the judgements of the professionals, but scrutinizes them to satisfy himself that methods and procedures are as efficient as possible in meeting the special needs of a research and development establishment.

On every important matter, he must begin discussions with the board, or with selected members (for example, the Deputy Directors on research matters, or the Secretary and Chief Engineer on labour matters), as soon as possible after its importance can first be foreseen, so that a policy can be agreed in good time. Constant foresight of this kind ensures that decisions are not needlessly delayed, and that more than one person is aware of an agreed policy and able to act if necessary in the absence of the others.

4. ORGANIZATION FOR CONSULTATION

In all matters concerned with staff or their work, the RAE tradition is that careful consultation of local and intermediate management must precede decision. The inferiority of management by decree to management by persuasion (where the power to decree if necessary remains in the background) is particularly marked where staff are engaged in original creative work.

An important example arises when the integration of an agreed establishment view on some technical question (which may arise in the first instance from new discoveries in the laboratories, or from new user requirements) is needed. The organizational pyramid itself can go far towards achieving this, if each member concerned with the question sees that he and those immediately under him discuss it as much as is needed to reach a common view in the light of all the experience and knowledge available to them, while he shares in similar discussion at the next level up, with all those under the direct management of the same person as himself. Then, the discussions at different levels interact on one another, and culminate, for the most important issues, as has already been said, at the level of the Deputy Directors and the Director.

The earliest stage in a scientist's or technologist's career at

RAE when such integration of technical opinion and his other management functions, absorb more than half his time, is that of Head of Division, a post usually held by a Senior Principal Scientific Officer, with an average of 30 Q.S.E.'s under him. The level above him in the pyramid (except in the two largest research departments) is Head of Department, and (without exception) the next is Deputy Director.

There are some fifty Heads of Divisions; evidently, the effective working of the Establishment depends critically on their choice. The acquisition of Heads of Divisions combining the necessary scientific or technological ability with the necessary qualities of leadership is one of the Director's most important tasks, carried out through the medium of an Appointments Board, on which he sits, and of which the Chief Scientist of the Ministry is Chairman; this board has the responsibility, under the Permanent Secretary, of making all S.P.S.O. appointments in the Ministry, after receiving, in most cases, a report from a small *ad hoc* panel. Most of these remarks apply with redoubled force to the even more important issue of the acquisition of good Heads of Department.

It may be tempting, sometimes, to select solely on scientific or technological ability, or solely on qualities of leadership, but both temptations need to be firmly resisted. Fortunately, the scheme for promotion on individual merit (without administrative responsibility) exists as a salary incentive for those outstanding individual research workers who lack inclination or ability for management.

Even with excellent intermediate management, the organizational pyramid alone cannot always achieve proper integration of an establishment view on technical questions (though sometimes it is the only method that time permits). This is because messages passing up or down the line acquire distortions additional to the legitimate ones resulting from the experience and knowledge of those making the transmissions. For various reasons the distortions are generally in the direction of 'over-optimistification'. To minimize distortions that have their origin in human failings present to some extent in everybody, as much personal contact and direct communication cutting across links in the chain should be maintained as is consistent with other essential needs; this also greatly assists staff management.*

In particular, the Director, alongside his extremely close contact with the Board of Management and with Heads of Departments, must get to know all his Heads of Divisions well, and must seize every possible opportunity to become properly acquainted with members of their staff, and to discuss work in detail with them. To spend, fairly regularly, half a day walking round one of the divisions is an excellent way to achieve this end, without which a sound grasp of the Establishment's activities would, indeed, be hard to achieve, and the staff's confidence in the management seriously weakened. Similar remarks apply to Deputy Directors, who, for example, continually need to hold small meetings of experts from different departments to make effective the Establishment's contribution to particular projects.

Staff management is also assisted greatly, in RAE as in any large organization, by formal joint consultation machinery. All matters affecting staff on which management decisions can be taken at RAE can be, and to the greatest possible extent are, discussed with the Staff Association's elected officers, either informally or at one of the regular meetings of the Whitley Committee; similarly, matters affecting industrial personnel can be, and to the greatest possible extent are, discussed with members of the Shop Steward's Committee, either informally or at one of the regular meetings of the Joint Factory Committee; furthermore many matters are regularly and simultaneously discussed by the management with representatives of both staff and industrial personnel at meetings of specialist standing

---

* But note that, whereas steps in the chain may be bypassed by the flow of information, executive action must not bypass them.

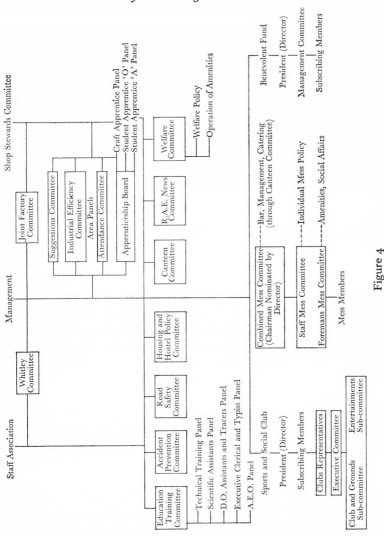

Figure 4

committees, indicated in Fig. 4, which shows the complete joint consultation machinery. The RAE management attaches great value to this machinery, and is seen so to do —which, indeed, is the principal condition necessary to make it work.

Geographical dispersion interferes with the management and organization of RAE to some small extent, greatly reduced by the rapidity and ease of communication afforded by air transport, but it does not distort the basic organizational structure. Admittedly, half of Aerodynamics Department (including the highest-powered wind-tunnels and the aerodynamic research flight) is at Bedford, together with the whole of the Blind Landing and Naval Aircraft Departments. Flying visits to Bedford by the Deputy Director (Aircraft) need therefore to be very frequent, and by the Director frequent, to enable them to consult adequately with the Bedford staff on the large and important volume of work done there. The Head of Aerodynamics Department has most of all to be in two places at once, planning and co-ordinating the wind-tunnel programmes at Farnborough and Bedford, research in manned flight at Bedford, and mathematical and free-flight research, and project studies, based on Farnborough. Similarly, the Head of Instrumentation and Ranges Department co-ordinates the work of the Aberporth, Llanbedr, Larkhill and West Freugh outstations with that at his central Farnborough laboratory, as do the Heads of Radio Department for Ambarrow Court and Lasham, and of Mechanical Engineering Department for Cardington (see Fig. 3). The Director, and appropriate Deputy Director in each case, must keep in touch to a degree largely proportionate to the outstation's size.

At the same time, the senior individual at each outstation performs, as officer commanding the outstation, certain duties parallel to those performed by the Director for the Establishment as a whole; particularly in respect of joint consultation, and of locally provided common services. The Board of Management's main task in respect of these officers commanding outstations is to create conditions in which they are all fully aware of the advantage of membership of the Royal Aircraft Establishment.

5. CO-ORDINATION WITHIN THE MINISTRY OF AVIATION

The remainder of this chapter is concerned with how the detailed research and development work done at RAE is co-ordinated and controlled. It would be out of place, of course, in a book on organization, to attempt the difficult analysis of the modes of original scientific or technological discovery. Nevertheless, the vital importance of the contribution of highly individual talent and experience cannot be over-emphasized, and is, indeed, the reason for the great significance which must be attached by the management of a research and development establishment to staff selection and career planning. It means that, however important leadership may be in providing co-ordination, direction and control, the organizational pyramid is ineffective unless those near its apex recognize that true creation springs mainly from its base—in the laboratory (using the word in its broadest sense).

Another implication is that the qualified scientist or engineer, whose creativity is so crucial to the Establishment's work, must be so supported by ancillary staff of different kinds that he has the facilities, and the time, to use his special talents to the full. Laboratory assistants, draughtsmen, clerical staff are all important; still more so are excellently equipped and managed workshops, and craftsmen of a high degree of skill and experience to work in them. RAE is fortunate in the quality of its ancillary staff, of which it has rather less than five per cent. Q.S.E., distributed among the various categories as in Table 1.

It must be recognized, however, that, beyond the problem of the proper support of individual research and development staff by scientific leadership and ancillary workers, lies the problem of ensuring that the sum of all their efforts constitutes such a body of research and development work as will further to the greatest possible extent the Ministry of

Aviation's tasks, particularly those in respect of the continued development and procurement of aircraft and missiles for the Services, together with supervision of the associated industries and of British civil aviation. The co-ordination aspects of this problem, which include co-ordination at

Table 1

	Totals	Totals per Q.S.E.
Q.S.E.	1,505	1·0
Laboratory assistants	425	0·3
Drawing Office staff	330	0·2
Administration		
(executive, clerical and allied grades, and police)	1,261	0·8
Skilled labour		
(including supervisory staff and 450 apprentices)	2,850	1·9
Unskilled labour		
(and its supervisory staff)	2,065	1·4

MOA Headquarters of its complete research and development programme, at RAE, several other establishments, and at a great variety of industrial firms (and, to a minor extent, universities) on whom contracts are placed, must now be briefly described.

The executive fulfilment of the Minister's functions in respect of aircraft is in the hands of the Controller of Aircraft. Any adequate account of how, under the Minister (and, beyond him, the Minister of Defence and the Cabinet), and subject to the continuous scrutiny of the Research and Development Board (with the Permanent Secretary in the chair), he formulates policy in respect of military and civil aircraft development, would be lengthy and out of place here. It must suffice to say that he has his own headquarters organization of scientists and technologists, divided into major groups responsible for airframes, engines, equipment, etc., and further subdivided; these are concerned with evaluating the technical merits of different lines of development (whose differences may be very complex and extensive, or very subtle) and of different firms as candidates to do the development, and with keeping in close technical touch with users and with parallel organizations in friendly countries with whom various collaborative or commercial arrangements may be in force or desired. This technical organization (there is between this and the establishments frequent and valuable interchange of staff) includes Serving Officers who are able to improve appreciation of the detailed needs of their Services within the Ministry, and works in parallel with a secretariat concentrating on contractual and financial implications.

The Controller of Guided Weapons and Electronics operates similarly in respect of guided missiles (mainly military developments, but, again, also civil, for example, development of sounding rockets for scientific research or assessment of satellite systems for commercial communications), and electronics (including, in the airborne equipment field specially relevant to RAE, all equipment operating at radio frequencies). Both Controllers have the responsibility for maintaining research programmes adequate to ensure continued ability to carry out their development functions. In addition, the Chief Scientist is professional head, and responsible for overall career planning, of the Ministry's 1,137 members of the scientific class and 1,835 of the experimental (of which, incidentally, 527 and 807 respectively are at RAE), is responsible for the scientific health of the establishments, and for overseeing (through the Controllers' scientific staff, together with the Heads of Establishments) the Ministry's scientific research programme as a whole.

In the light of the above very brief sketch of the headquarters technical organization, and of the fact that RAE carries out a large part of the required research work, in close association with other establishments, firms and universities, together with a major volume of development and testing work, and technological support and monitoring of development projects in industry, it will be evident that three separate processes of co-ordination of RAE's work with that of the Ministry as a whole must take place; or, in each area of the work, two: one by the appropriate Controller and one by the Chief Scientist. These co-ordination processes are continuously in operation, as will now be described, but are brought into coincidence once a year at the Annual Review of RAE, when the Controller of Aircraft is in the chair and the Controller of Guided Weapons and Electronics and the Chief Scientist are also present.

The co-ordination process used by either Controller involves him in personal consultation with the Director of RAE only when one of the biggest issues is involved; more commonly, one of his senior technical staff consults with a deputy director; more frequently still, the consultation is directly between a specific department at RAE and the corresponding headquarters technical staff, in the form of requests for work to be done, results described or opinions given. Where difficult issues are involved, the level of discussion can be raised to include the RAE management. For each RAE department, however, this happens on a regular basis (about three times a year, on the average) at the Departmental Programme Meeting, when the complete programme of work of the department (with, occasionally, related work in progress in other establishments) is reviewed jointly by an appropriate senior member of the headquarters technical staff together with the appropriate Deputy Director and/or the Director. These meetings are attended by many members of the department's staff and representatives of other departments, with good representation from headquarters, other establishments and, often, the Service Ministries, and afford excellent opportunities for issues of importance, including problems of the balance of effort in different areas of work, to be argued out by those principally concerned. In addition, they spread valuable information about the work actually in progress in the department, in the form of a 'Departmental Programme', or list giving current information on every job of work that is going on, and any of this (admittedly, rather extensive) information can in principle be discussed at the meeting.

In parallel with all this, the Chief Scientist keeps under constant review the Ministry's scientific research work proper by a variety of means, including an annual cycle of meetings devoted first to compiling a written account of all research carried out in the Ministry's establishments, or by firms and universities under contract to the Ministry, and then to discussing the resulting document in detail to highlight deficiencies or overlaps. Furthermore, the Aeronautical Research Council, which reports direct to the Minister, and the bulk of whose membership, and that of its committees and sub-committees, is divided about equally between Ministry technical staff (including RAE staff) and independent aeronautical scientists, largely from the universities, with some representation of the Society of British Aircraft Constructors and of other ministries, makes a comprehensive effort to keep the whole British aeronautical research picture under review (reporting deficiencies to the Minister) and provides a series of very valuable forums for detailed discussion between Ministry and non-Ministry workers. This often leads, for example, to systematic application to practical projects by establishments of some basic research carried out at a university. Similar functions in respect of electronics are performed by the Electronics Research Council.

All the extremely valuable procedures described above, linking RAE's work to the programme of the Ministry as a whole, and to British aeronautical research as a whole, are advisedly described here as co-ordination, since, on the one hand, the Controllers and the Chief Scientist recognize the importance and value of individual initiative at the Establishment, including a massive volume of close, informal contact with scientists and engineers in industry, and, as mentioned on page 29, with those involved in formulating future requirements for the Services and other users, and, on the other hand, headquarters technical staff in giving guidance to RAE departments accept that direction of the Establishment must in practice be carried out by the Director (through his organizational pyramid), although the Research and Development Board can, if necessary, give him instructions. Conversely, when research work at RAE needs to be supported or followed up by contracts on industry, and substantial sums are involved, RAE recommendations to headquarters, with whom in this case the direct executive authority rests, are required.

An interesting feature of RAE's work and of the associated aeronautical development work in industry is the close interaction of military with civil aviation developments. In particular, discoveries made for military purposes are later applied to commercial aviation developments of great economic significance. Furthermore, much aeronautical research work benefits both military and civil aircraft. It is at present estimated (from statistics described below) that the benefits to military and civil aviation of the aeronautical part of RAE's work are in the ratio of 3:2.

It will by now be self-evident that the pressure on RAE from a great variety of quarters (as well as arising from its own staff's new ideas) to take on new jobs acts as a constant incentive to terminate other jobs, preferably those that are proving less fruitful. It is sometimes suggested that research establishments are prone to continue lines of research long after the likelihood of their usefulness has dwindled away. This would be a serious state of affairs, but the author's experience at RAE (admittedly during a period of severe understaffing) indicates the contrary; the blazing light of professional discussion in which all work is carried on, and the pressing demands on scientific manpower to undertake new work, cause promising investigations to be dropped, if anything slightly too readily, when something more immediately promising comes along.

6. THE USE OF STATISTICS AT RAE

The rest of the chapter is devoted to the use made by the RAE Board of Management of manpower and financial statistics in controlling the work. There are two main aspects of this: budgetary and analytical.

Of these, the first, though outstandingly important, may here be discussed only very briefly, because every branch of Government is subject to the same annual discipline of making estimates, broken down by sub-heads, and in due course receiving a grant for the financial year, broken down similarly. To ensure that expenditure during the year remains within the grant, the Board of Management first determines what proportion of each separate class of expenditure will be required to make continuing payments resulting from commitments entered into in previous years. This is done by statistical analysis of past experience in respect of that class, which indicates also what proportion of the cost of new commitments made during the year will be borne during that year. Figures for the new commitments which can be entered into in that class are then arrived at, taking into account representations from departments relating to their needs; authority for these new commitments is then allocated to departments, a running check of expenditure against allocation kept during the year, and warnings issued in time to avoid overspending. Departments normally adopt a similar allocation of resources as between divisions. It is only necessary to add that some flexibility exists, permitting transfer of funds, as the year wears on, between classes of expenditure or between departments; and that a separate method exists (the so-called Complement) for control of expenditure on man-power, which represents about half the total expenditure of the Establishment.

Supplementing the control afforded by budgetary and

complementing statistics is a more analytical body of statistical data about RAE, compiled for the first time in the financial year 1961–62,* after a rigorous study of what type of cost accounting and estimating system would best meet the needs of a research and development establishment. It aims, like other such systems, to encourage cost consciousness, and long-term planning ahead, at all management levels in the Establishment, and, over and above this, to exhibit quantitatively how the work of the Establishment is related to the major objectives of the Ministry.

For this purpose, a major objective is taken to mean a class of related projects for which the Ministry has responsibility. For example, 'Objective 3: vertical and short take-off and landing aircraft' is one, and 'Objective 12: air-to-surface guided weapon' is another, of the nineteen such major objectives to which the work of RAE is regarded as applied.

The system recognizes, what the reader should by now have noticed, that two main modes of application of RAE work to objectives exist. In one, which the system calls 'immediate', the work is in immediate contact with the project, contributing creatively to it, aiming to get it out of difficulties—whether in the assessment, 'feasibility study', design, production, proving, modification or accident stage—or keeping work in industry under technical surveillance, and the staff involved would be immediately released for other work suitable to their qualifications if the project were abandoned. Much of this 'immediate' contribution is made by a number of widely separated small specialist groups, coordinated by methods which have been described.

On the other hand, when a group is not being required to contribute to a project in this way, its all-important expertise is as far as possible maintained in a state of readiness for future calls upon it, by careful direction of its research work

* The Board of Management used in December 1959, however, the earliest form of the system, which already was able, very valuably, to identify defects of balance and suggest the corrective action needed.

along lines aimed at identifying and combating difficulties of the kind foreseen as likely to arise when some particular objective or objectives is further pursued. Indeed, the art of directing applied research lies in this mobilizing of small groups, as their effort becomes available, on research jobs chosen as likely either to reveal the troubles which may be encountered on the way to some desired objective, in time to have the solution ready, or to reveal such improvements to existing solutions as may be possible.

Accordingly, the system defines 'aimed research', that is, research 'aimed at' a particular objective, as research work initiated or expanded with the aim of contributing to the objective by bringing to light unforeseen problems or the solutions to foreseen ones. There would normally be a considerable time lag before a group engaged in this type of activity, with its important additional aim of maintenance of expertise, could properly be transferred to other work in the event of the objective being abandoned.

The proper categorization of this 'aimed research' work is partly a matter of judgement, a judgement similar to that involved in the actual process of direction of the research with the future needs arising from objectives in mind, and the responsibility for it is accordingly given to heads of divisions, who have the immediate responsibility for such direction. Furthermore, to stimulate their interest in the statistical data they are required to collect, all final tables of data for the RAE as a whole are sent to them, data which helps them, incidentally, in their management responsibilities. On the other hand, from scientists and technologists below this first true management level, the system involves practically no effort; this is one of its advantages.

The work of each division is accounted for quarterly in respect of (i) the numbers of Q.S.E. and (ii) the cost (split up into Q.S.E. salaries, materials, workshop effort, flying, range trials, and a separate overhead rate per Q.S.E. in each division), to be allocated as the 'immediate' and 'aimed research' contribution to each objective (the 'immediate' being further sub-divided according to the actual projects concerned, except that those on which effort is marginal are lumped together as 'other projects'), all 'staff' overheads such as management, leave, etc., being apportioned pro rata. The remaining two categories to which manpower and cost figures are allocated are 'General Research and Development' (work important in a wide range of objectives, or looking forward to a number of possible, imperfectly defined objectives of the future) and 'Research, Development and Maintenance of Experimental Equipment'. Each of these last two categories absorbs about thirteen per cent. of the total current cost of RAE.

In addition to this quarterly accounting, an annual process of estimation by objectives and projects takes place. Starting from the grant for the ensuing year, and using cost statistics for the current and past years, the total RAE cost of Q.S.E. salaries, materials, workshop effort, flying and range trials is estimated, each total allocated among departments and by them among divisions. Heads of divisions then estimate how each of these elements of cost will be spread among objectives during the year (and, within objectives, between 'aimed research' and 'immediate' work on individual projects). Costs branch then prepares tables in several different forms, including estimates broken down by departments only, or for the RAE as a whole.

Later in the year, the process of comparing estimates with out-turn, and of uncovering the reasons for discrepancies, takes place; this is found to be an invaluable tool of management, not replacing the others described earlier in this chapter, but supplementing them, and, in particular, encouraging cost consciousness and planning ahead. When the estimates for RAE as a whole are available, the Board of Management, in consultation with heads of departments, forecasts for the five years ahead, in respect of RAE as a whole, simply the Q.S.E. employed on, and total cash cost of the 'immediate' work and 'aimed research' on each objective. For similar reasons to those just noted, this long-term forecast is found to be an extremely valuable exercise, and, together with the list of assumptions underlying the forecasts, forms the main material which is discussed at the Annual Review of RAE.

The full fruits of the new analytical statistics of RAE's work are doubtless not yet all apparent, but it has already proved of great value internally, in the balancing of the Establishment's effort proportionately to the importance of different objectives, and externally, where the quantitative picture it gives of the Establishment's contribution to the Ministry of Aviation's work has been widely welcomed.

7. CONCLUSION

If, following a survey of the RAE organization, one tries to formulate some general question regarding research and development establishments, to which the survey seems to point, the simple one that tends to emerge is: 'Is size a good thing?' The author's RAE experience makes him answer without hesitation that there are almost no limits to the benefits that size can confer, given homogeneity of aim and an organization designed to avoid fragmentation.

Thus, we have seen that RAE's notably homogeneous aim, of aircraft and missile research and development, supports an almost encyclopaedic wealth of scientific and technological disciplines and activities. All these interact on one another extensively and valuably, and the conviction that whatever subject comes up there will be 'someone at RAE who knows all about it' gives the Establishment all the best qualities of a university. Again, as with a university, size brings into existence large and expert groups in almost every one of those spare-time activities that help to make life interesting—orchestra, drama society, team games, field and track sports, gliding, sailing, bridge, to name only a few, while social life throughout the year is extensive, complex and entertaining.

All this sharing of interests, and of a great tradition founded on Farnborough's involvement with every British aeronautical achievement since 1905, a tradition with which the new and in some cases outstandingly equipped stations of RAE are proud to be associated, leads to an extraordinarily fine spirit throughout the Establishment, each member, whatever his job, vying with all the others to produce work up to RAE standard. The organization which has been described in this chapter is designed above all to promote this consciousness of RAE as a whole, and of its standards and traditions, in all its members, and to make RAE, as a whole, contribute creatively and efficiently throughout aircraft and missile research and development.

4

THE ATOMIC ENERGY RESEARCH ESTABLISHMENT, HARWELL

by F. A. Vick,* O.B.E., Ph.D., M.I.E.E., F.Inst.P.

INTRODUCTION

The Atomic Energy Research Establishment was founded in 1946 and took over what the Air Ministry had intended to be a permanent R.A.F. station half-way between Oxford and Newbury, at the edge of the Berkshire Downs, only about five miles from the Thames and about sixty miles from London. The new establishment was soon shrouded in an air of mystery and of glamour. Preparations for its work had been made by a team of scientists and engineers working in Canada under the leadership of (Sir) John Cockcroft, who became the first Director of AERE. Most of the team moved to Harwell, and they were joined by a rapidly increasing number of scientists, engineers and supporting staff.

For the first few years the main task of Harwell (then under the Ministry of Supply) was to provide much of the scientific knowledge and understanding needed to design and construct plants for producing fissile material in establishments further north, but the horizons were soon widened. There were first the growing applications of radioisotopes, then the prospects of the production of electricity by nuclear power. As is well-known, the Calder Hall and Chapelcross reactors were designed to produce power as well as plutonium. The choice of reactor design was based on studies by a group of engineers and scientists at Harwell, and these design studies

* Now Member for Research, UKAEA.

55

were then taken over by the Industrial Group of the UKAEA, as it became in 1954 when the U.K. Atomic Energy Authority was set up to take over from the Ministry of Supply responsibilities for the development of atomic energy.

The Calder Hall and Chapelcross reactors led to the U.K. 'magnox' power reactor programme, and Harwell became increasingly involved in an ever-widening scientific programme in support of this reactor system. At the same time, explorations were made of the potentialities of other reactor types and of other peaceful applications of nuclear energy. Over the years, many Harwell staff left to take up positions in other atomic energy establishments, in industry, in the universities, in Government departments and in a variety of organizations overseas, but still AERE grew— from 600 to 6,000 total staff in about ten years. More demands were made on the Establishment, due partly to the accelerated and expanded nuclear power programme decided upon at about the time of the Suez crisis.

Fearing that the Establishment would become too big and the area saturated, a measure of dispersion was decided upon. The majority of the former AERE Reactor Division moved to Dorset between 1958 and 1960 to found the Winfrith Atomic Energy Establishment. Most of the Accelerator Division became the nucleus of the Rutherford Laboratory of the National Institute for Research in Nuclear Science and formally became NIRNS staff in January 1961. The processing and marketing of radioactive isotopes were added to the responsibilities of the Radiochemical Centre at Amersham. Soon, too, all the plasma physics work (CTR) will have moved out to the new Culham Laboratory, six miles away. (The staff already there also include a group from AWRE, Aldermaston.)

In April 1961 the Authority was re-organized into the Weapons, Reactor, Production, Engineering and Research Groups. The new Reactor Group took over AEE Winfrith as well as Dounreay, Culcheth and other laboratories at Risley and Windscale and is responsible for the development of reactor systems included within the Authority's programme. The Research Group thus comprised AERE (Harwell and outstations), the Culham Laboratory (plasma physics), and the Radiochemical Centre, Amersham.*

THE TRANSITION PERIOD

Restrictions on staff numbers

These decisions concerning re-organization and the setting up of new establishments coincided with the end of the period of rapid growth of the Authority. Together these factors presented Harwell in the years after 1958 with a number of problems and a rather difficult task of re-orientation. The formation of AEE Winfrith and of the Rutherford Laboratory of NIRNS, and later of the Culham Laboratory, led to the removal of substantial numbers of staff and also of responsibilities for important areas of work. Also, the reorganization of responsibilities for isotopes and labelled compounds had a number of repercussions. All these changes were unsettling. Some parts of the Establishment became unbalanced (because the majority of staff transferred were experimental and theoretical physicists and 'scientific engineers'). There was a feeling that much of the interesting and promising work had been removed—what was there left for Harwell to do? I may say at once that these problems and uncertainties have largely been resolved (though one or two others have emerged), but it will be of interest to look more closely at some aspects of the transition problems before discussing present work and future prospects.

During a period of continuing expansion new ideas could be followed up by just adding staff and resources without interfering with existing programmes. This obviously could not continue, and the initial phase had to be transformed to one in which new items could be added to the programme

* From April 1964 the Radiochemical Centre no longer forms part of the Research Group but continues to be closely associated with it.

only by curtailing or closing down old ones, new equipment brought into use by replacement of old or by running the older equipment with fewer staff. In consequence programmes and priorities had to be reviewed more frequently and with even greater care. I felt it to be of great importance that staff at all levels should be brought into discussions leading to decisions on what changes should be made and when. To some extent this had always been done, of course, but in the changing circumstances more positive and regular arrangements had to be made. In this way staff felt they had opportunities to take part in decision-making, and they were informed of the circumstances making changes (particularly contractions) necessary. Even so it took some time for the Establishment to get used to the new conditions. Where the allocation of major fractions of available resources had to be decided, we took care and time to formulate by discussion an 'Establishment view', which meant that I could truly say when presenting the case for a capital grant that the whole Establishment was behind it. One example was the decision to build a variable-energy cyclotron for materials research.

AERE was hit particularly hard by the way in which the transition from expansion to fixed complements (and later contraction) of the Authority as a whole was carried out. At first the expansion was curbed by limiting it to eight per cent. per year. In principle this was perfectly reasonable, but in the Research Group practically the whole of the eight per cent. was reserved for the newly-founded establishment at Winfrith and for the Culham Laboratory. Moreover it so happened that the professional staff we wished to recruit to restore a reasonable balance between the disciplines after the moves already mentioned were those particularly difficult to find, for example theoretical physicists. We were quite determined not just to fill places by taking on people below top quality for the job. So our strength fell below complement, and places were kept open for good recruits, some of whom were earmarked for the future. We knew it would take some time to fill various posts, and we were planning well ahead. This policy made our problems temporarily more severe when, as part of the central Authority plans to restrict and reduce manpower, Harwell complements were reduced to be approximately equal to the strength at the time. Thus we were not able to fill the vacant posts until reductions could be made elsewhere in the Establishment; these reductions could not be made rapidly, and in consequence our plans for balanced recruitment were completely upset. Indeed the effects of these central decisions have not yet been fully overcome. The lesson is that if changes in overall staff numbers of a research establishment are to be made, sufficient warning should be given to enable forward planning to be effective.

Towards the end of the earlier period of expansion steps had been taken to move staff from the main Harwell site in addition to the formation of major new laboratories at Winfrith and Culham. Some electronics and engineering activities went to Bracknell (near Reading), isotopes research to Wantage (seven miles from Harwell), contracts and some finance staff moved to a rented office in Oxford, and parts of the Analytical Chemistry Branch remained in existing outstations at Woolwich and Chatham. Though the formation and retention of these outstations seemed reasonable at the time, they did not increase scientific and administrative efficiency (except perhaps in the case of recruitment of some junior staff), and the changes brought about in the transition period caused us to review the future of the outstations. Plans for the return to AERE of some of these staff are now well in hand.

The changing nature of Harwell's work

Even within the divisions that remained in AERE, considerable changes were taking place because of the evolution of the Authority's programme and Harwell's responsibilities

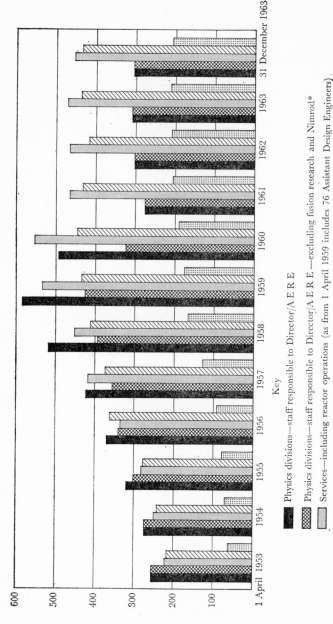

Figure 5   Professional strengths by discipline—AERE and RCC.

in it. One way of showing these changes is to examine the numbers and distribution of professional staff* in the main areas over the years. Fig. 5 shows these changes by discipline for AERE together with RCC Amersham (isotope production and marketing). The large changes in the number of physics professionals are very evident (the main reasons have been mentioned above). The AERE physics professional strength is now back to about the same level as in 1955, at which date there were slightly more physics professionals than there were corresponding staffs in the chemical and metallurgical fields. Now the latter are about 40 per cent. higher. (These figures have to be used with some reserve, because, for example, appreciable numbers of staff in the Metallurgy and Chemistry Divisions are doing work which many people would describe as physics!) The proportion of effort on services has increased, a major factor being the bringing into operation of the two materials testing reactors, DIDO and PLUTO. The figures should be regarded only as a general indication of the position; for example, changes from one year to the next may reflect changes in definitions, and the relative stability of numbers in the isotope field since 1961 in fact hides an increase on the production side and a decrease on research.

Fig. 6 shows the changes in distribution of professional staff at AERE over the main areas of work (as distinct from subject disciplines), adjusted roughly to exclude work later transferred out of AERE (for example to Winfrith and Culham). Isotope production, reactor operation and supporting services are also excluded, so the diagram refers to professional people engaged on research in its broadest sense. Basic research includes both 'pure basic' and 'objective basic' as defined by the Zuckerman Report,† most of it

* At Harwell, professional staff include the Scientific Officer grades (P.S.O., S.S.O., S.O.), the Experimental Officer grades (C.E.O., S.E.O., E.O., A.E.O.) and the Engineer Class (E.I, E.II, E.III and, since 1959, Asst. Design Engineer).

† 'The Management and Control of Research and Development', H.M.S.O. (1961).

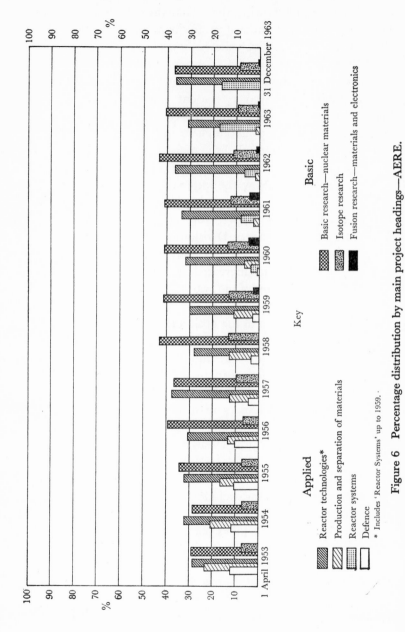

Figure 6 Percentage distribution by main project headings—AERE.

being objective. The proportion of basic research to applied increased up to 1958, and it is now about 40 per cent. of the work of the Establishment; of course, the boundary between objective basic and applied research is arbitrary and hard to define (and defend), and this may partly account for the drop between 1962 and 1963.

Work for defence has practically disappeared, and Harwell is no longer a defence establishment. Most of our 'secrets' are now of a commercial kind, though we are entrusted with a certain amount of confidential information from other places. In this we are no different from a great many other organizations, and the almost complete removal of work for defence has enabled us to segregate confidential work and information in defined areas of Harwell and permit much more free movement in the rest of the Establishment.

In the late 1940s and early 1950s Harwell was closely linked with getting the chemical plants in the north into operation, for example through problems connected with producing and processing uranium metal. Since then not only have the research and development branches in the north expanded greatly (as is reflected in Fig. 6 by the decline in Harwell's work on production and separation of materials), but the problems have changed also. With economic power as the goal instead of fissile material for defence purposes at almost any cost, it is necessary to examine much more closely all the factors, such as fuel and canning materials, moderator materials (and their interaction with cooling gases), nuclear data, etc., which are involved in going to higher temperatures and higher burn-ups and in predicting much more precisely the behaviour of nuclear power reactors. This has meant marked changes in areas of work and also a change to a more basic approach (to obtain fundamental understanding upon which to base longer-term predictions and planning) rather than efforts to meet immediate requirements related to defence.

Organization of Research Establishments

Organization and communication

Faced with problems of the kind outlined in the previous section, my first thought was to ensure that we had the right kind of machinery and organization to tackle them. The first step was to form a Directorate, consisting initially of the Deputy Director (Dr R. Spence), Assistant Director (Mr L. Grainger), Chief Engineer (Mr R. F. Jackson) and General Secretary (Mr T. B. LeCren). We set aside every available Monday afternoon to discuss quite informally items of policy, arising not only from current problems but also as parts of forward planning. We brought to our discussions different backgrounds, different points of view and different responsibilities and developed a common policy and outlook. The divisional structure of Harwell at that time is shown in Fig. 7.

As Director I was advised by the Harwell Council, comprising the members of the Directorate and four or five heads of scientific divisions who served in rotation. Major questions of scientific policy and proposals for expenditure on capital equipment, extra-mural research contracts, etc., were discussed at their monthly meetings with the increasing thoroughness and frankness that is possible between friends and colleagues with a common aim. The discussions were based on papers presented by a member of the Directorate or by an initiating division; if a division concerned with any item was not represented on the Council at the time, the division head was invited to attend. Sometimes special meetings were held to discuss particularly important proposals. Often a proposal was hammered into acceptable shape at several meetings. Recommendations for expenditure of capital sums above about £25,000 or for important changes in policy went from the Harwell Council to the Research Group Management Board.

Each Group of the Authority has a management board

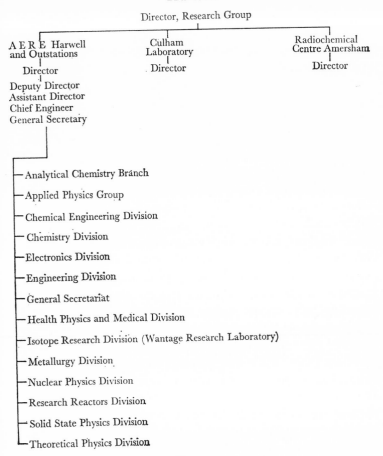

Director, Research Group

AERE Harwell and Outstations	Culham Laboratory	Radiochemical Centre Amersham
Director	Director	Director
Deputy Director		
Assistant Director		
Chief Engineer		
General Secretary		

— Analytical Chemistry Branch

— Applied Physics Group

— Chemical Engineering Division

— Chemistry Division

— Electronics Division

— Engineering Division

— General Secretariat

— Health Physics and Medical Division

— Isotope Research Division (Wantage Research Laboratory)

— Metallurgy Division

— Nuclear Physics Division

— Research Reactors Division

— Solid State Physics Division

— Theoretical Physics Division

Figure 7

UKAEA Research Group organization, April 1961 to June 1962.

with the Authority member concerned as chairman. During the latter part of the period now considered, Sir William Penney was Deputy Chairman of the Authority as well as Member for Research. All members of the AERE Directorate, the Director of the Culham Laboratory (Dr J. B. Adams), representatives of each of the other Groups and of the London office (Finance Branch) are members of the Research Group Board (RGMB). The Board has delegated powers of up to £50,000 for each capital item. It makes recommendations to the Member for Finance and Administration for expenditure on items between £50,000 and £100,000, and through the Atomic Energy Executive (AEX) to the Authority Board and Treasury for larger sums.

A very important task of the RGMB is the consideration of forecasts of expenditure under the various sub-heads, recurrent and capital, of the Authority vote, with some precision for the following year and in more general terms for the succeeding four years. These forecasts are then incorporated in forecasts for the Authority as a whole as a basis for overall planning and Treasury approval. When approval is obtained, the group is allocated a budget for the financial year, and the RGMB receives quarterly reports on actual expenditure under the various sub-heads. The Board enquires into any major discrepancies between actual and planned expenditure and into any unexpected trends and recommends action where necessary. Associated with budgets are, of course, ceilings of manpower under the main heads—professional, ancillary and industrial.

Within the approved budget and subject to specific approval of capital items in the ways outlined, Harwell has considerable autonomy to manage its own financial affairs, provided that broad lines of Authority policy and standards are adhered to. By agreement with the Member for Finance and Administration, the Director of AERE delegates financial powers up to approved limits to members of the Directorate and to division heads. Within the overall budget there are divisional budgets broken down into the various sub-heads, and the division heads are regularly provided with information on expenditure incurred and commitments entered into, so that they can plan the optimum use of their resources in relation to the scientific programme and exercise control. Thus division heads hold very responsible positions.

In addition to the Harwell Council there is a Division Heads' Committee, which meets quarterly and consists of the Directorate, all division heads and some other senior officers. The Committee discuss general (that is not specifically scientific) matters of concern to the Establishment, such as the fellowship scheme, education and training, housing and hostels, overseas relations, publications policy, public relations, information services, etc. After each meeting division heads normally lunch together and sometimes discuss over coffee a topic of general interest.

The machinery of RGMB, Harwell Council and Division Heads' Committee had existed for some time, but during the period under review much thought was devoted to defining their functions more clearly, to selecting and preparing subjects for discussion, to ensuring that proposals from anywhere in the Establishment were properly examined and that the various points of view were adequately expressed. The main emphasis throughout was on the maintenance and improvement of the scientific liveliness and efficiency of the Establishment and its effectiveness in the Authority and national programme. But those taking part in the deliberations so far outlined are normally of division head status and above. I felt that more should be done to bring in other experienced members of staff. So each quarter, during the afternoons following the meetings and lunches of the Division Heads' Committee, I talked in the Cockcroft Hall to all available members of staff of Principal Scientific Officer and equivalent status and upwards (about 250 attended), not about what had taken place but of problems under discussion (in the Authority as a whole when relevant, but primarily at Harwell), of the difficulties that faced us, of plans for the future and of changes that might take place. No one from outside AERE was admitted (I hope!), and I was able to speak quite freely and frankly, and sometimes in confidence. As far as I am aware, this confidence has always been respected, and no embarrassment has been caused by premature leakage of plans, etc. Questions and comments were encouraged. I have found these in general very useful, though not all the discussions have been as full as I would have liked. But the main aim, to enable a wider range of staff to feel 'involved', has probably been achieved. I am not sure that all group leaders have subsequently discussed with their more junior colleagues the less confidential aspects of the Cockcroft Hall talks and discussions, and I think more might be done in this respect.

In addition the Harwell Lectures were placed on a more regular basis. Open to all members of staff who applied for tickets early enough, they were given by visiting lecturers, by senior staff from other parts of the Authority and by division heads. Sometimes very lively discussions have followed the lectures.

Of course there has always been a wide range of discussions of scientific work and problems—colloquia, divisional lectures, conferences, symposia and all the other much-used methods, not excluding the arguments over mugs or beakers of tea. But additional steps were taken to discuss major sections of the programme and areas overlapping several divisions. For example there is an Inter-divisional Committee on Reactor Materials Research involving the Chemistry, Chemical Engineering and Metallurgy Divisions regularly, joined sometimes by other divisions, such as Solid State Physics. In principle the advantage of having a wide range of scientific and technical divisions on one site is the opportunities for wide-ranging discussion, but in practice such discussions have often to be stimulated by one means or another. One feature of recent discussions has been the bringing to bear on specific problems of importance of a wide range of knowledge and experience. Gradually it is becoming less common to seek elsewhere in the world for advice when at least one of the recognized experts on the subject is on the Harwell site!

AERE takes full part in Authority-wide discussions in which technical and scientific factors are important. There are the meetings of the Authority Reactor Programme

Harwell

Committee, the Reactor Development Policy Committee
(with various steering committees and working parties),
the Authority Health and Safety Committee (with its Health
and Safety Research Committee and sub-committees) and, of
course, the Research Policy Committee, all reporting in one
way or another to the AEX. To the Research Policy Committee report the Reactor Chemistry Research Committee
and the Physics of Reactors Research Committee. Through
the discussions of these and other bodies Research Group
staff are enabled to contribute to Authority policy and to
identify problems and priorities to be taken into account
when formulating and reviewing our own programmes.
Quite a number of significant changes have been brought
about in this way, though of course Harwell still has the
freedom to initiate. On the whole collaboration with the
'Northern Groups' is good, and the response times are
reasonably short.

Some particular problems

Against this general framework of a machinery for consultation, policy-making and decision-taking, let me quote
a few examples of particular problems of fairly general
interest that we have tackled. Some of these have already
been hinted at in previous paragraphs, while others it was
not possible to tackle until decisions on the future organization of the Authority enabled us to look further ahead than
had previously been possible.

Thus we began in 1960 a thorough review of the accommodation on the Harwell site. Much of this was an inheri-
tance from the R.A.F.; there were also some hastily erected
temporary post-war buildings—as well as some excellent
purpose-built, but temporarily very overcrowded, laboratories, etc. Some of the buildings would be vacated by staff
moving to Culham, and some substandard accommodation
would have to be pulled down; on the other hand some new
buildings would be essential to house new plant and to locate

staff close to experimental facilities. To reconcile these various factors we undertook a detailed appraisal of the accommodation available and of probable needs for the next five years, and this appraisal is kept up-to-date by annual reviews considered in detail by the Harwell Council and in less detail by the RGMB. Our work here has enabled us to plan carefully the location of new buildings in the light of probable future developments, and—though the staff who have been waiting in unsatisfactory accommodation for the Culham staff to depart may regret the delay in finding them good accommodation—it has undoubtedly helped to ensure that full use is made of the accommodation now becoming available. A small number of large buildings is, in general, more efficient, more flexible and more economic than a large number of small ones.

Another problem faced at AERE has been the allocation of staff within a pre-determined establishment complement (see page 66), and in association with this the joint discussion by directorate and division head of the programme of work to be undertaken by the staff concerned. Such reviews of divisional programmes and complements have been undertaken annually at Harwell for some years. The Directorate and division heads of course frequently discuss particular aspects of the scientific programme and special needs for altering the pace, scale or emphasis of part of the programme, but it is helpful to be able annually—within a space of about three months—to review the overall scientific programme and staff deployment of all divisions in the Establishment. This helps to identify, both to the Directorate and to individual division heads, the need, and the scope, for transfer of staff to permit the opening up of new areas of work where required (or expansion of existing areas) by closing down other work in the same, or another, division. There can be no doubt that such regular reviews have assisted me, as Director, to exercise my overall responsibility to allocate the staff available to me and thereby shape the work of the

Establishment in the way in which (in the light of Authority policy) it has seemed to me that it should go. I also believe that these regular discussions have assisted division heads to appreciate the difficulties facing the Director of the Establishment (and the reasons for staff reductions where required) and themselves to exercise corresponding oversight of the activities within their divisions.

Over the past few years it has at last become possible, now that movement from the site is slowing down and changes in organization are over, to review thoroughly the technical and administrative services provided and to seek to find ways to streamline them. Two approaches are possible, and both have been adopted. First, as Director, I have told my colleagues on the Directorate that I expect them by good management to be able to reduce the numbers of staff in their divisions without affecting the quality of the service they provide to the scientific divisions. Second, and the natural corollary to this, the Chief Engineer and the General Secretary have instigated, and discussed with the other members of the Directorate, a number of reviews of the individual services they provide and the staffing of their various departments to see where economies can be made. In addition, reductions in operating economies can often be achieved by installing new capital equipment to replace obsolete or inefficient facilities of various kinds, and a number of such capital schemes have been and are being introduced. As a result of such measures the total complement of the General Secretariat, for example (which provides for a wide range of administrative services from transport, messengers and cleaning to personnel and finance), has been reduced from about 1,450 at the end of 1961 to about 1,380 at the end of 1963, with a target for the end of 1964 of 1,360.

In the case of the Engineering Division other factors also need to be taken into account. The demands of the scientist for support tend to grow, both because equipment is becoming more complex and because with experience the division is able, despite the increasing complexity, to take over from the scientist more and more that he otherwise used to do for himself. We have therefore in recent years sought to ease the problems these demands create both by reorganizing the supporting services to attach engineering staff (designers and workshop staff) as closely as possible to the scientist in the laboratory and by discussing—quite frankly and with no holds barred—with division heads and others the adequacy of the services provided to them. In this way we hope to ensure a reasonable service and at the same time avoid criticisms from the scientific divisions that too much of the scarce resources (in terms of men and money) of the Establishment is allocated to the 'service' divisions.

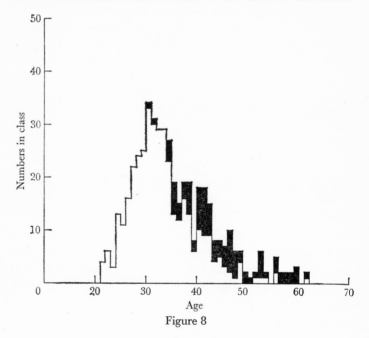

Figure 8

■ Senior and Banded Staff
□ P.S.O., S.S.O. and S.O

UKAEA Research Group (excluding RCC, Amersham): age distribution of the S.O. Class at 31 December, 1963.

In the supporting divisions and, more important, in the main research divisions also, a key factor is the need for flexibility. The needs of the Authority's programme change; this means a change in the research programme, a switch of staff and a rapid response from those designing, making and operating the equipment needed. Flexibility is the key too when it is remembered that research has now been going on at Harwell for almost twenty years; so we have been trying to anticipate and overcome the inevitable and in some places, I think, exaggerated problems of an aging scientific population. We have not found the phenomenon of the 'burnt out' scientist to be a very real problem, because we have found difficulty in locating the men in question! Yet we have taken steps to ensure that the age pattern of the Scientific Officer Class (Fig. 8) stays about the same, though the staff themselves get older, and Table 2 is evidence of the measure of our success.

Table 2. Research Group (excl. RCC Amersham);
Average age of the S.O. Class (excl. Senior and Banded posts)

	1.7.61	1.7.62	1.7.63	31.12.63
P.S.O.	38·1	38·1	38·5	38·6
S.S.O.	31·2	31·3	31·7	31·6
S.O.	25·8	27·2	26·3	26·1
S.O. Class	32·6	33·3	33·6	33·6

In an increasingly competitive market we have tried to recruit the best young men for Harwell, and as I have said we have refused to debase the coinage in our efforts. The annual North American 'trawl' is established—and much publicized!—and in addition we have instituted Open Days at Harwell, when undergraduates and post-graduate workers are invited to come and see us at work in the right atmosphere for an informal, mutual assessment. To ensure maximum freedom of movement we have tried to increase the range of employments for which transferability of pension from the Authority's scheme is possible. We have encouraged exchanges and attachment arrangements both with universities and with other institutions here and overseas. This means we must be able to assimilate our staff when they return, and this applies more strongly where we have encouraged younger staff to study and improve their qualifications, possibly even to change their specialization. The Harwell Reactor School, under the Post-Graduate Education Centre which I set up last year, has taken on to some extent the role of a dissemination centre for knowledge of other disciplines or specialized and novel techniques recently developed in an effort to break down further the arbitrary barriers between disciplines or between divisions, as well as to ensure that what is known is known widely enough to be of full value. So in all this we need the flexibility to plan ahead and to meet changes in order to produce the right atmosphere for fruitful research.

But whatever steps are taken to encourage staff mobility and wider experience, the director of a research establishment, and the division head, are faced with the fact that to a very large extent they must do the best they can with their current staff with their varied, but perhaps limited, capabilities. This too means flexibility—in organization and in the selection of tasks. From time to time, for example, it will be appropriate to form new divisions or scientific groups; since I came to Harwell we have founded the Research Reactors Division, set up the Solid State Physics Division and created an Applied Physics Group (dealing mainly with special problems on the direct conversion of heat to electricity). In these cases, and in others, the precise organization, and indeed the nature of some of the work done, will depend on the capabilities of individuals. We at Harwell cannot hope to do everything, and so we must be selective, building on our strengths, and wherever possible relying on other research teams to cover areas relevant to our work which they are better fitted to tackle—for example NIRNS for high-energy physics, Winfrith for power reactor physics, the universities for particular problems of basic research where they have suitable expertise and facilities.

INTERACTIONS WITH UNIVERSITIES AND COLLEGES

There have always been close and friendly relations between Harwell and the universities and colleges, especially those in the region. Indeed many of Harwell's scientific and engineering staff in the early days had been professors or lecturers in universities. In more recent years the net flow has, naturally, been the other way, and in the U.K. alone at least fifteen holders of chairs have been on the Harwell staff.

At present (January, 1964) AERE has about 134 extramural research (EMR) contracts with universities and colleges of technology to the total value of about £830,000. Over the years such contracts have helped universities and colleges establish new lines of research and give experience to graduate students in a wide range of problems related to atomic energy. Care is taken to ensure that there are no clashes with the provision by DSIR of research studentships and grants for special researches. We have gained much from the continued collaboration with university research teams, and in general if a university is able and willing to undertake basic work of value to our programme, we encourage it to do so and devote our own resources to those aspects that demand our special experience, equipment and immediate contacts with the needs of the civil programme.

Harwell also draws on the knowledge and experience in universities by appointing senior members of their staff as consultants; there are about seventy at present. These consultants spend days or weeks at a time at Harwell talking to and working with the scientists concerned. With a few exceptions we do not expect them to attend formal advisory committee meetings. In addition to the consultants, Vacation Associates from universities spend a few weeks

75

working at the Establishment and receive subsistence allowances and fees according to their academic status and length of stay; there were 22 Associates at Harwell in the summer of 1963. There are also Vacation Assistantships for post-graduate workers and Vacation Studentships for undergraduates; the number of studentships awarded is at present limited to about 60 at any one time to ensure that each student is adequately supervised by a member of the scientific staff during his stay.

Harwell Research Fellows are chosen very carefully. They normally have post-doctorate experience and carry out research on topics of their own choosing within our general field of work. They are appointed for three years, and many of them go on to university staffs, though some are appointed to our own. In addition to Fellows we appoint Temporary Research Associates, usually scientists of established reputation who can make special contributions to our work.

Attachments to Harwell may vary in duration from a few days to two or three years. At present, for example, about 70 graduate students and members of staffs of U.K. universities come to Harwell for recurring short visits which together amount to three months or more. Many of them carry out experimental work on our accelerators. The recent percentage of time of operation of three of the accelerators by university teams has been approximately as follows:

12 MeV Tandem Van de Graaff	44 per cent.
5 MeV Van de Graaff	17 per cent.
110 in. Synchrocyclotron	25 per cent.

In addition the synchrocyclotron is used quite considerably by joint AERE and university teams. There is, too, an increasing use of Harwell's research reactors by university visitors, and discussions are now in progress to work out ways and means to make this easier. Another and quite different method of collaboration now being discussed is the attachment of senior students and members of staffs of universities and colleges to design teams to enable them to take part in a design project from conception to commissioning.

Many of the courses held at the Reactor and Isotope Schools have been attended by members of universities (and we have sometimes been helped by visiting lecturers from the universities), and to an increasing extent courses are being specially devised for them. The recently instituted Post-Graduate Education Centre has already been mentioned.

Our staff help universities in several other ways—by giving courses of lectures, by examining for higher degrees, by holding seminars, attending colloquia, etc. There is no doubt that all these activities benefit our own staff as well as assist universities, and the climate of opinion seems now to be becoming more favourable to closer collaboration between us, helped partly by the fresher outlook and the needs of the newer universities and C.A.T.s.

CONCLUSION

Harwell is still a busy place. For some of the problems arising directly from the Authority's civil programme we find great difficulty in meeting target dates owing to the calls on those staff having the necessary knowledge and experience. In spite of the size of the Establishment the range of activities is so wide that many scientific groups are quite small. Care must be taken, therefore, to reserve enough effort to lay the scientific foundations for the needs of the 1970s and 1980s, especially in those regions where we have unique resources, some of which have potential applications that are wider than our present programme. So I have every confidence in the future of Harwell. There are no signs of its becoming stale or underemployed. With a period of reasonable stability it should become even more efficient and an even greater national asset.

It is a pleasure to pay tribute not only to my present colleagues, but also to my predecessors as Director, Sir John Cockcroft and Sir Basil Schonland, to whom so much of the success of the Establishment is due.

5

THE NATIONAL INSTITUTE FOR MEDICAL RESEARCH*

by Sir Charles Harington, K.B.E., F.R.S.

HISTORICAL

One of the first decisions to be taken by the Medical Research Committee (the predecessors of the Medical Research Council) when they were appointed in 1913, was to set up centralized research laboratories in which should be employed full-time investigators, and to the implementation of this decision they were prepared to devote their first year's income. Negotiations were started forthwith for the purchase of the Mount Vernon Hospital, Hampstead, with a view to its conversion into a research institute. These negotiations were delayed by an abortive proposal by the governing body of the Lister Institute that the latter should be handed to the nation for use as the central research institute of the Medical Research Committee; time was also spent in considering whether or not to incorporate a research hospital with the new institute. As the result of this the purchase of the building in Hampstead was deferred until just before the outbreak of war in August 1914; the building had to be taken into use as a military hospital and so it remained until 1919; actual occupation for the purposes of the Medical Research Council was delayed until April, 1920.

The work of the Institute grew rapidly in extent and it was

* This chapter was written in 1962 when the author was still Director of the National Institute for Medical Research; the account has been brought up to date (1 January 1965) with the aid of notes kindly provided by the present Director.

not long before the need for more accommodation made itself felt. This was first met by additions to the Hampstead building and by the acquisition of a site at Mill Hill on which some small buildings were erected, principally for work on the large number of dogs that were required for the studies of virus diseases to which reference will be made later. By 1936, however, it had become apparent that more drastic measures were needed if the Institute were to be enabled to fulfil its proper function. The decision was therefore taken by the Medical Research Council to build a new and larger building on the property that they had acquired at Mill Hill.

Once again the plans of the Medical Research Council for the National Institute for Medical Research were disorganized by war. By the spring of 1940 the new building had been erected, but authority could not be obtained for its internal completion. It was therefore lent to the Admiralty by whom it was used as a training depot for W.R.N.S. until 1946. In the event it was not until the end of 1949 that the internal construction and equipment were completed and the building could be taken over for its proper use.

In the meantime the work of the Institute had been continuously carried on at Hampstead and had indeed been expanded to the limit imposed by available space. Nor was the delay enforced by the war entirely disadvantageous, since it afforded an opportunity of re-planning, which was utilized to bring the internal arrangements of the new building into closer accord with the demands of medical laboratory research as they had developed since the original design was made. The re-planning included for example the provision of a Biophysics Division which had not been allowed for.

It had been the intention of the Medical Research Council to dispose of the Hampstead building when the new institute at Mill Hill was completed. When the time came, however, other demands had arisen which made it necessary to retain the Hampstead laboratories for a variety of purposes,

79

including some of the work of the National Institute itself; at the present time the Hampstead laboratories are used almost entirely for the purposes of the Institute; the latter therefore now comprises the main building at Mill Hill, with its very extensive ancillary buildings for experimental animal work and the original Hampstead building. This makes the Institute much the largest establishment of its kind in the British Commonwealth.

WORK OF THE INSTITUTE

The Medical Research Council have consistently taken the broadest view of their responsibilities and in particular they have been at pains to avoid the prescription of projects of research to their staff; moreover they have regarded it as necessary that their scientific staff should have the greatest degree of freedom in the choice of their field of work that can be provided within their very broad terms of reference; in the general selection of problems an eye is kept particularly on subjects that are at an early stage of development but show promise of increasing importance in the future. These principles are well illustrated by the way in which the present activities of the National Institute have developed.

The purpose of the Medical Research Committee in establishing a central institute was to provide a place where full-time scientific workers might study any subject in the field of non-clinical medical research. This object has always been kept in mind, so that the growth of the National Institute and the expansion in the range of work undertaken there that have occurred during the first forty years of its existence are reflections of the increasing recognition over the same period of the contribution that laboratory research can make to medicine.

For the implementation of their object the Medical Research Committee appointed medical and scientific men of high standing in the subjects of physiology and pharmacology, applied (environmental) physiology, experimental pathology and bacteriology, chemistry and biochemistry. This choice was just what would have been expected in the scientific climate of the time except that, in retrospect, it seems that the Medical Research Committee and their advisers showed unusual prescience in the importance which they attached to chemistry and biochemistry. These then were the scientific foundations of the work of the Institute, and on them has been built the present organization which comprises fourteen divisions and two special laboratories in which are employed a total staff of about 675 of whom about 160 are professionally qualified in science or medicine.

There would be little purpose in describing the growth of the Institute step by step or in giving a catalogue of its present activities. On the other hand there is some interest to be found in tracing the development of a few of the major themes of interest that have been, and in some cases still are being, studied, particularly because they serve to illustrate the type of development which the present principles of organization of the Institute are designed to promote.

Physiology and Pharmacology

Before H. H. (now Sir Henry) Dale was appointed to the scientific staff of the Medical Research Council he had acquired what was to prove a lasting interest in the physiological properties of simple basic substances (several of which were first isolated as constituents of ergot) as the result of the distinguished work that he had done with the late George Barger in the research laboratories of Burroughs Wellcome Ltd. The development of certain aspects of this work, with special relation to the properties of histamine and acetylcholine, remained one of the principal themes of research at the Institute for many years.

The similarity of some of the effects produced by the administration of histamine to animals with those observed in anaphylactic shock had already been noticed by Dale and interest in this compound was further stimulated by the suggestion, first made by the late Sir Thomas Lewis, that histamine, owing to its power of dilating blood capillaries and increasing their permeability, might be responsible, at least in part, for the reactions of the skin to injury. This conception was, however, without experimental support, since the only site in the animal body where the presence of histamine had actually been demonstrated was the intestine, and here it was almost certainly a product of bacterial action.

The biochemists in the Institute therefore took up the search for histamine in the normal animal body and were in fact successful in showing that it was widely distributed in a bound form in many tissues, in some of which, such as lung, it occurred in surprisingly large amounts; moreover it was liberated from its bound form by tissue injury. In this way objective evidence was provided to support the hypothesis that histamine played an important part in anaphylactic shock and other allergic manifestations and also in local tissue reaction to injury. It is reasonable to regard this research as having provided the stimulus for the development elsewhere of the antihistaminic drugs that are now so widely used in the therapeutic treatment of allergic conditions.

A somewhat similar situation existed in the case of acetylcholine. Here also the compound was first observed by Dale as a natural product in examining an abstract of ergot, but physiological studies, especially the work of Otto Loewi, had shown the likelihood that a substance with the properties of acetylcholine was concerned in the effects produced by stimulation of para-sympathetic nerves.

In this case again reality was given to the conception by the finding of acetylcholine in normal body tissues and research work was stimulated which occupied the physiologists in the Institute for many years. This research, which brought to Dale the award, jointly with O. Loewi, of the Nobel Prize for Medicine, led to one of the great generalizations of physiology. This is that acetylcholine is the substance responsible for the transmission of nervous stimuli from the peripheral ends of parasympathetic nerves to plain muscle through the ganglionic synapses of the sympathetic nervous system, and at the nerve endings of motor nerves to voluntary muscle; that is to say it is the chemical transmitter for the effects conveyed by the whole of the efferent fibres of the peripheral nervous system except the post-ganglionic fibres of the sympathetic system for which a similar part is played by noradrenaline.

This generalization formed a new chapter in neurophysiology and its implications for neurological medicine have been significant. In the present context, however, it is worth noting that the work lay at the basis of one of the greatest advances in therapeutics for which workers at the Institute have been responsible. The way in which this came about incidentally affords an excellent example of the effectiveness of interweaving of scientific disciplines in the advance of medical research.

Mention has already been made of the importance attached by the Medical Research Council to chemistry. The primary reason for this was the desire to advance the study of chemotherapy, and reference will be made to this later. In accordance with the liberal policy of the Council, however, the chemists were not discouraged from pursuing their own interests as opportunity offered and it happened that one of these interests lay in research on alkaloids. One group of alkaloids, namely the curare group, were known to block neuromuscular transmission and these were therefore of special interest in view of the physiological work that has been described. The result was a research that led to the isolation of *d*-tubocurarine, its identification as the active principle of the South American arrow poison tube curare, and the elucidation of its chemical constitution.

The isolation of *d*-tubocurarine was itself of immediate medical importance because of the usefulness of the compound as an adjuvant in anaesthesia, where its muscle-relaxing properties were of value. However, the matter went much further. The constitution of tubocurarine suggested the desirability of studying the pharmacological properties of simple straight chain aliphatic compounds having trimethyl-ammonium groups attached to their terminal carbon atoms and a series of such compounds was therefore synthesized. It was in fact found that the member of the series in which the terminal groups were separated by ten carbon atoms (as is the case in tubocurarine) had a powerful muscle relaxing effect superficially mimicking that of the alkaloid, although, curiously enough, detailed physiological analysis showed later that the effect was produced by a different mechanism.

More interesting results attended the examination of the lower members of the series, for it was found that those with five and six carbon atoms were powerful ganglion-blocking agents and thus had the effect of lowering the blood pressure; these two simple compounds could in fact be used thera-peutically and they were so to speak the founder members of the group of methonium drugs that provided the first effective drug treatment of hypertension in man.

In recent years the interest of the Division of Physiology and Pharmacology of the Institute has shifted largely to the central nervous system, a new approach to the pharmacology of which has been developed as the result of the discovery of a method of studying the action of drugs applied to the inside of the brain. In addition, a considerable research has developed jointly with the Division of Biochemistry, on biologically active peptides.

Chemotherapy

At the time when the Institute was opened the only effective chemotherapy, apart from the centuries-old treatment of malaria with quinine, consisted of the treatment of syphilis with organic arsenicals. There was indeed a feeling of defeatism about the prospect of effective drug treatment of infections other than those caused by protozoa and perhaps metazoa (for example helminths) and this persisted until the

84

discovery of the sulphonamides followed by that of the anti-biotics. For a country with the extensive overseas responsibilities that Great Britain carried forty years ago, however, infections by protozoa and helminths provided a sufficiency of medical problems to justify an effort by the Medical Research Council; this was the more so in that chemotherapeutic research as then understood was not a subject likely to attract attention in university laboratories, nor had the modern pharmaceutical industries that have since made great contributions in the form of new chemotherapeutic drugs made more than a beginning with their research developments.

In the early days of the Institute chemotherapeutic research was pursued along the conventional lines of testing organic compounds for their action on experimental infections in animals, with little or nothing in the way of biological clues to guide the search in a profitable direction. Although research of this kind at the Institute met with no greater success in proportion to the effort devoted to it than did similar research elsewhere, it nevertheless undoubtedly influenced the course of later studies in other laboratories which produced some of the successful antimalarial drugs that are in common use today; moreover in another field it led to the development of the amidine drugs which are still the best treatment for kala-azar. More important, however, than the direct search for new drugs were the attempts to explain the mode of chemotherapeutic action of those already known, and in this matter some useful progress was made.

In recent years, as the result of a deliberate policy decision, the whole approach to chemotherapeutic research in the Institute has been re-orientated. Little effort is spent in the direct unguided search for new drugs and much more emphasis is laid on studies of the biological aspects of the subject. Chemical work is still undertaken, but so far as possible on the basis of biological clues. Research is carried out on the metabolic behaviour of infective micro-organisms in the hope of revealing promising directions of chemotherapeutic attack, and the considerable effort that is devoted by the bacterial physiologists in the Institute to the study of induced enzyme formation in bacteria is directly relevant to the problem of drug resistance, the development of which constitutes the chief obstacle to successful chemotherapy. Here again therefore the attempt to advance the subject depends not on the effort of a single specialized group of workers but on the combination of the efforts of several groups, each having a different approach.

Virology

The growth of the subject of virology as it is understood to-day is contemporaneous with the history of the Institute, and it was here that some of the important early discoveries in virology were made; mention may be made in particular of the isolation of the virus of dog distemper, followed by that of influenza. The first studies of virology were undertaken by men with training in pathology and bacteriology, as was natural at a time when the subject was regarded as an extension of bacteriology; it soon became apparent, however, that further progress required the use of new physical and optical techniques; the requirements of virologists provided in fact the stimulus for the early development of membrane filtration as a measure of particle size and of ultra-violet microscopy, as in recent years virology has offered one of the most profitable fields for the biological application of electron microscopy. Moreover the interplay between virological and biochemical research has become very close; such a discovery as that of interferon, recently made in the Institute, although arising from purely biological considerations could not have been properly pursued without the application of biochemical methods, whilst conversely a viral infection of cells has provided a system that has proved of great value for the biochemical study of protein synthesis. A history of the continuous research in virology that has been carried out in the Institute over the past forty years would afford many other illustrations of these points.

Apart from work on the more academic aspects of virology attention is paid in the Institute to virological problems of more direct practical importance; mention may be made in particular of the long-continued research on the common cold, and of studies of the arthropod-borne viruses which are the cause of much illness in tropical countries.

Biochemistry

At the present time the Division of Biochemistry is one of the largest in the Institute; this is the result not only of the growth of biochemistry as a scientific subject in its own right but of the ever-increasing impact of biochemistry on all aspects of medical and biological research.

So far as the Division itself is concerned the centre of interest, as in so many biochemical laboratories throughout the world, lies in the general problem of biosynthesis of protein, but the tentacles of biochemistry penetrate into a large proportion of the scientific activities of the whole institution.

Mention has already been made of the growing importance of biochemistry to virology. Similarly the essentially biological subject of immunology, interest in which has increased greatly in recent years and which has now been recognized as a major activity in the Institute by the establishment of an independent division, depends in many of its aspects on biochemical thought and technique. Biochemistry grew in part out of physiology and still impinges on this subject at many points; as an example we may recall the work of the last few years, and which is still proceeding in the Institute, on biologically active peptides. This could only be done by the close co-operation of physiologists and biochemists. Chemotherapy is profoundly dependent on biochemistry, through the study of metabolic function, enzymic constitution and structure of micro-organisms. Other examples could be given, but sufficient has been said to indicate the key position that biochemistry has attained in medical research and which it seems likely to hold.

Environmental Physiology

Most of the work of the Institute that has so far been mentioned consists of long-term research projects, undertaken with no immediate practical objective in view but with the faith that increase in scientific knowledge will inevitably lead to results of practical benefit. Examples of such results, some obvious and some less obvious, are not wanting.

Research is, however, also undertaken in fields where the problem is clearly defined and answers to questions of immediate practical importance are required. This type of research is well illustrated by the work of the Division of Human Physiology. The objective of the work, defined in the broadest terms, is to study the reaction of man to his environment. In practice the questions to which answers are most frequently required relate to the effects of alterations in environmental conditions on human performance; these questions are of obvious importance to the Armed Forces, whose members may be called upon at short notice to operate in climates to which they are totally unaccustomed, and to civilian workers whose efficiency may be greatly influenced by the suitability or otherwise of the environmental conditions in which they carry out their tasks.

The execution of the work requires first of all the development of methods for the quantitative measurement of the performance which it is desired to assess and secondly the availability of facilities for practical tests, first under defined artificially produced conditions, and later under the conditions actually prevailing in the office, factory or field. The Division of Human Physiology is provided with climatic chambers in which conditions either of heat or cold extending to the limits of human endurance can be produced; the staff of the Division also take such opportunities as arise, either in the course of expeditions or in service field trials to test the validity of the laboratory observations under natural conditions. In this way a wealth of factual knowledge and experience is acquired which should not only improve present conditions but which should provide the necessary basic information to deal with environmental problems of the future.

It is of interest to observe that although the questions to be answered by this type of research appear at first sight to be simple they seldom turn out to be so when more closely examined, and in the course of their practical solution inexplicable facts are revealed which invite examination. Thus we find the reverse of what is the normal situation in the Institute, in that an investigation undertaken with an immediate practical objective may lead back into paths of basic research.

Official responsibilities

The Medical Research Council undertake certain official responsibilities, on the international level for the World Health Organization and at the national level for the Ministry of Health. These responsibilities relating to standards and control of therapeutic substances and to the epidemiology of influenza are discharged through the Institute.

Standards and control. In contradistinction to chemical drugs, the purity of which can be defined in chemical and physical terms, there are an increasing number of therapeutic substances of biological origin which have to be assayed by intrinsically variable biological tests and whose activity can therefore only be defined in terms of a standard preparation. The Division of Biological Standards has the responsibility for the preparation, assay, custody and distribution of International Standards of all such biological therapeutic agents (other than serological products). The work does not involve a large organization because members of the scientific staff of the Institute, outside the Division of Biological Standards, assist with work on standards of which they have special knowledge; moreover it combines well with pharmacological or immunological research, to which indeed the standards are themselves important.

Control. The control of biological therapeutic substances in this country is exercised by the Ministry of Health under the provisions of the Therapeutic Substances Act, and the role of the Division of Biological Standards is to maintain the standard preparations as described above and to advise on the formulation of regulations governing individual preparations. Actual laboratory control is not usually called for, being rendered unnecessary by the system of inspection and licensing of manufacturers by the Ministry of Health and by the close relations maintained between the Division of Biological Standards of the Institute and the scientific staffs of the manufacturing organizations.

These circumstances do not, however, hold good for antiviral vaccines, such as poliomyelitis vaccine, and a new Division of Immunological Products Control has recently been formed within the Institute which has the responsibility on behalf of the Ministry of Health of checking by actual laboratory studies the safety and potency of all manufactured batches of antiviral vaccine.

World Influenza Centre. The World Influenza Centre is a laboratory established on behalf of the World Health Organization within the Division of Virus Research. The work consists of the maintenance of type strains of influenza virus with the aid of which strains isolated from new outbreaks of the disease may be rapidly identified; such strains are sent to the World Influenza Centre for identification by corresponding laboratories in other countries. The objects of the work are to maintain a continuing general study of the epidemiology of influenza, to facilitate the production of appropriate vaccine by early identification of a strain causing a spreading epidemic and to keep a watch for the appearance of a strain of unusual virulence.

Similar reference work is now being undertaken on viruses that cause other respiratory diseases and on arthropod-borne viruses.

ORGANIZATION

The stated purpose of this volume being to describe the organization of research institutes, it may well seem strange that the word organization has so far scarcely been mentioned. In point of fact it is right that this should be so, since it has hitherto been an accepted principle, so far as the National Institute for Medical Research is concerned, that the sole purpose of administrative organization is to provide the most favourable conditions possible for scientific work and that any extension beyond this purpose is deleterious. This being so it has seemed better to allow the picture of the organization to emerge through a description of the development and work of the Institute before proceeding to a brief discussion of the actual administrative arrangements.

The description of the work of the Institute that has been given is of course no more than a sketchy outline and highly selective at that. Apart from the sections, included for the sake of completing the picture, on the more practically orientated research in environmental physiology and on work involving official responsibilities, the selection has been made with one object; this is to emphasize the great part that collaborative efforts between workers in different fields have played and continue to play in the work of the Institute. The joint efforts of physiologists, pharmacologists and chemists over many years leading to great advances in neurophysiology and eventually to the practical outcome of the methonium drugs, the combination of chemists, parasitologists and microbiologists in chemotherapeutic research, the dependence of virological work on help from physicists and biochemists, the way in which biochemists find themselves drawn into a variety of research problems outside their own sectional interest—all these illustrate the point that is being made.

Although the limitations of space have made the selection a narrow one, it must not be supposed that the examples chosen are unrepresentative. There are many other researches that are remembered as achievements of which the Institute may be proud and which provide evidence in the same direction. The work that led to the isolation and identification of calciferol, the contributions to knowledge of the sex hormones, the studies of the biology of hypothermia, the discovery of a new thyroid hormone, the production of permanent diabetes by hormonal means—each of these is properly associated with the names of one or two people who were the initiators; it is fair to say, however, that a retrospective glance will show that in every case the development of the work owed much to help from colleagues in other fields, some of which were far removed from the original investigation.

The organization of the Institute is therefore planned (1) to provide the most favourable background for the work of the institution as a whole and (2) to make it not only possible but easy for collaborative work to develop between any members of the staff who see profit in combining their efforts. To this end the formal administrative arrangements are as follows:

The Director is responsible to the Medical Research Council for the overall operation of the Institute. Under him the scientific and technical staffs are grouped into fourteen divisions of which nine are occupied with full time scientific research, two carry some official responsibility in addition to research, one is primarily concerned with control and two are principally service divisions (Table 3). At the head of each scientific division is a man appointed to the Council's scientific staff for his ability in the field of work that it is desired to pursue; the work of the divisions is naturally much

Table 3. Divisions of the National Institute for Medical Research

Research	Research & Official Work	Control & Research	Service & Development
Bacterial Physiology	Bacteriology and Virus Research	Immunological Products Control	Engineering
Biochemistry	Biological Standards		Laboratory Animals
Biophysics			
Chemotherapy & Parasitology			
Experimental Biology			
Human Physiology			
Immunology			
Organic Chemistry			
Physiology & Pharmacology			
Special laboratories:			
Cytopathology			
Human Biomechanics			

coloured by the interests of the men who lead them, but a large measure of freedom in choice of research projects is enjoyed by the more senior members of the scientific staff.

All matters, whether scientific or personal, relating to the scientific staff are dealt with in the Director's own office; as are also matters concerning the staff of the library and the divisional secretaries.

Reporting to the Director are a Finance Officer and a Personnel Officer, each with their own deputies and secretarial staff. The Finance Officer is responsible for accounting, purchasing and preparation of estimates for consideration by the Director, together with the management of the stores and maintenance of the inventory of equipment. The Personnel Officer takes charge of the day-to-day matters concerning the technical, maintenance and estate staff; he is also responsible for the general housekeeping of the Institute.

The Superintendent of the Works Division is responsible for maintenance of the buildings and fixed equipment and reports to the Director thereon.

This simple system (Fig. 9) therefore constitutes the framework of the administrative arrangements within the Institute and it will be observed that it is designed to keep the Director in the closest possible touch with all branches of the work of the institution, in the hope that this may have a unifying effect on the overall effort.

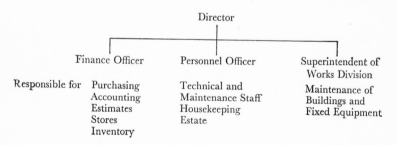

Figure 9

National Institute for Medical Research administration.

Institute for Medical Research

The provision of an appropriate administrative framework is, however, only the first step towards the collaborative method of working that is aimed at. The natural tendency towards segregation of special interests and lines of work in a large research institute is strong and has to be continuously guarded against. The first safeguard against this tendency is acceptance of the principle, which is insisted upon, that the grouping of scientific staff into divisions is little more than an administrative convenience. It is necessary for the orderly operation of the institution; it is advantageous in that appropriate groupings accelerate advances in the different branches of the work; it is entirely deleterious if it is allowed to induce a sense of scientific self-sufficiency.

Wide dissemination of information about the scientific work that is going on in the institution as a whole is another means of preventing intellectual isolation; attempts are made to achieve this in the Institute by two methods. In the first place frequent colloquia are held at which all members of the scientific staff are invited to hear and discuss an account by one of their colleagues of his current research. Secondly, at less frequent intervals, open days are held by the divisions; on such days the whole technical staff are invited to hear a general talk from the Head of the Division on the work going on in the laboratories under his care and are shown appropriate demonstrations; the scientific work of the Division is also fully displayed for inspection by any member of the scientific staff who wishes to see it.

With such facilities available therefore there is no reason why any member of the staff should remain in ignorance of what is going on outside his own division; it is indeed from the proper use of these facilities and out of the discussions to which they give rise that interdivisional research interests may grow and, with good fortune, lead to joint research projects; the existence of such joint efforts in the actual conduct of research is the third and most powerful influence that can be brought to bear against scientific insularity.

Organization of Research Establishments

It seems obvious that the only justification for the existence of a research institute is that it should constitute a scientific instrument more effective as a whole than would be the sum of its separate parts. The gathering of a number of scientific groups under one roof with common services will not alone achieve this end. The object of the simple administrative framework of the National Institute for Medical Research and of the other measures of organization that have been adopted there is to ensure that so far as possible the institution should work as a corporate body rather than as an assemblage of disparate groups of scientific experts. The quality of the scientific work of a research institute clearly rests primarily on the talents of its scientific staff; these talents may, however, be stunted or may expand according to the conditions of the work. It is the function of organization to make these conditions as favourable as may be; all that is claimed for the system that has been described is that it represents one approach towards this end which has had some measure of success.

6

THE MEDICAL RESEARCH COUNCIL SOCIAL PSYCHIATRY RESEARCH UNIT

by Professor Sir Aubrey Lewis, M.D., F.R.C.P.

Psychiatric research extends over a very large field. Since psychiatry is concerned with disorders of human behaviour, its investigation must rest on psychology and the social sciences generally. Since it is also concerned with the pathology of mental disease and the changes in the body which can affect behaviour, its study must depend on the biological and physical sciences which provide the basis for medical research. The roll call of its fundamental sciences is therefore almost absurdly long—anthropology, sociology, psychology, physiology, pathology, genetics, epidemiology, biochemistry, pharmacology. In each there are conventional subdivisions especially relevant to the problems of mental disorder—most such subdivisions have to do with the workings of the nervous system. In psychology the relevant subdivisions are, of course, particularly numerous; they include social, developmental and comparative psychology as well as the psychology of perception, thinking, personality, and learning and motivation.

Obviously no institute can compass the whole range of potential fields of research applied to psychiatry. This sort of limitation holds good for medical research generally; but psychiatry, at its present stage of development, cannot pretend to the same confidence about which are rewarding and which are barren fields for it to till as has been securely attained in many other branches of medical research. Consequently there is an extensive, weakly patterned mosaic of methods; the divisions between them are apt to be blurred, as is suggested by such terms as 'psycho-pharmacology' 'physiological-psychology' and 'neuro-endocrinology'.

In any one institute, because of the manifest futility of trying to be comprehensive, there is concentration on one line of research (for example, the biochemical), or workers trained in diverse basic sciences attack relatively small psychiatric problems. Although it may be true to say of a particular research centre that it is engaged in large 'multi-disciplined' study of schizophrenia, in practice this usually means, not that a number of diversely equipped investigators are busy on the same precisely formulated problem but that by methods as different, say, as those of pharmacology and educational psychology, varied aspects of schizophrenia (such as anomalies of reaction time and of fantasy-formation) are being examined, sometimes in conjunction, sometimes independently. Progress in settling one narrowly defined question may have to wait until technical or theoretical problems in a different area of discourse have been disposed of: thus an epidemiological inquiry into the prevalence of obsessional neurosis, or into the association between arterial hypertension and emotional abnormality may be held up while means are being devised for making the necessary measurements and diagnoses reliably, or for ascertaining the social and psychological factors that characterize the background, and determine the accessibility to study, of the population under scrutiny.

A research institute in psychiatry needs two kinds of contact: with a hospital, and with a university. Its contact with a hospital is essential because illness provides the stimulus and the testing ground for study of its crucial problems; the further the research gets from recognizable bearing on clinical issues, the less justified is its location in a psychiatric institute and the less intimate will be its link with mental illness. Moreover, clinical research cannot be conducted without observations on patients made under controlled conditions such as a hospital affords; and the phenomena of illness constantly suggest questions to the mind of a trained and inquiring observer which can be the starting point for a fruitful investigation.

The research institute's contact with a university is necessary in order that it may be able to attract men who as undergraduates have shown their capacity and promise—psychiatric research has suffered in the past from its relative failure to attract first rate people. It must also have access to workshops, libraries, computing, and other services rarely available on a large scale to isolated research centres; and it needs the spur of extraneous criticism, intellectual forays, and uncovenanted reinforcements to its stock of ideas and methods.

The attainment of satisfactory contacts and alliances entails a rather complex structure. This is illustrated by the relation of the Social Psychiatry Research Unit to the Institute of Psychiatry and to the Maudsley Hospital, in whose building it is located. The Research Unit is maintained by the Medical Research Council; the Institute of Psychiatry is maintained by the University of London; the Maudsley Hospital, jointly with Bethlem Royal Hospital, is maintained by the Ministry of Health. The Honorary Director of the Research Unit is the Professor of Psychiatry in the Institute, who also, as Honorary Physician, has charge of beds in the hospital. There are, on the staff of the unit, besides the Director, four psychiatrists: three of these have honorary clinical appointments on the staff of the hospital, giving them access to patients, and the other has a similar appointment to the Regional Board of the area of South Wales, where he is conducting his investigations. Psychologists and other senior scientific members of the Unit are Honorary Lecturers in the Institute, and supervise Ph.D. students occupied with research in the Unit. Members of the Unit use the same refectory and common rooms and library as the staff of the Institute and of the Hospital.

THE M.R.C. SOCIAL PSYCHIATRY UNIT

Though the main aims of the Unit cannot be defined in terms of method or precise subject-matter, there is a general understanding that it seeks to elucidate the social causes and the social effects of mental abnormality, and the application of social influences to treatment. Within so wide a field, only restricted areas could be cultivated: delinquency, psychopathic personality, group psychotherapy, drug addiction, marital problems and other important aspects of social psychiatry have not been studied in the Unit (though some of these are studied in the Institute). In the first few years after its establishment industrial problems dealing with the relation between neurosis and working efficiency were among the main interests of the Unit, and led to a sub-group hiving off temporarily to do field work in Manchester, where suitable opportunities offered for study in factories; but in 1954 this line of inquiry was brought to an end, in order that work more intimately related to psychiatry might be pursued. Whereas in the first six years mental deficiency was the form of abnormality focused on, in the succeeding years schizophrenia has been likewise made a primary concern of the Unit; and in the period now beginning, the social problems of abnormal development in children will become a cardinal interest.

Social studies of the kind the Unit undertakes make it necessary to put up with the disadvantages of having to establish sub-groups, or outliers, pursuing a semi-independent existence. Having decided that we wanted to compare psychiatric morbidity in two areas that would be geographically near each other but socially diverse, we found that this could best be done in South Wales, where another unit of the Medical Research Council had made valuable socio-medical investigations and established confidence between investigators and the population studied. As the general conditions for an epidemiological approach to the psychiatric problems seemed so satisfactory in these areas of South Wales, a pilot study was made from which it was concluded that the mining area differed significantly from the agricultural area in respect of several indices of maladjustment or illness. On the strength of these preliminaries, a detachment from the Unit went there and for the last five years has been working in the two districts collecting social, psychological and clinical data. Contact with the parent unit is maintained chiefly by discussion with the Director and attendance at Unit colloquia, at which progress is reported and problems examined.

The setting up of an outlying group in another part of the country is a serious matter both for the work of the Unit, and for the staff members affected. They have to move house, change their children's place of education, and forge new academic and personal links without being assured that this will be their permanent place of work. Hence the need for pilot surveys and much consideration before such a policy is adopted, and then only if there is a practical certainty that the work of the outliers will continue for a period of years, sufficient to justify the personal upheavals entailed.

A body such as the Social Psychiatry Unit cannot expect to be able to make opportunities; it must contrive to avail itself of opportunities as they arise. It is, for example, impossible to prevail upon so complex an organization as a mental hospital to alter its admission and discharge policies, its nursing practices, or its therapeutic procedures at a given time, to oblige research workers. During the last decade, however, a minor revolution has occurred in the mental hospitals in this country—and to some extent elsewhere—leading to striking changes in these matters of policy and treatment. To investigate the social causes and social effect of the changes required some prevision of where they would take place and some diplomatic approaches to those in charge so that the state of affairs before the reforms could be assessed by the same methods and observers as the aftermath would be. Similarly, advantage was taken of a fortuitous chance to study the impact of social change, when the people of Tristan da Cunha were brought to England after the destruction of their isolated home by the volcano. In 1937 a group of Norwegians had made extensive medical and social observations on the islanders, in the course of which a curious epidemic of hysteria had been recorded in detail, with particulars about each affected individual. The ground had thus been prepared for a comparative study showing how these and other members of the island community reacted to the separation from their tiny rock, with its bare and primitive means of subsistence, its enforced intimacy and narrow range, and their introduction to the complexities of modern urban life in Southern England.

Whereas research in the natural sciences is largely carried out in the laboratory, social research must be carried out in society and psychological research must be carried out in part on human beings where they congregate. Studies of the mentally ill and the mentally defective can most conveniently be conducted in the hospitals where they are cared for; the ward becomes a laboratory for the clinical investigator. No single institute can be depended on to provide or collect the numbers of patients and kinds of illness which the research worker may need for a particular social or psychological inquiry. The Research Unit has therefore had to make use of the resources of a considerable number of mental hospitals and institutions: though this arrangement entails some restraints and more than usual discretion, since the research worker is a privileged guest in the hospital, it has worked well. In many cases the hospital has not only willingly given the necessary access to patients and clinical data but has set up a psychological laboratory or a workshop which was required for the experiments, and members of the hospital staff have taken an active share in the investigations. This would not have been achieved if the research workers had been maladroit or unmindful of their permissive footing in the hospital—a minor but not trivial consideration in choosing staff for such studies.

For its studies in mental deficiency the Unit has taken the defective person as a member of society, and examined the ways in which he is excluded, accommodated or accepted. His ability to learn has been studied in educational and workshop experiments, paying regard to his working potential, his ability to support himself, his handicaps and personality, and the effect of various teaching methods based on psychological analysis of his abilities and limitations. How social and psychological attitudes affect his care was the object of an extensive field study in which the situation in the families of severely subnormal persons who had been admitted to an institution was compared with that of families who kept their handicapped relative at home, in spite of all the minor and major stresses this could occasion: the subnormal *propositi* in the two groups were approximately the same in intelligence level and social class. For this study a sociologist who had had the specialized training of a psychiatric social worker was an invaluable member of the Unit; for the studies of learning capacity, psychologists who had an intimate acquaintance with the experimental approach to cognitive attainment were needed. Since, however, the borders between the social sciences, and divisions within particular social sciences, are loose and arbitrary, the psychologist is not so specialized that he cannot turn from studies of educational capacity to experiments in motivation, say, nor is the sociologist so attached to the theory and methods of his subject that he is unfamiliar with the psychological procedures requisite for validating a personality inventory, standardizing a test, or ascertaining social attitudes. Psychiatrist, psychologist and sociologist adapt themselves to the varying complexion of the Unit's interest, though of course the more expert member will be appealed to by the rest for advice and assistance when they get into the higher reaches of the relevant discipline, just as they turn to the statistician when something less within their competence than *t* tests, chi-square and simple analysis of variance is called for. It is then also that the advantages of close association with the university may be most evident and most availed of.

For the study of chronic schizophrenia—the most serious and obscure of mental illnesses—which has been a major concern of the Unit, intensive investigation of small numbers of patients has run *pari passu* with analysis of the social factors and clinical history of large groups. For the former, very detailed records, such as those of the Maudsley Hospital, were requisite, and for the latter systematic observations made over many years in the mental hospitals where most patients with inveterate schizophrenia are to be found. The collaboration of an industrial rehabilitation centre had to be obtained, in order that controlled experiments in the rehabilitation of these patients might be carried out.

Since schizophrenia is a subject of incessant inquiry and is the most widespread of incapacitating mental disorders, it might be assumed that it is easy to assemble any number of patients for a particular investigation, and that the techniques for measuring the severity of their symptoms have been fully developed. It is not so. Available numbers are quickly reduced when the investigators have to eliminate patients who are outside a given age-range, or have a complicating physical disease, or are receiving a special form of treatment, or absolutely refusing to co-operate: therefore for some studies the population of several mental hospitals has to be drawn on. Measuring the severity of the illness raises many problems; in certain cardinal areas of function it has turned out to be a research undertaking in itself, which the Unit had to carry through in conjunction with psychological studies of reaction-time and work-curve. These, in turn, have led to the experimental study of problems in perception, arousal and communication.

Social Psychiatry Research Unit

If a unit is to deserve its name, the members of the scientific staff must have common interests, but it is almost inevitable that their lines of work will tend to diverge as the years go by. It is legitimate and in the nature of research that individuals will follow their bent, but the so-called unit can become a loose association of people busily engaged in centrifugal movement if the individuals feel no obligation towards a common or central undertaking. Different units obviously handle the problem in very different ways, according to their purposes and stage of development, and the achievements and personalities of their members. In this Unit there has been a steady effort at compromise: it is recognized that X and Y are specially concerned with certain approaches to the study of mental subnormality, while A and B are absorbed with their interests in certain problems of chronic schizophrenia, and C and D have still other chosen lines of inquiry; but it is also recognized that they must contribute to the common pool of experience and ideas and techniques in the Unit, and that though their investigations may for a time lead away from direct or discernible bearing on psychiatric problems, it is highly desirable that they should return. A kindred difficulty, familiar in most clinical units, is that of the medical worker who needs to keep abreast of clinical advances in his field: he is afraid he may grow rusty and out-of-date if he gives up all clinical work, and that he will in consequence be of less value to the unit, *qua* clinical worker, or that he will later find it difficult to revert to a clinical career, or take up an academic clinical appointment, if he should wish to; or, strongest reason of all, he may like clinical work with patients as much as he likes research, and so he deplores any necessity to choose between them. To meet these legitimate wishes the psychiatrists of the Unit have obtained honorary appointments as Consultants or Senior Registrars and spend a small proportion of their week (say, an afternoon) 'keeping their hand in' clinically: this is distinct from the clinical work they may require to do in the course of their research and as part of it. Similarly one of the psychiatrists of the Unit had a particular interest in the psychopathology and morbid consequences of grief; he was given facilities for pursuing this study, alongside his main investigations into problems with which the Unit had been busy before he joined it, but since his departure the theme of grief-reaction has not been pursued.

The Unit has no committees of any kind. Informal discussions and colloquia have served its need. Guests who come to the Unit, visitors, attached workers staying for a year or more—for example Fulbright scholars and post-graduates from abroad—contribute to the lively exchange of ideas and methods, which is also furthered by visits to workers in related fields elsewhere. Arrangements are flexible. A recent appointment to the Unit was of a psychiatrist who has a dual attachment to this Unit and to the M.R.C. Unit at the London School of Economics; another psychiatrist in the Unit is responsible for teaching psychiatric aspects of social medicine and public health at the London School of Hygiene.

The Director of the Unit is Professor of Psychiatry in the Institute. His duties as a Clinical Professor necessarily make such demands on time and thought that he can obviously not play the same part in the work of the Unit as a director can who has no other calls upon him. Since he is therefore less intimately involved in the day-to-day work of the Unit than a whole time director is, it might be supposed that an honorary director of this sort tends to become a passenger in the research coach, or a fifth wheel, or even a drag. No doubt this can happen, and no honorary director will be the right person to judge whether it has happened in his own case. He has to make the best adjustments he can to his varied opportunities and obligations, which are in one sense competing, in another complementary. The research unit becomes an extension, perhaps the major part, of the research activities of the department for which he is responsible, and the wisdom of the dual appointment will be tested, not by judging whether the director is deploying his time and abilities in the proper proportions and the right directions, but by the liveliness and quality of the research.

In a subject still at an early stage of development, as psychiatry is, issues of scientific policy elsewhere taken for granted are subjects of vigorous controversy, and the Director may have to take difficult decisions on whether to relax scientific rigour. As Thorpe has recently said 'we all want greater precision and better design of experiment; but psychology is not physics, and if we pretend that the methods of physics, and only the methods of physics, are adequate for the study of behaviour we shall miss much of vital importance to the subject. Indeed to restrict ourselves completely in this respect would be obviously stultifying.' This is an acceptable statement, but its application in psychiatric research comes up against risks and uncertainties that await anyone who forsakes safe roads for bypaths notoriously beset with pitfalls. Psychoanalytic findings and concepts illustrate the difficulty: they have exerted a powerful influence on psychiatric theory and practice but are insusceptible of validation by controlled experiment and other procedures which have been the sheet anchor of research in the natural sciences. Psychoanalytic methods are being used in some centres of psychiatric research: but in the Social Psychiatry Unit they are not. It seemed that findings arrived at by these methods were too uncertain to be depended upon for the kinds of inquiry with which the Unit has been occupied. Where experiments could not be carried out, empirical observations have been resorted to and found fruitful.

The selection of staff (including technical and clerical workers) is, as always, crucial. The field is not large from which one can choose. It is easy to list desiderata, and hard to devise and apply criteria for those that matter most. Academic attainments, publications, relevant experience, interest in the problems the Unit studies, and personality attributes are weighed as carefully as they can be, and a man of proved capacity presents no problem: but no one knows better than the psychologist and the psychiatrist that selection is often a chancy, intuitive affair.

The medical members of the Unit need to have had a good clinical training in psychiatry; they want it for full appreciation of the facets of whatever psychiatric problems they are investigating, and for direct observation of patients. But psychiatric training alone will not be sufficient (unless they are juniors only temporarily engaged in the research). They require also an adequate familiarity with the subject matter and methods of sociology or anthropology or psychology. This they gain, in most cases, by tenure of one of the Clinical Research Fellowships of the Medical Research Council, or a Travelling Fellowship from the Council, the Nuffield Foundation, or a university: in rare instances they have attended the necessary courses or participated in relevant research before they took up medicine. The question is often asked: which is better, to take the clinician and give him a scientific training say, in biochemistry or psychology; or to take a biochemist or a psychologist—or a biologist or geneticist or pharmacologist—and help him to get a medical training appropriate to his field of research? Instances of both, and advantages in each, can readily be pointed out, but the former is the commoner route. Some medical schools and particularly some teachers foster in their students a habit of mind, in the face of clinical and scientific problems, which leads to their steady development into research workers of undeniable capacity. It has proved a sound policy in the Social Psychiatry Unit, to choose men from among the psychiatrists who have been at the Maudsley Hospital for several years and whose training, interests and abilities are therefore pretty well known, and to ensure that at suitable stages in their post-graduate career they will be helped towards requisite further training in some scientific field either at the Institute or elsewhere. Of course, sometimes a

Social Psychiatry Research Unit

man who seems suited to such a career decides that he prefers
to engage in clinical work and teaching, and he is therefore lost
to research; but it can be argued that his heart was evidently
not in research anyway, and that the dividing line between
the whole-time research worker and the man who combines
day-to-day clinical work with teaching and perhaps a
modicum of research should not be hard and fast. At all
events it has been possible to find among the psychiatrists
in training at the Institute a series of men who have made
psychiatric research their main concern. It is probably
superfluous to remark that whereas junior members of the
Unit receive much supervision and guidance, the senior
members have a high degree of autonomy. Thus a psychologist who has been a member of the staff since the Unit was
set up has recently received with the blessing of the Council a
large grant from a foundation for a five-year study of
various problems of institutional care for handicapped
children: this, under the administrative wing of the Council,
will enable him to conduct, substantially on his own responsibility, research which is closely relevant to the main business
of the Unit and supplements cognate lines of research which
he is pursuing in the Unit.

Through the M.R.C. Scholarships for training in research
young psychologists and sociologists are introduced to the
special problems and methods of psychiatry or of medicine
generally. Some psychologists come via the course of
preparation for the post-graduate Diploma in Abnormal
Psychology that is provided at the Institute. Another probable route of entry will be through the new unit set up at
the London School of Economics for the study of environmental factors in mental and physical illness.

One of the outstanding advantages of a research unit is its
assurance of continuity: a programme of research can be
worked out which will cover a period of years, in contrast
to projects supported by *ad hoc* grants which may have a short
life. This is clearly of prime importance in studying chronic

diseases and social change. Many of the inquiries with which the Unit has been concerned, in respect of mental deficiency and schizophrenia, would not have been embarked upon, or if undertaken could not have been brought to any useful stage, if there had not been this sort of stability in the research programme—which serves moreover to offset the delays and upsets which may arise when a key member of a small unit leaves it for another post. Since, however, the research programme looks ahead for some years, particularly where the effect of social change is to be observed, commitment to a mistaken plan can be very wasteful: the corrective has been by way of the pilot study. Without pilot studies there would have been much misconceived effort, and where the pilot study has been skipped or skimped in a social investigation there has mostly been subsequent cause for regret. The time schedule for some psychological experiments has been different: here faulty design may be corrigible in good time, and there is less occasion for wringing the hands over lost opportunities (as when measurements later recognized to be indispensable were not made during the first phase of a continuous socio-clinical study of patients with schizophrenia).

The optimum size for a unit is dictated by its aims, stage of development, and degree of integration. Psychiatry has such diverse problems that a large research unit could turn into a comprehensive institute with little to account for the juxtaposition of strangely assorted departments. A Research Unit, properly so called and set up with a special aim—in this case to study the social aspects of mental disorder—is too big if the members do not meet easily and often, and know what each other is doing. The Social Psychiatry Unit has been small enough to keep local administrative arrangements to a minimum. There are fifteen members of the scientific staff, besides six post-graduate scholars and attached workers, and nine technical and clerical staff.

The growth and size of the Unit has been inevitably

influenced by the activities of the Institute of Psychiatry, with which it lives in comfortable symbiosis. It was desirable at the time when the Unit was established by the Medical Research Council, to give distinct support to the advancement of a branch of research that had been neglected by the majority of psychiatric investigators. Since then the situation has changed greatly for the better; the recent increase in epidemiological inquiries attests the altered outlook. As social studies get a firmer footing in the universities and strengthen their theoretical foundations, the impetus towards applying them to throw light on the dark places in psychiatric etiology and prevention will no doubt become still more powerful. This would not remove the need for strong support for such studies by the research councils, but it would make it reasonable to incorporate much of the work now being done by the special unit into the regular activities of the Institute. It is therefore relevant to consider briefly the structure and work of the Institute, which is very largely occupied with research.

The Institute comprises professorial departments not only of psychiatry but also of its main basic sciences—psychology, neurophysiology, biochemistry, neuropathology, and experimental neurology. Within the departments (which vary considerably in their amount of responsibility for teaching and clinical services) there are subdivisions: in the Department of Psychiatry these are concerned with research in pharmacology, endocrinology, metabolism, and epidemiology as applied to psychiatry. There is, located in the grounds of the Institute, also a Medical Research Council Unit in Psychiatric Genetics. Collaboration between departments in research is common, especially where direct observations on patients are necessary or where quite diverse methods need to be deployed, as in 'psycho-pharmacological' studies of the behaviour of experimental animals receiving various drugs.

A large part of the income of the Institute (40 per cent.)

comes from research funds: sixty per cent. of this derives from British, forty per cent. from American sources. It is obviously an unhealthy state of affairs when so much of the work of an institute predominantly concerned in research depends on short-term grants and when barely two-thirds of the budget of a university institute comes from the university. But in the current predicament, unfortunately familiar in most academic centres of the United Kingdom, much research in the university would be hamstrung or crippled if it were not for the support of the research councils and the foundations. It will be disastrous if university resources are not before long made adequate to the work universities do. This applies not only to their funds for salaries and expenses but still more to the accommodation they can provide.

It may be expected that some, probably a large part, of the work and staff of the Research Unit will be absorbed into the Department of Psychiatry of the Institute within the next five or ten years. This measure (which would be in keeping with the general policy of the Medical Research Council) will not entail any radical readjustment or administrative dislocation since status, salaries and conditions of work in the Medical Research Council Unit and in the university are closely equated. Nor would it entail a lessening concentration on research because of the claims of teaching. It would, in large measure, confirm a relationship already well established, and fulfil aims which are as much those of the University Institute as they have been those of the Medical Research Council Unit.

7

THE AGRICULTURAL RESEARCH COUNCIL INSTITUTE OF ANIMAL PHYSIOLOGY, BABRAHAM

by SIR JOHN GADDUM, F.R.S.

The Agricultural Research Council (ARC) is a corporate body, established by royal charter, responsible to the Committee of Privy Council for Agricultural Research. It consists of not more than eighteen members, of whom three represent the Ministry of Agriculture, Fisheries and Food and one the Department of Agriculture and Fisheries for Scotland. The remaining members are appointed by the Committee of Privy Council for Agricultural Research. Of these, not more than five are selected on account of their knowledge of agriculture; and not less than nine are chosen, in consultation with the President of the Royal Society, for their eminence in one or other of the basic sciences underlying agriculture.

There are two Agricultural Improvement Councils—one for England and Wales and one for Scotland, which provide the formal means of bringing to the notice of the Council the problems of the industry and of handing on to the farmer the results of research, but the research workers are, of course, also in direct touch with farmers.

The Council's main functions are to review and facilitate research in progress and to promote new research. It is responsible for the oversight of research at 31 institutes.

Some of these, such as the ARC Institute of Animal Physiology, are directly administered and financed by the Council and others are controlled by governing bodies and receive annual grants from the Council covering the greater part of their expenditure.

The Council has set up a number of units, almost all of which are closely associated with universities, to provide distinguished university scientists who have established reputations in fields of science of potential interest to the Council with greater opportunities to develop their researches. The Council also makes a number of grants to support promising research projects and awards research studentships and training grants to honours graduates for training in research. A few fellowships are also awarded to enable young scientists of outstanding promise to undertake independent research.

The arrangement by which this independent Council is responsible for fundamental research in agriculture means that scientists who work for them are freer than most civil servants to study problems of general scientific interest.

During the last twenty years farming has become much more scientific than it was. For example, some farmers calculate their success in fattening animals in terms of the conversion factor, which is equal to the ratio of the weight of the food to the increase in the weight of the animals. The successful farmer must always be looking out for ways of reducing his cost and increasing his output. The farming journals, agricultural shows, and the Agricultural Improvement Councils provide information about new machinery, new fertilizers, new insecticides, new weedkillers and new ways of growing crops and multiplying stock. Such advances are the result of experiments in farms and laboratories the world over, but the practical farmer does experiments himself all the time to find out what suits his own conditions best. The experienced man, who gets a better crop, may know by instinct whether it was due to a new fertilizer or better weather or better seed, but, if he wants to be certain, and to convince others, he must arrange a controlled experiment, and this may be complicated by the fact that two plots of land are never quite the same as one another.

The design of this type of experiment occupied the attention of Sir Ronald Fisher at the Rothamstead Experimental Station in Hertfordshire for many years and the result has been an important advance in the general theory of experimental design. Many of the methods used by doctors to assess the results of trials of new drugs are based on methods developed at Rothamstead, so that medicine, together with other branches of knowledge, is indebted to agriculture for a new research tool. This is one example of the value of fundamental investigations. The best kind of scientist tries to add to the general stock of knowledge that is of value to all the sciences, although this may mean that the practical results of his work may be slow to come, and the credit will be shared with others. The Institute at Babraham is particularly concerned with fundamental problems, some of which have no obvious immediate application to agriculture.

HISTORY

The early history of the Institute has been recorded by its first Director, Dr I. de Burgh Daly (1957).* In 1945 the ARC decided that progress towards the improvement of animal health and production was impeded by the lack of knowledge of the fundamental physiology of farm animals. It was, therefore, decided to start a new institute to study these problems, with facilities for breeding, feeding and housing farm animals on a scale which would not be suitable for a university department. During the last few years of his life, Sir Joseph Barcroft was head of an ARC unit, which made fundamental discoveries about digestion in the rumen and the nutritional significance of short-chain fatty acids in the sheep. When Barcroft died in 1947, Daly became director

* *Proc. Roy. Soc. B.*, 146, 194–205.

of the unit and was asked to find a suitable site for an institute.

Babraham Hall and 450 acres of the surrounding land were purchased by the Council in August 1948. It is situated about six miles south east of Cambridge beyond the Gog Magog hills, near the place where the Roman Via Devana crossed the prehistoric Icknield Way, about 80–100 feet above sea level. The soil varies from deep loam to a light soil on gravel and chalk; the river Granta runs through the grounds. Babraham Hall had belonged to the Adeane family since it was built, between 1832 and 1837, but at least two earlier houses had stood on the same site. It is a solid building in the Jacobean style and houses the library, the administrative offices, the Director's flat, a hostel for ten junior workers and the refectory.

In the grounds there are five houses for the farm manager and some of his staff, three lodges and 38 other small houses in the area known as The Close. These are let to members of the staff and to visitors who come to work in the laboratories. The laboratories consist, at present, of single storey buildings scattered over a wide area. Some contain a pen in which animals can be kept during experiments, and other special facilities for work on large animals.

The operating theatre is well equipped and a hospital for operated animals is attached; it is in the charge of a trained nurse. There is also a larger building where operated sheep are kept, two buildings for small animals, and various other buildings, including a workshop. In 1961 a new laboratory was constructed, especially for experiments on the effects of climate on pigs.

STAFF

The total staff, including cleaners and labourers, numbers just over 200. There are, at present, about 40 graduates and this number is likely to increase slightly. There are about 55 technicians working directly with the scientists in the laboratories, and about 30 more working in central services, such as the workshops, photography, the animal houses, etc.

There are three main departments. The largest of these is the Physiology Department, which includes a subdepartment of Chemical Physiology. The Biochemistry Department was started by Sir Rudolph Peters after he had retired from the Chair of Biochemistry in Oxford. The Experimental Pathology Department was started by Sir Alan Drury, who had been Director of the Lister Institute in London. The Institute owes much to these two men, who were on the staff for five years and attracted a number of first class scientists to Babraham. There is also an independent Pharmacology Unit, formed to provide opportunities for one particular outstanding scientist. These divisions are not rigid and there is much collaboration between the different departments. About half of the graduates are senior scientists carrying out their own research, each of whom would like to have several junior workers under him. This need has been partly supplied by visitors, most of whom come with scholarships and training grants from abroad. There are generally over a dozen of these staying for a year or more, and others coming for shorter periods to learn techniques. There should be more young British scientists being trained at Babraham, where the facilities are in some ways unique, but there are difficulties. Newly qualified graduates commonly wish to acquire a Ph.D., but, except for those few who have been eligible to take external degrees from their own universities, it has proved difficult to arrange that work done at Babraham should count for a Ph.D., since the University of Cambridge regards Babraham as too far outside the city to be permitted to take research students for the Cambridge degree. This is particularly unfortunate since it deprives the senior staff of the stimulation that comes from contact with young people; certain members of the staff have left because they wanted more opportunity to teach. It also deprives newly qualified graduates of a good chance of learning to do research.

During the last ten years about ten graduates have left the Institute to work in universities, other official institutes and commercial laboratories. The recruitment of new staff to fill vacancies and to provide for expansion is not easy. The most important attraction is likely to be the scientific reputation of the Institute, and this takes time to build up. The opportunity is great, since equipment is rather good, experimental animals of all sizes are readily available, and the ratio of technicians to scientists is higher than in most universities. These attractions appeal to the scientist who is devoted to research but there is a danger that he may eventually suffer from lack of contact with students.

The recruitment of technicians is also difficult. Sometimes it is possible to offer a house in The Close and this may prove a powerful attraction. Young people join the staff as scientific assistants straight from school, having obtained the General Certificate of Education at the ordinary level. Promotion depends on passing this examination in two subjects at the advanced level, or on obtaining a degree, the Higher National Certificate, or some other similar qualification. Most of the younger technicians attend classes to work for the necessary examinations. This may mean that they are absent for as much as a whole day each week, and this interferes with the work of the Institute and means that the amount of technical assistance available is less than appears at first sight. On the other hand, it would be difficult to attract young people to work in the laboratories without this chance of advancement.

ADMINISTRATION

The details of the administration are in the hands of the Secretary, who is responsible for building and maintenance, the actual spending of the money granted by the ARC each year in the estimates, and the engagement of junior staff. The Laboratory Superintendent is responsible for the purchase of apparatus, the store and much of the early designing in connection with internal changes. He has worked most of his life as a technician in physiological laboratories and has an intimate knowledge of laboratory design. He discusses proposed changes with the scientists and then prepares plans which show the position of each bench and tap, and from which the Clerk of Works makes the final drawings.

Small committees or individual scientists are responsible for the library, the photographic section, the workshops, the histology section, the electron microscope, radioactive isotopes, the animal houses, the experimental farm and the refectory. These general services are equally available to members of all the departments.

THE SUPPLY OF ANIMALS

The success of the work of the Institute depends on the supply of large numbers of animals. The demand is difficult to forecast accurately and is liable to change unexpectedly at short notice. It is important that the animals should be healthy and uniform and, for this reason, the Institute tries, as far as possible, to breed all its own animals. Sheep and cattle are bred on the farm which occupies about 350 acres and is run so that it largely pays for itself. The farm manager engages his own staff of about a dozen agricultural workers and breeds the animals which are needed by the scientists, and also animals for the market. The farm has a flock of Clun Forest sheep which has won many prizes in lambing competitions and shows, and a herd of Jersey cattle which has also won prizes. The maintenance of a well-known pedigree herd of animals is good for the morale of the farm staff and does not interfere with the main function of the farm.

When animals are used for acute experiments they are sometimes transferred directly to the laboratories, but, more often, they are transferred to the Experimental Farm, where they may remain for long periods. The Experimental Farm has a staff of five technicians skilled in the art of handling animals, taking samples of blood, etc.

Smaller animals are kept in special buildings where goats, cats, rabbits, guinea pigs, rats and mice are bred. Other animals, such as dogs, are bought. Pigs are bred by a stockman, who comes under the farm manager, but works with the scientists. After weaning, they grow fat in a special house where the food supply and the sanitation are almost entirely automatic. A veterinary surgeon is responsible for the health of all the animals.

SCIENTIFIC WORK

The ARC has laid down that the work of the Institute is to be devoted to the physiology of normal animals, with especial emphasis on farm animals. The Director and his scientific staff prepare a programme within this framework, which is submitted to the Council for approval. This programme is designed to advance physiology; the study of infectious diseases is excluded as far as possible. Small animals, such as rabbits or rats, are used when these are more suitable or convenient than farm animals for the solution of a particular problem. At intervals of about five years a visiting group comes to the Institute and spends a few days discussing problems with the staff. Their report to Council reviews the research programme and discusses the needs of the Institute for the next few years. Members of this visiting group are also available for consultation at other times. They help the Director to decide what is needed, and the Council to decide what to give.

The results of the Institute's work are published in scientific journals. They are seldom likely to be of interest to the ordinary farmer, but parties of farmers do visit the Institute from time to time to see the farm and learn something of the purpose of the work in the laboratories. Colloquia are held at fairly frequent intervals dealing with the details of the work and these are attended by scientists from Cambridge. The staff also attends colloquia in various departments in Cambridge.

Institute of Animal Physiology

It will not be possible to do more than give a brief account of some of the problems studied in this Institute. The most convenient method of studying internal functions in the whole animal is to anaesthetize the animal in order to attach suitable recorders, or to collect samples, but the anaesthetized animal may be very different from the normal animal and it is, therefore, often desirable to prepare the animal under an anaesthetic and then to take the record after it has recovered. Such animals must be trained to cooperate calmly since emotion may affect the result. The Institute is well equipped for this type of experiment. For example, the temperature of sheep has been recorded by a small telemetering device on the sheep, which transmits information through a radio transmitter.

The unit which Barcroft started in Cambridge was concerned with chemical changes in the contents of the rumen, samples of which can be collected through a tube inserted in a preliminary operation. In this organ a great deal of fermentation takes place under the action of microorganisms, so that the material which actually reaches the animal is quite different from the material which it eats. Cellulose is broken down, acetic acid is formed, ammonia is formed, amino acids are changed, new proteins are formed, fats undergo great changes so that new fatty acids and new phospholipids are formed in the rumen. These changes have been followed at Babraham by means of such techniques as gas chromatography, paper chromatography, and automatic aminoacid analysis. A surprisingly large proportion of the microorganisms in the rumen are protozoa, and these are being cultivated and studied *in vitro*. The products of this digestion are eventually passed to the true stomach and to the intestine, where they are subjected to digestion similar to that which occurs in non-ruminant animals. Some of these processes are studied at Babraham on sheep which have been operated upon so that it is possible to collect their pancreatic juice and their bile separately, and the factors controlling the secretion of these juices have been studied.

Organization of Research Establishments

There are two schools of thought regarding the maintenance of body temperature in mammals. According to one school it depends principally on temperature sensitive receptors in the brain; according to the other, these receptors are chiefly peripheral. Evidence on this point has been obtained by experiments on sheep. A thermocouple is placed in the artery going to the brain so that the temperature of the blood going to the heat centre can be accurately measured. The sheep is then exposed to high temperature and it pants, although there is no change in the temperature of the blood going to the heat centre. This experiment suggests that this particular mechanism is not due to central control but to peripheral heat-sensitive receptors; further experiments have thrown some light on the details of this mechanism.

Experiments have also been done on heat exchange in pigs. Total heat gain is estimated from the basal metabolism. Attempts are being made to determine in what part of the body heat is formed, by measuring the temperature in various blood vessels. The loss of heat can be divided into loss by radiation, loss by evaporation, loss by conduction, and loss by convection. These different ways in which heat can be lost are being measured separately. Experiments have been done with small pigs in the laboratory. A special house has now been constructed, so that these experiments can be extended to larger pigs and carried out over a long time and the effects of acclimatization can be studied.

A number of experiments have been done on the blood flow. The total cardiac output in the whole animal can be estimated by injecting a known quantity of a dye into a vein and then measuring the concentration of the dye in a series of samples of blood in an artery and plotting the concentration against time. Another method, which was devised at Babraham, is to inject known quantities of cold salt solution into a vein and then to measure the temperature of the blood in an artery with a thermocouple. The blood flow can be calculated from the area of the curve relating temperature to time. This method is convenient and accurate and can be used repeatedly in a conscious animal. It has been adopted in other laboratories in various parts of the world.

A series of experiments has been carried out on the biochemical changes associated with lactation. For this purpose, goats are used; they are more convenient than cows, being smaller. Interesting results have been obtained by removing the udders from anaesthetized goats and perfusing their blood vessels. For this purpose blood is obtained from a flock of goats which act as blood donors, and pumped through the isolated udder so that milk continues to be produced for a period of twelve hours or more. In this apparatus it is possible to control the conditions exactly so that one can get information about the biochemical changes taking place. It has been found that if acetic acid is missing from the blood, the fat content of the milk is low, but that if glucose is missing there is no milk at all. This result was somewhat surprising as it had previously been thought the energy for the processes like the production of milk in ruminants was largely derived from acetates. In these experiments a mixture of about twenty separate amino acids is added to the blood. These acids are removed by the gland and converted into milk protein, but they are not all removed equally quickly and data are being accumulated about which amino acids are removed in this way.

In another series of experiments the causes of early foetal loss in pigs are being studied. It is possible to estimate the number of ova liberated by exposing the ovary at an operation and counting the number of corpora lutea. It has been found in this way that a large number of ova are liberated, and that the number of piglets born is less than might have been expected. The causes of this early loss have been studied and the conclusion has been reached that it is largely due to failure of implantation.

The factors controlling the absorption and excretion of

magnesium are being studied partly in the hope of developing a method of preventing the disease known as hypomagnesaemia, which causes serious loss among sheep and cattle. In these experiments it has been shown that magnesium is not absorbed in the rumen or the true stomach, but lower down in the intestine. A mild degree of magnesium deficiency can be produced by feeding sheep on a diet of young grass. Under these conditions the absorption of added radioactive magnesium from the intestine is deficient.

The metabolism of acetate is particularly important in the sheep. This has been studied by giving continuous infusions of acetate labelled with radio-active carbon and measuring the radioactivity of the CO_2 in the expired air.

Experiments have been carried out on the absorption of proteins from the intestine of young calves. It is known that young calves acquire immunity by absorbing proteins containing immune bodies during the first few days of their life. In this respect they differ from some other animals which absorb their immune bodies through the placenta before birth. The absorption of these proteins in calves has been shown to be due to an abnormal permeability of the mucous membrane of the intestine, which disappears after the first four days or so. At this time it is not only the immune proteins which are absorbed, but various other proteins are also absorbed and their presence has been detected both in the blood and in the urine. In another series of experiments blood groups in sheep have been studied. Observations on these may settle questions of paternity, but this has no immediate practical application since the paternity of sheep is known if precautions are taken in advance, and if proper records are kept. Another series of experiments has shown by various methods that red blood corpuscle of a sheep normally survives for about 120 days.

The establishment of a herd of pigs provides excellent material for the study of the effects of such factors as age and pregnancy on the walls of arteries, and full advantage is being taken of this. Supplementary observations have been made on the arteries of sheep, goats, rats and mice. It has been shown, for example, that multiparous sows develop marked thickening of the intima and medial fibrosis in the uterine arteries. These histological changes have been correlated with biochemical measurements of substances present in the arterial wall.

The study of genetics is not one of the prime purposes of this Institute, since this subject is studied in other institutes under the Agricultural Research Council. A few observations in this field have, however, been made. For example, it was found that the Jersey cattle at Babraham contained a hæmoglobin which was different from that present in other cattle, and was distinguished by the fact that when it was placed on paper and subjected to an electric potential, it ran faster than the normal hæmoglobin. It was shown that this particular hæmoglobin was genetically inherited, and that very few of the cattle in this country contained it, except Channel Island cattle. Samples of blood were obtained from France, from Africa and from the Middle East. It now seems probable that the gene responsible for this effect was originally derived from India. These observations confirm the view that Channel Island cattle are closely related to the native cattle of India.

Most of the experiments which have been described so far have been concerned with the whole animal. In addition to these, more academic studies have been carried out on some of the mechanisms of physiology. Experiments have been done on the biochemical pump which can maintain a low concentration of sodium and a high concentration of potassium inside mammalian cells. This is important for the excitability of the tissues and for the health of the animal.

A number of observations have been made of the importance of electric charges at surfaces such as those between fat and water, and between cells and tissues. These are important in the action of enzymes such as the water-soluble enzyme lecithinase, which acts on suspensions of lecithin. They are shown to be important also in the clotting of blood, and apparently in the action of Vitamin A, and in the action of poisonous substances upon the liver. Experiments have been done on the effects of electric potentials on spermatozoa. Claims have been made by others that it is possible by passing suitable electric currents to separate male sperm from female sperm. This would obviously be an important discovery, but the claims have met with much scepticism. Experiments have, however, shown that when mammalian spermatozoa are exposed to electric fields under suitable conditions some of them face the anode and some of them face the cathode, and when the current is reversed the spermatozoa turn round. It appears that each sperm contains a negative charge but under suitable conditions some of them contain it in their heads and some of them in their tails. There is, at present, no evidence that there is any relation between this phenomenon and the sex of the sperm.

A number of people at Babraham are studying the central nervous system from various points of view. It is known that some nerves produce their effects by liberating acetylcholine at their endings. This can be shown in several different ways. Devices can be applied to the surface of the brain or to the inside of the brain of an anaesthetized animal so that the tissue is continually washed with a salt solution. Acetylcholine can be detected in the salt solution afterwards and the effect of nervous stimulation on its release can be studied. In other experiments the effect of applying acetylcholine and other substances is studied in a five-barrelled electrode. In this instrument five fine tubes are pulled out together, a central tube is used to record the electric changes produced in the tissue, and the other four tubes contain different drugs, which may be applied by means of an electric current passed down the tube. In this way very small quantities of drug can be applied in an accurately measured time and their effects recorded in the immediate neighbourhood of the place they are applied. This device has been pushed into the cerebrum of anaesthetized animals and the effects of drugs have been tested in this way. It is found that most cells respond to the application of glutamate by giving an electric discharge. The electrode is pushed in slowly and tested with glutamate, and when a sensitive spot has been found in this way other drugs are applied through one of the other electrodes. In this way it has been found, for example, that the Betz cells in the motor area of the cortex are mostly sensitive to acetylcholine, and that the effect of acetylcholine on these cells can be antagonized by atropine. In this way it is hoped to build up a pharmacological map of the brain.

The acetylcholine which is liberated is formed by the enzyme cholineacetylase which is present in the nerve trunks. The enzyme is actually formed in the body of the nerve cell and is pushed down the trunk. This can be shown by obstructing the nerve, in which case it is found that the enzyme disappears from the peripheral part of the nerve and accumulates in the central stump. The distribution of this enzyme is also being studied by mincing the brains of guinea pigs in a solution of sucrose. This suspension of the broken parts of cells is then centrifuged and it is divided into a number of fractions. By suitable devices it is possible to separate a fraction which appears to consist entirely of nerve endings. The properties of this fraction are being studied by means of the electron microscope, and it has been found that much information can be obtained by taking advantage of the new technique of negative contrast, which shows a number of details which hitherto have not been visible.

It seems unlikely that acetylcholine is the only substance liberated in the central nervous system. A number of other pharmacologically active substances have been found in extracts, but there is no good evidence that any nerve liberates any one of them. The evidence regarding their importance is indirect. It depends, for example, on their distribution in extracts of the tissues, and on the effects of various factors upon this. Some active substances such as noradrenaline, 5 hydroxytryptamine and Substance P have been found to be especially concentrated in the nerve ending fraction. This suggests that they may be liberated by nerve endings but there is no direct evidence that this is so. Experiments of this kind depend on the development of suitable methods for the estimation of small quantities of these active substances, and much work is being done on this problem. Quite apart from the known substances it seems probable that other unknown substances play a part in controlling the central nervous system. Search is being made for such substances.

Besides all this, much work of more specialized interest has been done at Babraham. An adequate account would do justice to important researches not mentioned here, but it would occupy much space and would not attract the general reader. The present account is only intended to give a general idea of the objectives followed.

8

THE EMPIRE COTTON GROWING CORPORATION AND THE ORGANIZATION OF RESEARCH ON RAW COTTON*

by SIR JOSEPH HUTCHINSON, C.M.G., Sc.D., F.R.S.

and

D. F. RUSTON

HISTORY OF THE CORPORATION

The Empire Cotton Growing Corporation was established to develop the production of raw cotton in new areas, and thereby to increase the supplies available to the Lancashire cotton industry. The sudden drop in world production of cotton at the beginning of the First World War (from 28 million bales in 1914–15 to 21 million the next year) coupled with shipping difficulties and increased consumption in American mills, had placed the cotton industry in this country in a parlous position. As a result, at the request of the industry, the Board of Trade appointed a Committee in 1917 to investigate ways in which cotton growing in the Empire might be developed. Following the report, it was decided that an independent organization should be set up, and the Empire Cotton Growing Corporation was established under Royal Charter in 1921.

Briefly, the objects of the Corporation were to extend and promote the growing of cotton. The powers given to the

* This chapter was written in 1962, but although there have since been a number of changes in detail the broad outlines of the work and policies remain the same.

Corporation were wide and could be carried out either alone or in conjunction with agents, not only in the Empire, but in any part of the world, provided that such work would assist cotton growing in countries where the Government had any mandate, control or special influence.

The management and control of the affairs of the Corporation are vested in the Administrative Council, consisting of representatives of Government departments and of the cotton trade. From this Council is appointed a small Executive Committee with power to act for the Council in all ways and to appoint sub-committees; whilst the investment of the Corporation's funds is in the hands of the Board of Trustees.

The Executive Committee, like the Council, is composed of representatives of the cotton trade and of Government departments, and it is an important feature of the management of the Corporation that over the period of 40 years there has been continuity of membership. For most of this period there have only been two Chairmen, Sir Richard Jackson (1922–44) and Mr James Littlewood (1946–62) and three members of the present committee have completed over 25 years' service, whilst the ten most senior members have averaged fourteen years' service. This continuity of membership, and particularly of the Chairmanship, has been especially valuable, as it has cut down the need for lengthy explanations and paved the way for quick despatch of the Corporation's business.

The Executive Committee has, from the beginning of the Corporation's existence, allocated important responsibilities to a sub-committee of scientists—first called the Research Committee, and now the Scientific Advisory Committee—which has grown in importance with the progressive development of the Corporation's research interests and has become its chief policy-making body. The Committee has always been small, so that meetings have been easy to arrange and attendances have been full. Here again, continuity, and a membership with wide knowledge of the Corporation's work and policy and of the staff itself, has been of the greatest importance. Of the members of the Committee in 1962, two have been associated with the Corporation in executive or advisory capacities since 1922, and three began their careers as Corporation students and have spent between 20 and 30 years working on the cotton crop, either on the Corporation's staff or in the Colonial Agricultural Service. The Director of the Shirley Institute has always been a member, and the remaining two places are now filled by directors of Agricultural Research Institutes in Britain. One member of the recently established Overseas Advisory Board sits with the Committee as opportunity offers. In addition, the Director of the Plant Breeding Institute at Cambridge, the Professor of Agricultural Botany at Reading University, the Reader in Statistics at Aberdeen University, and the Head of the Physics Department at Rothamsted, act as scientific consultants in their own subjects. Between them, these members combine a specialized knowledge of nearly all branches of agricultural science, not only in this country, but in many areas overseas. In addition to their advisory function, the contacts they provide with universities and research institutes are of the greatest assistance to the Corporation's overseas staff.

The proceedings of the Committee have been greatly facilitated by the fact that trivial and formal business has always been kept to the minimum, and in consequence major scientific questions and principles have been the chief concern at its meetings. The papers prepared for the Committee have been, while duly informative, brief enough and few enough to ensure of their being well studied by members in preparation for meetings. A further great help has been the excellent standard of brevity, scientific accuracy, and lucidity maintained in the Annual Progress Reports.

Organization of Research Establishments

The day-to-day management of the Corporation has always been conducted from a small administrative head office in London. The chief officers when the Corporation was started were Sir James Currie, Director; Mr L. G. Killby, Secretary, and Mr J. C. May, Assistant Secretary—three men who gave between them 82 years of service to the Corporation and to whom a very great debt of gratitude is owed. With the help of the Executive and Scientific Committees, they were largely responsible for building up the Corporation from a small beginning to the successful independent and inter-territorial cotton research organization which it is today.

FINANCE

The Board of Trade Committee recommended that funds should be provided from three sources—the British Treasury, local revenues from cotton growing areas, and the cotton industry. In the early years, since cotton was not an established crop in any of the areas where the Corporation worked, funds were provided only from the Treasury and the industry—the first by way of a capital grant of nearly one million pounds, and the second by means of a levy on cotton entering the United Kingdom, this levy giving place later on to a grant from the Cotton Board.

These two sources provided all the funds from 1921 until after the 1939–45 war, at which time, with cotton a firmly established crop in many overseas countries, grants from the third source—local revenues from cotton growing areas—began to take the place of money provided by the cotton industry, so that today the work is financed from interest on investments made from the capital grant (totalling just over £70,000) and grants from the governments of the cotton growing countries in which the Corporation works (amounting to just over £150,000). The capital grant made by the British Treasury has been of inestimable value to the Corporation, since it has given it a measure of financial independence that has made possible prompt and effective implementation of scientific policy.

It is interesting to note that when the Corporation was first formed, it was estimated that the annual expenditure would total approximately £200,000, of which £25,000 would be required for the central office in London. Forty years later the financial forecast for the year 1962 was for an estimated expenditure of £223,500, with commitments in the United Kingdom totalling £24,000.

During this period of 40 years the Corporation has spent nearly £4 million on the work of encouraging and helping cotton growing overseas. Of this, one quarter was contributed directly by the United Kingdom cotton industry. In that time the annual value of the cotton crop in the territories in which the Corporation works increased (at conservative valuation based on the price of American Middling) from £2 million to over £60 million.

THE RESEARCH ENTERPRISE

The history of the Corporation's research work may be divided into four periods, which were in turn Exploratory, Development, Redeployment, and Expansion.

Exploratory

In 1921 little was known of the potentialities, and less of the problems, of cotton growing in territories then within the Empire. The exploratory period was therefore devoted to the establishment of research units in areas that were deemed likely for cotton production, and to the organization of a research team.

Since the improvement of the cotton crop in India was in the hands of the Indian Central Cotton Committee, the interest of the Corporation was directed primarily to Africa. The choice of places in which to work was determined by two considerations: first the assessment by the Corporation of the potentialities of the territories for the production of cotton, and secondly, the wishes of the local Government. The Corporation has never undertaken work in a territory without an invitation from the Government to do so, and has never exercised more than an advisory function in determining local policy. On these considerations, work was begun in four areas: southern Africa (including the Union, the Rhodesias and Nyasaland), the Sudan, Uganda and Nigeria.

Recruitment of staff was a serious problem. Owing to political changes in India it was possible to attract a number of senior men with Indian experience, but there was no system whereby young graduates in agriculture and the agricultural sciences could be attracted into overseas service with the Corporation. A training scheme was therefore started to provide the men needed for the Corporation's service, and also to supplement the staffs of the Colonial Agricultural Departments. This scheme, involving postgraduate work at Cambridge and at the Imperial College of Tropical Agriculture in Trinidad, was so successful that it was soon adopted by the Colonial Office, and was still in force in 1962. The Corporation still awards one-year studentships tenable in Britain, usually in Cambridge, but, with the closing of the Cotton Research Station in Trinidad, and with a mature and experienced staff of their own in Africa, it is no longer necessary to send students for a second year in Trinidad. Nearly 130 graduates have been awarded Corporation studentships since the scheme started.

Development

The prospects for the development of a cotton crop under rain-fed conditions seemed best in southern Africa, and in the early years more than half the staff was posted to the southern group of territories. After early abortive attempts to grow cotton on an estate scale it was decided that research was the need that the Corporation could meet, and research stations were established at Barberton in the Transvaal, Gatooma in Southern Rhodesia, and Domira Bay in

Nyasaland. Barberton became the most important, but no hierarchy was formed, each station being responsible direct to the London office.

In the other three African regions, aid for the development of cotton growing was provided through the territorial Departments of Agriculture. In Uganda, young agricultural officers were provided and were paid for so long as their posts were in excess of the establishment the Government was able to provide. In Nigeria, a seed farm was opened and was staffed until the Government could take it over.

It was soon realized that if an adequate irrigation system could be provided, the Sudan was one of the countries with the greatest possibility for cotton development, and the Corporation undertook to staff the Cotton Breeding Section of the Research Division of the Ministry of Agriculture.

Members of staff were posted to other territories besides those in Africa. The Corporation worked for a time in Iraq, Fiji and Queensland, and has throughout its history maintained one or more members of staff in the West Indies.

The wisdom of the decision to devote the Corporation's resources to research on cotton growing was soon evident. Cotton growing in all the territories with which they were concerned encountered major problems of varietal suitability, farming practice, and pest and disease attack that were only overcome by patient and imaginative research. Moreover, the establishment of a remunerative cotton crop in an African peasant economy involved its integration with the other crops, and with the stock, on which the peasant depended for his living. Hence, it became an essential part of the Corporation's policy to regard cotton growing as a component of an agricultural system, and to undertake in their research programme the study of the wide range of husbandry problems that this entails. There have been important consequences of this attitude. First, the types of cotton bred, the methods of husbandry, pest control, etc., devised, have been well suited to the circumstances and needs of every locality. And secondly, new knowledge from research on cotton has frequently had direct and valuable application to the general agriculture in a locality, this being perhaps most notably the case with the conservation of soil water.

The first station in point of time was the Experiment Station at Barberton in South Africa. From it much information of use to cotton growers elsewhere was obtained, and seed of the U4 variety bred there for jassid resistance was sent to numerous other countries. Seed of local selections from the U4 stock was issued from Gatooma and Domira Bay and advice was given, based on critical experimental work on cultural practices and on disease and pest control.

Soon after the establishment of the Barberton station, the Corporation set up a station in Trinidad in the West Indies for long range research into the genetics and physiology of the cotton plant. Trinidad was chosen for the station, in spite of the fact that the island does not grow cotton commercially, because of the existence there of the Imperial College of Tropical Agriculture. At that time, 1926, the conditions that make for good scientific research—the proximity of other scientists, the existence of other laboratories, with equipment and facilities for servicing equipment, and access to a good science library—were hardly to be found in the tropical parts of the British Empire, and the choice lay between Trinidad with the facilities of the Imperial College, and the cotton growing territories with no more of the milieu in which research prospers than could be provided on the station itself. In the event, it turned out that another advantage of Trinidad—the comparatively advanced education system of the island—contributed enormously to the success of the station in making it possible to recruit technical assistants who, with training, became first-class laboratory technicians. At this station a collection of some 1,400 types of cotton and cotton relatives was built up. A series of Research Memoirs was published. The genetic research, published in 27 memoirs, culminated in the publication of

Organizations for Research on Cotton

The Evolution of Gossypium. The physiological research, published in seventeen memoirs, made a fundamental contribution to the understanding of the transport of nutrients in higher plants.

By force of circumstance, the Corporation's work in the Sudan became more closely related to that in Trinidad than to that in southern Africa. The able and experienced Corporation officers attached to the Cotton Breeding Section of the Research Division of the Ministry of Agriculture had considerable success in breeding better Egyptian-type cottons for the irrigated Gezira, but for many years their strains did not go into commercial production because as a matter of policy only the two established varieties were accepted for marketing. What might have been a frustrating situation was redeemed by the decision to set about the control of the devastating bacterial blight (or blackarm) disease of cotton by breeding for resistance. The potentialities of a breeding system proposed by the Trinidad geneticists were recognized and, relieved by the inflexible marketing policy of the need to produce a quick commercial answer, an analysis of resistance to this particular disease was conducted. This analysis is a classic in genetics, and has led to the synthesis of stocks that were later recognized as fundamental to the continued success of cotton growing in the irrigated regions of the Sudan.

The work overseas was supported by a strong home base. The importance of the head office in London was very great, with its direct contacts with the Colonial Office and the Foreign Office on the one hand, and with the cotton industry on the other. The recruitment and training scheme, and the special needs of a research staff working in considerable isolation made it important to maintain close touch with English universities, and the particular needs of agricultural research in a crop grown for industrial use made contact with technological research an essential part of the business of the London office. In the interests of research contacts, and of staff training, regular grants were made to Rothamsted Experimental Station and to the universities of Cambridge, London and Manchester. Technological research on cotton is in the hands of the Cotton, Silk and Man-made Fibres Research Association's Shirley Institute, and a close association was built up with them which has led to a much improved understanding between grower and manufacturer. Facilities for the testing of experimental samples were developed at the Shirley Institute, and these have been greatly extended and improved over the years to provide for the Corporation a spinning test service that has been invaluable in maintaining a quality check on the products of plant breeding research.

Redeployment

About 1938 the Scientific Advisory Committee reached the conclusion that a comprehensive review of the Corporation's work was called for, and that some redeployment was likely to be necessary. The Executive Committee encouraged them to undertake the review. Progress was slow during the war, but by 1944 the committee was ready with proposals for redevelopment when the war was over. The position as it appeared in 1944 was that, largely as a result of the Corporation's work, the areas in which cotton could be grown economically had been defined, and the main limiting factors governing the crop had been identified. Two major diseases, bacterial blight and leaf curl, and one major pest, jassid, had been countered by the breeding of resistant varieties, and much had been learnt of the ways in which such major pests as stainers and bollworms might be controlled.

The prospects for further improvement were evidently great, and in particular it was felt that the long-range research in Trinidad had reached a stage when it could profitably be integrated with the more directly applied work in the cotton growing countries. The committee were faced with a major difficulty, in that it was now clear that the countries in southern Africa in which the greater part of the Corporation's resources had been deployed were unlikely to become important cotton producers. Prospects for development and for the exploitation of the products of research lay in the Sudan, Uganda, Tanganyika and Nigeria, and of these four territories the Corporation had a research team in the Sudan only. Moreover, the effects of the war had been considerable. Barberton was kept going by a minimum staff, the rest being away in the Forces. The Gatooma staff had been transferred to Tanganyika to help the depleted Agricultural Department, and were working on war-time duties on stations that were not equipped for research. In other places cotton research had given place to more urgent work on food crops. When the war was over, the problems of redevelopment in a time of acute staff shortage were universal, but the Corporation faced them with the considerable advantage of having their plans matured and ready for execution.

On the advice of the Scientific Advisory Committee the Executive Committee decided to close their station in Trinidad, and to hand over to the respective Governments the stations at Barberton and Gatooma. On the invitation of the Uganda Government they undertook to build a new major research station in Uganda, to which they would transfer the work in progress at Barberton and Trinidad. The staff moved to Tanganyika during the war remained there, and in co-operation with the Tanganyika Government, proper research facilities were built up. A few years later, on the invitation of the Nigerian Government, a research team was established at Samaru in Northern Nigeria.

The new pattern of work took time to develop. Land was difficult to acquire in Uganda, and clearing, building and development were slow. Plans were changed as circumstances dictated. Some of the genetic work transferred from Trinidad was located in the Sudan instead of Uganda, as conditions there were more suitable for the maintenance of the cotton collection. In the Aden Protectorate, the establishment of cotton as a commercial crop led to the posting of members of the Corporation's staff to the Protectorate at the request of the Government.

By 1950, however, the Scientific Advisory Committee's plan for redeployment had been carried out, and indeed pushed further than was contemplated in 1944. The new station at Namulonge in Uganda fulfilled expectations in combining research in applied genetics and crop physiology with attention to the needs and the problems of the local crop. The group of able and experienced colleagues at the Tanganyika station at Ukiriguru across Lake Victoria was close enough for the two stations to exercise a powerful influence on each other. In the Sudan, changing conditions in the cotton market, expansion in the cotton acreage, and changes in policy following independence, led to the acceptance of blackarm resistant strains in commerical cultivation and a demand for further products of the breeder's work. In Nigeria, the advent of a research team with experience of cotton in other parts of Africa led very rapidly to a new assessment of the problems and prospects of the crop. In Tanganyika, the Sudan and Nigeria, the crop increased greatly in size. In Tanganyika and Nigeria the whole crop, and in the Sudan and Uganda a substantial and increasing part of it is grown from seed of improved varieties bred by the Corporation's plant breeders.

Expansion

The period 1950–62 was one of rapid expansion, the overseas staff increasing from 28 in 1950 to 47 in 1962. This is the more remarkable in that it coincides with the time when in general expatriate staff have been leaving Africa. So far at least, as the countries became independent, the Corporation's work has tended to increase. The Sudan, Nigeria and Tanganyika successively, on obtaining independence, all asked the Corporation to continue to supply trained staff, and in the Sudan the Corporation's staff have increased from five to nine since independence was achieved in 1956. This year (1962), in co-operation with the Department of Technical Co-operation, a plant breeder and an entomologist have been sent to Western Nigeria on a full-time basis. A part-time cotton adviser has been appointed to help the Swaziland Government, and a plant breeder is being trained for posting to that country next year.

The Corporation's activities have never been confined to Imperial or Commonwealth territories. Work was undertaken in the Sudan very early in their history and has gone on continuously. This interest in cotton growing territories outside the Commonwealth is now to be extended, and a cotton specialist has been appointed to spend the next three cotton seasons in Thailand.

It should be noted that the Cotton Research Station at Namulonge is the only one which belongs to the Corporation. The land is leased from the Uganda Government, and the buildings were erected with funds contributed by the Corporation, the Colonial Development and Welfare Fund, the Uganda Government, the Raw Cotton Commission and the Cotton Industry War Memorial Trust. In all other countries, and at Serere in Uganda, Corporation staff work on Government Research Stations where, by agreement, houses, laboratory accommodation and equipment, and field and technical assistants are all provided by Government. The Corporation for its part provides the cotton research officers and pays their salary, superannuation and leave passages. The system works well, and having Corporation staff on Government stations working with other members of the Departments of Agriculture, ensures the closest co-operation and enables the results of research to be put into practice with the least possible delay. The distribution of overseas staff at intervals during the Corporation's history is set out in Table 4.

Organization of Research Establishments

Table 4.   Distribution of Staff

	Pre-war			Post-war			Proposed end 1962
	1928	1933	1938	1948	1953	1958	
Fiji	1	1					
N. Rhodesia	2	1	1				
S. Rhodesia	3	4	4				
Swaziland	1	1	2				
South Africa	8	11	11	4			
Nyasaland	5	3	4	2	3	1	1
West Indies	4	6	5	1	2	1	1
Sudan	4	3	3	6	6	5	9
N. Nigeria	2	2	1		4	5	7
Tanganyika				3	6	6	7
Uganda				6	13	14	16
Kenya					1	1	1
Aden						3	2
W. Nigeria							2
Thailand							1
	30	32	31	22	35	36	47

Up to 1945 communication was much easier with London than between stations in Africa, but since the war air travel, short tours of service, and interchange of visits have greatly changed the situation, and there is now frequent visiting and extensive correspondence between stations. Research problems are discussed and techniques exchanged. Moreover, opportunities for the staff to attend the annual Summer Meeting in England and meet the members of the Scientific Advisory Committee and Consultants, and to visit Namulonge at the time of the Advisory Board meetings in Uganda have fostered the development of a team spirit that was unattainable in the days of long sea journeys and long tours of service before the war. Hence the Namulonge Advisory Board, which was set up to consider and advise on the research programme at Namulonge only, has by natural development become an overseas research committee. It is now a forum where representatives of all the major cotton growing countries in which Corporation staff are working can discuss problems that concern them all. In recognition of this, the name has been changed to the Overseas Advisory Board and it is planned to hold the meetings in other territories besides Uganda as opportunity offers.

REVIEW

The organization of the Corporation has proved sufficiently flexible to allow major changes in structure and staffing without disruption. It is now a very different body, and a considerably larger one, than it was in 1940, and it will be convenient to summarize its salient features in these new circumstances.

In spite of the fall in the value of money, the income from the original endowment plus the reserves accumulated in earlier years, meet one-third of the expenditure on the current enlarged programme. The other two-thirds is contributed by the countries in which the work is carried on.

The Lancashire cotton industry no longer makes a direct contribution to its funds, but the interest of Lancashire cotton men persists. They have provided most of the members of the Council and the Executive, and have ensured continuity in the counsels of the Corporation. Their habit of mind has dominated the Executive, and has ensured that advice on scientific policy from the Scientific Advisory Committee has been translated into action in the field without administrative delay.

Hitherto, advice on policy has almost always come from the Scientific Advisory Committee, and to their influence must be credited the establishment of the Trinidad station, which was one of the first stations set up in the tropics exclusively for fundamental research, and later the redeployment of the Corporation's resources by withdrawing from Barberton and Trinidad and building the new station at Namulonge in Uganda.

The establishment of Namulonge initiated an integrative

process that has brought the overseas staff more closely together and has led to a most profitable association between the staff of the Corporation and their colleagues in government service. With independence either realized or imminent in all the territories in which the Corporation works, these are the associations on which their success will depend. The development of the Namulonge Advisory Board into an Overseas Advisory Board has therefore been appropriate and timely, and it is to be expected that it will increasingly act as a complement to the Scientific Advisory Committee in advising on scientific policy.

It is always difficult to measure the results of agricultural research, since much of it is long range and is unlikely to have any immediate impact on production. However, the Corporation has now been in existence for over 40 years, long enough for even long range work to have taken effect. As the object of all agricultural research is to increase production or quality, a study of cotton production figures should give some indication of what has been achieved. Table 5 shows the growth in cotton production in the eight countries in which the Corporation was working in 1961–62 —in total it has risen from approximately 100,000 bales to over $1\frac{3}{4}$ million bales. The main credit for the increase goes to the Departments of Agriculture and the growers themselves, but there is no doubt that the work of the Corporation's staff during this time has played a very important part. Most of the cotton varieties grown in the eight countries were produced by the Corporation's cotton breeders, and the resistance of these strains to pests and diseases has had a material effect upon the yield. Seed supply systems, cultural practices, ginnery practice, and pest and disease control have all been influenced by Corporation officers who, by the nature of their employment, have acquired a knowledge of the crop that enables them to speak with authority. While marketing has always been outside their terms of reference, the quality tests arranged at the Shirley Institute, and the

Table 5.   Cotton Production
(*1,000s of bales of 400 lb.*)

Season	Sudan	Uganda	Tanganyika	Nigeria	Kenya, Nyasaland, W. Indies, Aden	Total
1921–22	24	48	7	15	10	104
22–23	28	88	11	17	10	154
23–24	48	129	19	25	13	234
24–25	45	196	22	39	14	316
25–26	121	181	24	48	13	387
26–27	148	132	16	27	10	333
27–28	126	138	33	21	10	328
28–29	161	204	28	32	13	438
29–30	158	130	23	44	16	371
30–31	120	191	11	19	10	351
31–32	235	203	18	6	9	471
32–33	137	295	31	24	13	500
33–34	158	286	39	28	21	532
34–35	296	253	58	59	34	700
35–36	248	321	67	60	34	730
36–37	333	338	62	48	41	822
37–38	332	417	45	32	43	869
38–39	331	304	64	24	21	744
39–40	293	297	65	51	26	732
40–41	320	369	73	73	30	865
41–42	295	236	51	36	34	652
42–43	354	113	38	32	15	552
43–44	223	192	25	25	19	484
44–45	374	272	40	16	18	720
45–46	242	229	41	37	19	568
46–47	282	232	40	34	20	608
47–48	277	170	54	22	22	545
48–49	340	391	51	51	19	852
49–50	360	340	50	62	25	837
50–51	526	346	47	77	34	1030
51–52	313	380	78	113	42	926
52–53	476	320	51	96	40	983
53–54	498	398	103	143	54	1196
54–55	486	300	122	188	57	1153
55–56	528	364	134	154	58	1238
56–57	705	372	169	143	47	1436
57–58	273	351	171	241	56	1092
58–59	691	401	202	176	56	1526
59–60	704	361	189	171	75	1500
60–61	648	371	167	293	59	1538
61–62	1167	181	202	180	57	1787

information on them made available to the trade, have contributed to the successful marketing of a steadily increasing crop.

The Corporation has a high reputation for the quality of its staff and the standard of its research work. This is owed first and foremost to its founders, the Lancashire cotton men, the scientists on the Advisory Committee, and the first director, who had the foresight to base their plans on the recruitment of the best possible staff. In this connexion it is worthy of note that the object of the Corporation's postgraduate training scheme is to fit the staff for the work that they will be required to do, and not to give them further paper qualifications. The Executive Committee for its part has always endeavoured to treat the staff in the best possible way, for good staff will only stay if the organization and working conditions are good. In these matters the Corporation is fortunate. Firstly, it has a degree of financial independence (from the original capital grant) that has ensured continuity of policy and flexibility in the face of changing circumstances. It has enjoyed continuously the support and encouragement of the Cotton Industry in Great Britain, Government departments in this country, and the Governments, Departments of Agriculture, and Cotton Marketing Boards of the territories in which its work is carried out. Secondly, the continuity in the chairmanship, and the stability of membership of the Executive and of the Scientific Advisory Committee have resulted in prompt and decisive administrative action, and continuity and flexibility of scientific policy. Finally, continuity of staff in the London Office, and the comparatively small size of the organization have made possible close personal relations between overseas staff and headquarters.

With these advantages in organization it is able to offer a degree of security of tenure that cannot be offered to expatriates by the governments of the countries in which it works in these days of rapid political change. An expatriate officer in the Corporation's service is on a United Kingdom superannuation scheme, his interests are the responsibility of the head office in London, and the hazards of employment in rapidly changing political circumstances are mitigated by the considerable, and increasing, number of countries in which the Corporation is interested. Moreover, he is free to leave the service if it is in his interest to do so. If he wishes to go elsewhere for family or other reasons, no pressure is put on him to remain, and the Staff Assurance Scheme does not oblige him to stay for any specified length of time. On these terms of service, a large proportion of the staff have remained with the Corporation for many years.

Transfers from one country to another are made from time to time in the interests of the work and of the officer, since it is to the advantage of both that staff should have experience of cotton growing under different conditions. Every effort is made, however, to allow officers to stay at one station long enough to enable them to make an effective and individual contribution to its work.

Publication of the results of research is regarded as very important. Progress Reports are published annually, and in the last three years 48 papers and a number of shorter notes have been published in various scientific journals, including the Corporation's own quarterly publication—the *Empire Cotton Growing Review*. This contains original articles on all aspects of cotton growing, and agricultural experimentation related thereto, in addition to abstracts of important literature on cotton published in all parts of the world.

The future for an organization employing British staff in independent tropical countries is, of course, uncertain, but it is significant that at a time when expatriate officers are being replaced in large numbers by local men, the Corporation is finding it difficult to meet the number and diversity of the demands on its services. Its functions will doubtless change, but having achieved the extensive post-war redeployment with facility, it can face the changing demands of the future with confidence.

9

THE GLAXO RESEARCH
ORGANIZATION

by Sir Harry Jephcott, M.Sc., F.R.I.C., F.P.S.

The present Glaxo organization, which provides much of the experience on which this chapter is based, has evolved gradually. Beginning as a small department of Joseph Nathan & Co. Ltd, it grew to independence as Glaxo Laboratories Ltd. Today Glaxo Group Ltd, as a holding company, not only embraces Glaxo Laboratories Ltd, but also includes Allen & Hanburys Ltd, Evans Medical Ltd and the Murphy Chemical Co. Ltd, as well as a considerable number of subsidiary companies overseas. Clearly it is impossible to develop at length the histories of all the constituent units today included in the group: what I have written here has inevitably been conditioned by my long association with one of them. My colleagues in the others will certainly appreciate this and will not regard as a lack of courtesy any omission due primarily to lack of knowledge.

Research activities within Glaxo, doubtless like those in many other industrial companies, have evolved over a long period of time from small beginnings. At first, now over 40 years ago, research involved no more than one graduate and an assistant, whose work was almost exclusively that of quality control. However, at an early stage an element of research appeared because of the need to assess the extent to which the process of drying was affecting the vitamin content of the milk. The only procedures for vitamin assay then known consisted of tests on animals; these were also necessary

148

to demonstrate the freedom of the products from tubercle bacilli. An animal colony was therefore set up. This made us one of the first commercial firms in the United Kingdom to be licensed for animal work. There are now many industrial laboratories, using animals on a scale running into probably at least three million a year.

Shortly afterwards, the Company was faced with trading difficulties that led to the small technical staff and their commercial colleagues exploring some fresh avenues of investigation that could have marketing possibilities. They were especially attracted to the new knowledge about vitamins just then emerging. Development of procedures for manufacturing vitamin D as a pure substance led to some commercial success, which in turn made possible an increase in the technical staff. At that time, however, it was not possible to differentiate to any appreciable extent between production, the development of processes and what might more strictly be designated research. It was not, indeed, until 1936 that the construction of completely new premises at Greenford enabled production control to be separated from research and development and space to be allocated specifically for this. Of this space, about one half was for chemical laboratories and the other for the animal colony.

Although vitamin research and the control of vitamin contents in food and medicinal products were shortly to pass largely into the hands of the chemical analyst, this animal colony was destined to play a vital part in the future of the research effort. The Company's expanding interests, first in medicinal products as a whole and later in veterinary products, as well as its advances in the fields of antibiotics and immunology, meant that it was necessary to handle not only a much greater number of animals in field and laboratory, but also that the number of species was considerably extended beyond the guinea-pig and the rat, the two animals used for the early work on vitamins C and D. Nowadays the various control and research laboratories under the Company's control use annually tens of thousands of mice and rats, and a considerable number of hamsters and ferrets— animals of these four species being raised entirely in the Company's own breeding colonies—as well as a considerable number of rabbits and other animals and, in the field, chickens, pigs, cattle and sheep.

Much attention has always been paid to improving methods of analysing the Company's products and raw materials, whether by chemical or biological techniques. The Company's animal laboratories were almost certainly the first to advocate and practise the use of highly inbred laboratory animals for assay purposes, so reducing the number of animals required to give a particular degree of precision, or increasing the precision achieved with a given number of animals. In the field of chemical analysis, including physico-chemical techniques, the Company's scientific staff has made many contributions to analytical literature, reporting investigations conducted by themselves, individually or jointly, or as members of teams involved in collaborative investigations, with workers in other laboratories. It has always been the Company's policy to encourage publication of work on methods used for quality control.

Naturally enough, the kind of expansion to which reference has been made took place gradually, and over a period of more than thirty years, during which the laboratory colony has been moved en bloc no less than five times. Each transfer was made at the same time as some major expansion that was the result of the general research policy of the Company. This began to take shape in the early 'thirties, or even before, but it was at about that time that a consultative committee of distinguished academic scientists was formed to help determine research policy. In practice this did not prove satisfactory. After a period, a Head of Research was appointed, and he was given the responsibility for planning the programme in consultation with the academic advisers.

The Glaxo Research Organization

In 1938, an official enquiry was made into supplies of medicinal substances not then manufactured in the United Kingdom. The Company undertook to be responsible for producing some of them, and the research staff had the task of devising effective and economic processes of manufacture. This task was carried out to such good purpose that, although at the outbreak of war stocks of these substances in this country were low, no shortage ever arose—a state of affairs only secured by the research staff devoting themselves to production if necessary, using for the purpose whatever plant could be secured. Longer term research programmes necessarily gave place to short term national needs.

The desire of the research staff to apply themselves with all energy to national needs led to particular interest being taken in information then becoming available on penicillin. The success of their work on penicillin arose largely through preparedness to produce whatever might be possible with the restricted facilities that alone were available in wartime; as a result this relatively small group made useful and indeed substantial contributions to penicillin production in Britain. This led to official permission to increase the numbers of technical staff and to develop in the fermentation field, although the Company had not previously been active there.

Rapid expansion of the Company's manufacture of antibiotics took place at new factories remote from the Greenford headquarters, where the Research Division was then situated. The many problems of research and development to which these new activities gave rise made inevitable not only a considerable expansion of its research but also the creation of specialised research and development facilities at the individual factories. Subsequently, because building licences to extend the main research laboratories at Greenford could not be secured, a country house near Slough was acquired and converted to laboratories; here also a pilot plant was erected for antibiotic research.

Organization of Research Establishments

Some time later, special buildings were erected for virus research. Further, the research building at Greenford was extended to twice its size. More recently still, new buildings have been constructed at Greenford for immunological research, together with isolated premises for the preparation and biological control of vaccines for use in medical and veterinary practice.

This somewhat confused pattern of research and development facilities was imposed by the urgent nature of the work that had to be carried out and the speed with which new facilities had to be provided. A more rational pattern is now steadily developing generally, so that each individual factory has its own research and development team engaged on problems arising directly from the production with which it is concerned. Six such teams at different geographical points are now active in the United Kingdom and a seventh in India. In other oversea territories some development work, although at present limited, is being carried on, and it is probable that these establishments will need further extension.

As a result of this growth and also of the merging of other companies, each engaged likewise in research and development appropriate to its special interests, the total research and development staff of the Glaxo Group is now nearly 300 graduates with about 400 technical assistants.

The present intention is that research and development work not associated with current manufacture shall be centralized, though to accomplish this effectively newly designed research laboratories will be needed. As part of this scheme the centralized research has now been constituted formally in a Research Company (Glaxo Research Ltd). This separation enables it to delegate to those in charge of a particular section of the work a clearly defined responsibility. This for a time fell into four main parts—Chemistry, Biochemistry and Pharmacology, Antibiotics and Immunology. The heads of these sections often met together informally, and at a formal meeting once a month, each reporting on his own projects and agreeing upon any action necessary for the better integration of their several activities. Before the beginning of the financial year a budget and project meeting is held; at this, plans for research in the ensuing twelve months are discussed and adopted, together with estimated costs of the work in each section.

Recruitment of staff of appropriate background, training and calibre has not so far presented serious difficulty. It is true that openings within industrial organizations for research workers have greatly expanded, but it is also true that increasing numbers of such persons are leaving the universities. Provided the facilities for research are satisfactory, the reputation of the laboratory for the quality of its research is good and the terms of employment attractive, the young graduate in industry usually quickly finds himself in a congenial and stimulating occupation. The rapid publication of results may sometimes present a little difficulty, but it is soon appreciated that, in the interests of the organization as a whole, publication may sometimes need to be deferred until patent protection has been secured. Similar restraint is necessary in speaking to outsiders about work in progress. Nonetheless, no restraint has ever been imposed upon free interchange of information between members of the research staff; we have always considered it wise to trust our staff, and we have never had reason to regret doing so.

Subject to the limitations imposed by patent and commercial policy, the Company's policy towards scientific publications has always been liberal. Publication in the scientific and technical press is encouraged and we believe that this attitude has advantages for both the staff and the Company. Indeed in this manner the organization has been able to make contributions to the general advancement of pure and applied science. The improved status of industrial research, a marked feature of recent years, has, we believe, been in great part due to the publication by industrial laboratories of scientific papers of high quality.

It has likewise been the Company's policy to encourage its graduate staff, and indeed senior technicians also, to take an active part in the work of learned societies and professional institutions, even when this involved some absence from the Company's premises during 'working hours'. In our view this kind of contact is as important, and possibly even more so, for industrial scientists as for their academic colleagues. The latter have their lives diversified and their experiences widened by the teaching duties that almost always have to be undertaken alongside their research work, as well as by a certain amount of activity in the organizations outside. To the industrial scientist, teaching opportunities are as a rule denied; something must be found to replace them as a means of encouraging a broad and outward-looking attitude. To a certain extent this will be provided by day-to-day contacts with non-scientific colleagues, but his concern with the wider aspects of science, more easily catered for among scientists at the university or technical college, can be satisfied only in the national and international meetings of scientific bodies to which he belongs or should belong. The industrial scientist should, it is suggested, be even more active in these societies and institutions than his academic colleagues, simply to balance the lesser opportunities for looking all round that result from his lack of teaching activities. Too much self-fertilization, if practised because of an exaggerated desire for secrecy, can in fact easily lead to a gradual increase in mental sterility.

FINANCE

It is a difficult matter to determine the total amount that should be spent on research. This can only be met out of profits, so that the problem becomes to decide how much of the profits should be devoted to research. In doing this, the need to make a reasonable return to the shareholders must not be overlooked, and maintaining the general financial status of the Company is important to the research worker, no less than to other employees. To expend too high a proportion of trading profits on research could be as unwise as spending too little and could indeed be disastrous.

Trading profits fluctuate as a result of many factors. Among these are the general state of trade; the keenness of competition, not only at home but also in the international markets if there is any substantial proportion of export business; even the decisions of foreign governments on taxation, import licences and exchange. The last named are beyond the control of any individual company; because of them, however, profitability, out of which the cost of research must be met, may be seriously reduced by economic or even political circumstances.

On the other hand, an effective research organization is only built up over a period of years. It must be kept going at an effective strength and cannot be expanded or reduced at short notice. Its cost becomes a first charge on profits, irrespective of the ebb and flow of trade or its profitability. It is thus an overhead expense not to be spasmodically reduced, except marginally, without doing harm that can only be counteracted over a period of years, during which a loss of effectiveness will be continuously experienced. For this reason the problem of deciding the overall level of expenditure on research is a serious one, especially for any commercial organization narrowly based, or dependent on commodities that may be the subject of severe price competition and a resulting disastrous effect upon profits. These considerations must act as a deterrent to research by smaller companies with uncertain and fluctuating profits. It is significant in this connection that of the total industrial expenditure in Britain on research, 93 per cent. is by the larger firms, who constitute only 8 per cent. by number of the industrial companies. The pattern in the U.S.A. is much the same.

It might be easier to make long term decisions about research and development expenditure if a company that saw fit to constitute its research and development as a corporate entity (as our group has done by the formation of Glaxo Research Ltd) were free to exclude the accounts of the subsidiary research company from its consolidated accounts. It may be that the provisions contained in Sections 150 and 151 of the Companies Act 1948 permit such non-consolidation, but, so far as is known, no company has adopted this course.

This suggestion is not to be taken as advocating a system of hidden reserves; for good reasons this would be unaccept-able. It is a proposal to treat research and development as a separate corporate activity whose accounts do not require to be consolidated with other trading activities. Research might thus be protected against trading adversity and during periods of favourable trading might receive allocations of trading profits in excess of its current requirements in order to meet committed expenditure in subsequent periods. It would be necessary to be satisfied that such procedure would not lead to any tax disadvantage.

Without some safeguard such as this, expenditures on research and development may well be somewhat less than they would otherwise be, since the cost of research must not absorb so great a proportion of trading profits as to risk unduly denuding them in periods of unfavourable trading.

There have been numerous attempts in recent years to determine the total expenditures upon research by U.K. industry and to compare them with those of the only other country, U.S.A., about which reliable information is avail-able. Reports have been published by the Federation of British Industries (Industrial Research in Manufacturing Industry 1959/60) and by the Department of Scientific and Industrial Research (Industrial Research and Development 1958), and in America by the National Science Foundation (Funds for Research & Development in Industry 1955, 1959, 1960). These reports have been analysed with great care by the National Institute of Economic and Social

Research in that institute's journal—*National Institute Economic Review* No. 20, May 1962. After a careful assessment of the relative cost of research in this country and the U.S.A., the conclusion is reached that 'American industry's research expenditure is over five times as large as British industry's as an absolute figure, is nearly three times as large per employee and is twice as large as a percentage of net output'. That American expenditure upon research, in absolute terms, should be substantially greater than British was to be expected and reflects the difference in the size of industry in the two countries; but the other two comparisons are even more revealing and important.

Apart from the overall comparison for the chemical industry the conclusion is reached that American expenditure per employee is more than twice that in Britain and is one and a half times on a net output basis. The conclusion is unavoidable that, even within the chemical industry, which compares in this respect more favourably than most other industries with those of the U.S.A., expenditures upon research are higher in the United States than in Britain.

However, even these comparisons may not go to the root of the matter, especially in respect of individual companies. An endeavour to make comparisons on the basis of the information disclosed in the published accounts of American companies, which are somewhat more detailed than those of British companies, confirms the conclusion reached in the report of the National Institute of Economic & Social Research. In the particular sector of American industry studied, there is clear evidence that expenditure upon research represents a higher proportion of both turnover and trading profits than is believed to be customary in Britain. It must not, however, be overlooked that this can be met without adversely affecting the financial stability of a company because of the greater profit margins customary in the U.S.A.

Organizations with a wide spectrum of industrial activity

are clearly in a better position than the others to sustain a constant and relatively high level of research and development expenditure, for all sections of the business are unlikely to be adversely affected at the same time. Conversely, an organization that is narrowly based and mainly concerned with commodity trading is especially vulnerable. Within the business to which this chapter relates, the various influences have tended to counteract each other to some extent. The spectrum of trading is not broad; on the other hand the element of commodity trading is not unduly large, and there is a wide geographical spread.

Attempts have sometimes been made to compare the cost of research in different laboratories by dividing the overall cost by the number of graduates employed. Though this may provide a rough and ready measure of comparison, it can be most misleading, for the number of non-graduate technical assistants working with a graduate may vary from none to three or four. Moreover, the work upon which the graduates are employed may greatly differ. Thus a few of our graduates are engaged in assessing the effect of a spray in protecting a particular crop against the ravages of an insect pest: little is involved here but salary and incidental expenses. Other graduates are engaged with technical assistants in bench work involving the use of expensive chemicals. In consequence, though our average cost per graduate is a little more than £6,000 p.a., it ranges in the various laboratories from less than £3,000 to more than £8,000. Probably a better index is the cost per scientific worker, whether graduate or not. On this basis, the average cost for all the laboratories is £2,500. However, the validity of this figure is somewhat doubtful owing to the varied work upon which the staff is engaged in the several divisions.

What is probably much more significant is the steady increase in the cost, whether computed per graduate or otherwise, that has characterized the past six years, the longest period for which strictly comparable records have been kept. During this period there has been an increase in costs of ten to fifteen per cent each year over the preceding one. It is to be expected that, if the number of staff remains constant, costs will continue to increase; it is hoped that the rate of increase will be less.

One of the factors that seriously increases cost is the high level of instrumentation which is called for today. A chemical laboratory, for instance, that was well equipped twenty-five years ago with a few hundred pounds' worth of glassware and balances, may now need instruments to the value of £30,000 or more, which are expensive to maintain and have a high rate of depreciation. Moreover, they need specialists to use them effectively and to interpret the results. On the other hand, instrumentation has greatly increased the speed with which results are obtained; indeed, and more importantly, much of the new equipment has made possible work that would previously have been impossible, but all this has added to the cost.

THE RESEARCH PROGRAMME

In any industrial organization the research programme has to be realistic and to have clearly defined objectives. The pharmaceutical industry has not at any time had the support of government research or development contracts, such as have been placed on a large scale with aircraft and aero-engine manufacturers. That is the main reason why there is only one source of income from which research can be financed—the profits from sales of the company's products. To use an official phrase, 'taking one year with another' research must pay for itself by the sale of products resulting from it.

It is against this background that agreement must be reached on the programme of research; here, the nature of the industry with which the organization is concerned must be the dominant factor. Even though medical fashion does not seriously influence the use of drugs, new knowledge, the outcome of research or clinical observation, may have a dramatic effect on the use of a drug for which there is already an existing substantial demand. Even apart from such occurrences, medical thought, and consequently the usage of a drug or a group of drugs, may change over a period of years with the accretion of knowledge and experience. Comparing successive editions of the Pharmacopoeia vividly demonstrates this fact. There still remain a few drugs of historical origin that have survived basically unchanged, although they may now be available in a more highly purified state or a more convenient form than before. However, these are the exceptions: for the most part it will be observed that new chemotherapeutic products have replaced traditional medicaments. The effective life of a drug rarely exceeds 25 years, and its period of substantial usage may well be considerably shorter. Moreover, as soon as a new drug comes into use, the organic chemist will begin trying to improve on it, often to useful purpose, but with what may be disastrous effects on the first producer.

The instance of cortisone may be cited as typical of what takes place. Cortisone was discovered in 1936. The determination of its chemical structure led to partial synthesis in 1946; by 1948 a sufficient quantity had been synthesized to permit its first administration to a human subject in the autumn of that year. The use of cortisone was a major breakthrough in the treatment of disease. By 1950 cortisone acetate was available for general medical use; it was followed two years later by hydrocortisone—an improved form. Since that date numerous variants of the cortisone molecule have been prepared; many of these have proved either less effective or otherwise less desirable than cortisone, but a few of them have shown substantial advantages. Consequently, within ten years cortisone, whose production was a veritable *tour de force* in synthetic chemistry, accomplished only by great effort and at vast expense, has been almost completely replaced. Many of these cortisone developments have been made by firms other than the one responsible for the costly effort entailed in the first synthesis. This is only one illustration of the problem continuously facing the pharmaceutical manufacturer. He must expend a vast effort to maintain his place in the race, and on this depends the profitability of his operations, which in turn makes possible the continuance of his research effort.

It is against such a background that those responsible for framing research programmes in a pharmaceutical company need to work. When, as in our own, there are at least four major divisions of research—chemical, biochemical, fermentation and microbiological—the complexity of the issues involved must be considerable. A brief description of the machinery evolved to deal with them follows.

Before the annual meeting is held to determine budgets and programmes for the ensuing year, the responsible head of each division with his senior staff will have considered the proposed programme for his group and consulted with both his commercial colleagues and the heads of the other research divisions. The former may be unnecessary as a formal exercise, since from daily casual contacts he will have learnt what is commercially desirable; those responsible for sales are forthcoming as to their needs. With the heads of other research divisions, consultation and a degree of integration is essential. Rarely does a research project in one division fail to need the aid of another for its full accomplishment. A fermentation project may seek new precursors that have to be synthesized by the organic chemist; the organic chemist almost certainly will synthesize more new compounds than can be 'screened', even crudely, for effectiveness as antibacterial agents or for acute toxicity. Many compounds will be eliminated by a first screening before the lengthy and expensive task of pharmacological appraisal is begun. Unless the programme is reasonably well balanced, it is almost inevitable that work in one division will impose such demands upon another that some of it becomes impossible to carry out.

Fortunately not every project calls for such combined endeavour. Thus, within the Chemical Division itself there may well be, and usually is, need for research directed to a new and more economic synthesis of some known substance already in production.

The programme that has finally to be considered must take into account the various divisional interactions and demands, which will almost inevitably be greater than can be met effectively with the resources of manpower available. It will certainly entail a mixture of projects. Some will arise from existing commercial needs for an improved product or a more economic process, though these rarely present any difficulty in deciding the priority to be given; the urgency of the need is known, and the prospects of success can be roughly forecast from past experience.

It is in the newer fields of endeavour that difficulty arises. The projects that are completely novel and unrelated to any exising production of commercial interest may have arisen from a variety of stimuli—newly published research, conversation with academic workers, discussion with colleagues or the expressed desires of doctors for some specific problems to be solved. Each of these last mentioned will have been considered in relation to the frequency with which the condition to be treated occurs and the probable complexity of the project. Clearly if the disease, although of great medical interest, is a rare one, it may well be that, even though success is achieved, there will be little or no prospect of recovering the cost of research: all the same, the prestige attaching to a successful outcome in such circumstances, and also the desire to obtain experience in a particular field, may make the project acceptable.

Before any new project is set in motion, considerable enquiry will usually have been undertaken, and in all probability some preliminary laboratory investigation as well. Provision is specifically made for this by the practice of leaving 10 per cent. of the budget for each division unallocated, but to be spent by the responsible head at his sole discretion.

The foregoing description of procedure takes no account of the problems that arise in operating the programme resulting from the annual review. It is almost inevitable that some project undertaken proves to be much greater in scope and cost than was envisaged. I recall one that had had a large sum spent on it over many years and was then completely abandoned. Another cost £400,000 without any clear indication of a successful outcome. The project was, with some hesitation, voted a further sum because the leader of the team believed that before the further sum voted had been expended success would be attained; it was. More recently a total expenditure approaching £1,000,000 has been incurred upon a project and at least half as much again will probably need to be spent on it before the kind of commercial success necessary to make the effort worthwhile is in sight. There are prospects of this, but there is no certainty.

Though these sums are not large compared with the huge expenditures on defence projects, they are far beyond the resources of the small company. They are substantial in any industry of limited sales potential or whose profit margins are constantly under critical appraisal by government.

A project considered to be more appropriate to an academic institution is not undertaken except in special circumstances, but aid is frequently given to academic research in which there is a special interest. This aid may be financial, direct or indirect, or the undertaking of part of the project for which the academic institution has not the facilities, the supply of special materials, or the aptitude.

In general, the object of a project is clearly defined in practical terms before work on it is begun: this is in contradistinction to academic research, from which an addition to knowledge may be in itself an adequate end. Occasionally, however, there are calculated exceptions to this policy, as when academic advance in a field is considered to be approaching a point at which there may be a practical application. Here, if the techniques are highly specialized and difficult, work of a more or less academic nature may be undertaken in order to build up a team with the necessary expert knowledge and skill. This course was followed in the virus field before application of the techniques could be clearly foreseen. In the event, the practical uses developed with embarrassing speed.

An even more difficult problem is to determine when to abandon a project. Research workers are always optimistic about a successful outcome; indeed they would not be much good unless they were, for enthusiasm is an essential ingredient of good research. In consequence, there are occasions when work is continued after, and sometimes long after, there is any likelihood of success, simply because of the bad effect there would be on morale if the project were abandoned. I feel only sympathy with the staff concerned when a decision to 'abandon ship' has to be taken. To have spent months, possibly years, on a project, meeting and successfully solving a succession of difficult problems, and then, when success seems to be on the horizon if not actually in sight, to be defeated by an obstacle that proves insurmountable—this is indeed acutely disappointing and frustrating. Indeed, there may be good reason in such circumstances to maintain the effort for a time until repeated disappointment wears away the enthusiasm and the task is abandoned with a feeling of relief rather than of disappointment.

It is clear that the difficulty of bringing to an end some investigation thought no longer to have sufficient priority or possibilities to justify expending further resources on it is not confined to research in industry. It arises in possibly even more embarrassing form when public expenditure is involved. The problem is clearly one that occupied the attention of the Committee on the Management and Control of Research and Development of the Office of the Minister of Science (H.M.S.O., 1962), more familiarly known as 'the Zuckerman Committee'. I find there (pp. 31/32, par. 103): 'It may be difficult for a director to terminate a basic research project without wounding the amour-propre or shaking the confidence of some member of his staff. ... To lessen the danger of frustrating the research worker, however, it is always useful to allow those affected by a decision to bring their work on a project to an end reasonable time to write up and publish the work they have done—given that it merits this recognition.' I would only add that this is as true about applied as about basic research; for the former, as for the latter, the question of the worker's morale is of high importance. Moreover, what the Committee has written about publication is entirely in accord with our own policy, as outlined elsewhere in this chapter.

In practice the programme adopted at the beginning of the year is rarely if ever completed according to plan; indeed, it is inevitably subject to revision as progress is regularly reviewed during the year. Some projects may develop with unexpected speed and success; more likely, unexpected difficulties are encountered and necessitate a revision of the work. Still more likely is it that some unexpected development takes place, perhaps the result of new knowledge or a commercial urgency previously not foreseen. In these circumstances the whole programme in a particular division may need to be reviewed and its priorities redetermined.

From time to time a major task arising may prove to be no more than a defensive exercise of magnitude. The establishment of griseofulvin as being of value in the treatment of certain fungal infections immediately gave rise to the question whether its substituted compounds or analogues might prove more effective or have other desirable attributes. To leave the question unanswered might have resulted in others elsewhere in the world securing patent protection that would take from the originators the commercial advantage of work already accomplished. This task was treated as one of urgency; in the event over 300 derivatives and analogues were prepared, none of which showed any advantage over the parent substance.

Work of a similar nature constantly occurs in the fermentation field; there, for any process of major economic importance, there is a constant endeavour by strain selection and medium modification to improve yields. In the course of this work over a period of years, new techniques for producing mutants have been developed, with the result that many thousands of mutants have been isolated and screened. Success is considered to have been attained if one in five thousand proves to show some advantage. The problem, and it is constantly present, is to determine when this work should stop. To increase the yield of a new fermentation product tenfold from the laboratory to the factory may not be unduly difficult; past that point advances are hardly won, but may nevertheless be of material commercial significance.

When all aspects have been considered, the problem of deciding on a programme of research is not in itself unduly difficult; there exist practical criteria by which it can be assessed. As a result some interesting proposals may need to be deferred; others less attractive purely in terms of research activity may have to take precedence. In general, this is a fairly simple act of objective judgement. To settle the overall magnitude of the desirable research effort presents by far the greater problem.

It has frequently been stated in public, and recently at the meeting of the British Association, in Manchester, that too little is spent upon research. As a general statement this may well be true. As applied to an individual commercial organization, the limiting factor is the extent to which those responsible consider it wise to expend the Company's resources upon research with the uncertainty necessarily attached to it. Particularly is this so with long term research. The medium-sized company, such as my own, cannot afford to spend more than a modest proportion of its research budget upon a project that may extend over a long term of years. Moreover, research of this nature calls for men of outstanding research calibre, and such persons are rare; the limitation may be of men rather than of money.

None the less, if the project is well chosen and happily brought to a successful conclusion, the outcome will be rewarding both for the individual and the organization. The longest term speculative research project the Company has probably ever undertaken—it extended over a period of ten years—resulted in a material advance in medicine, a substantial demand for a new product and the recognition of the research worker primarily concerned by his election to Fellowship of the Royal Society.

(September 1962)

10

CO-OPERATIVE RESEARCH IN THE BRITISH IRON AND STEEL INDUSTRY

by SIR CHARLES GOODEVE, F.R.S.

Research organizations are of several types, but none have aroused such interest as those founded for co-operative research. The 'research associations', as they are called, were started with the underlying purpose of strengthening the national economy through the medium of technical progress. During the 1914–18 war it had been brought home to the Government that many parts of British industry were backward in contrast to their counterparts in other countries. In particular, industrial research needed intensifying to provide the foundation for more rapid technical progress. It was decided that co-operation between government and industry, and between private companies within a particular industry, would be an effective way to stimulate interest in research and to make the most economical use of the scientific resources then available. Accordingly, on the recommendation of the newly formed Department of Scientific and Industrial Research, Parliament voted in 1917 one million pounds sterling towards setting up a number of co-operative research associations. This partnership between Government and industry has been an important factor in the British economy.

A research association is essentially a voluntary association of private companies with common technical interests. Each company contributes financially according to an agreed formula and the DSIR makes a grant that is related partly to the association's industrial income and partly to the extent to which governmental support for co-operative research in that industry is judged to be appropriate. The arguments for industrial support are obvious. Government support is justified on the grounds that co-operation alongside competition is of great benefit to the national economy and is a good investment because the exchequer's funds originate in the activities of industry.

A research association has two main functions. One is to provide channels of information through which its members can be kept in touch with the latest developments in science and technology and also through which their own knowledge and experience can be pooled. The other is to conduct a search for new knowledge particularly related to their industry's problems by organizing collaborative research between members, by sponsoring research in universities and other research institutions, or by operating its own laboratories for the purpose. Most research associations employ all three methods in some proportion.

Today, there are in Britain about 50 research associations each serving a different industry. They differ widely in size, character and problems but have many things in common. The British Iron and Steel Research Association is the largest, but by no means the oldest: it is certainly not typical but a description of it may serve to illustrate organizational problems and solutions as found in some of the research associations.

THE STRUCTURE OF BISRA

The governing body of the Association is its Council, of whose members most are nominated by the British Iron and Steel Federation (the industry's trade association), some by the Iron and Steel Institute (the industry's 'learned society'), and one by the Department of Scientific and Industrial Research. Also co-opted on to the Council are one member of the Iron and Steel Board and one trade union official from the Iron and Steel Trades Confederation.

The Council exercises ultimate control of the Association's policy and work. It is guided in its research policy by six panels, related to main sectors of the Association's field of work. These panels appoint research committees, for whose work they are responsible, and they seek the allocation of funds to finance the research programmes put forward by the committees in conjunction with BISRA executive staff. The panels confirm or amend the research programmes put to them.

The executive staff of the Association is headed by the Director, closely supported by the Deputy Director, the Secretary and two assistant directors; this group forms what is known as the Centre. The remainder of the staff is organized within five divisions corresponding to five main technological sectors of the industry, namely, Ironmaking, Steelmaking, Mechanical Working, Plant Engineering and Metallurgy. In addition there are three departments responsible for scientific work in the fields of chemistry, physics and operational research. The secretary's department is responsible for various administrative matters and for the Development and Information Services. The three research departments and the five divisions are led by heads, who are directly responsible to the Centre, the two assistant directors themselves each being head of one of the divisions.

Each of the divisions and departments has a considerable degree of autonomy and they are free to organize their work in the way that best suits the needs of their particular section of the industry. They are linked at the centre by matters of general policy and through their ultimate responsibility to Council via its six panels.

As already mentioned, BISRA is in some ways not typical of the research associations. Being relatively large, it has been able to distribute its laboratories so as to be near to appropriate centres of the steel industry. Its largest laboratory group is in Sheffield and there are similar but smaller groups in Middlesbrough and Swansea close to centres of ironmaking and tinplate manufacture respectively. A fourth major group, being concerned with physics, chemistry, engineering and operational research, is placed in London where it is reasonably accessible to all. A central administrative group is also situated in London (though not at the London laboratories) so that it is close to other central bodies, notably its principal sponsors, the British Iron and Steel Federation, the Department of Scientific and Industrial Research, and the Iron and Steel Institute.

It has been found that by placing the laboratories close to the industry, the staff of member companies and of the Association can exchange frequent visits without the disincentive of a long journey. They also share in many local activities and this makes for close contacts and a sense of partnership in tackling the industry's problems.

The Association has steadily grown in size since it was started in 1945 and has now (1965) a staff of over 600, thirty per cent. of whom are university graduates. Largely because of the wide contacts that members of the staff have with industrial companies, there is a big turnover each year, amounting to over 25 per cent. A large proportion of the losses are to member firms; these losses are offset by the consequent gain in valuable links. The BISRA 'alumni' include ten professors and quite a few company directors.

The annual budget, including new equipment but not new buildings, is approaching £1,500,000. This represents about 15 per cent. of the total research carried out by the iron and steel industry, a percentage which is somewhere near the optimum in a balance between competition and co-operation. Of BISRA's income about twelve per cent. comes from the DSIR (the lowest ratio of any research association), six per cent. from sponsors of special projects, two per cent. from Commonwealth members, $2\frac{1}{2}$ per cent. from royalties, etc., and the remainder from industry, mostly through the British Iron and Steel Federation.

The Research Committees

Below the top level of the structure there are research committees responsible to the panels and, on the staff side, research sections responsible to the heads. The close relations between the research staff and the committees is one of the key points in the successful organization of the Association's work especially in the important matters of project selection and the application of research results.

There are nearly sixty research committees, sub-committees and *ad hoc* groups; they each meet about three times a year. Those who are familiar with the weaknesses of committees may wonder whether so large an administrative structure is a handicap. Given suitable methods of working with committees, however, there are more advantages than disadvantages in the system.

Most BISRA committee members come from member companies directly concerned with steelworks operations in one form or another. This makes their advice valuable, especially in identifying problems and specifying needs on which research projects can be based. For the same reason, their criticisms of research work in progress are also valuable, all the more so because they meet *in camera* so that discussion can be free and frank. Committee meetings perform the function of the colloquium in a university, only they do this more systematically. The most important contribution which the committees make is to foster close personal contacts between BISRA's research staff and the staff of member companies; the committees give the companies a real sense of involvement in the Association's work.

Prominent on the debit side is a committee's tendency to favour research on its immediate (and often evanescent) problems at the expense of bolder ideas that may take longer to develop and for which the immediate need is not so pressing. There is a danger that the long-term needs of the industry may suffer through failure of forward-looking projects to get on the active list or through 'revolutionary' ideas being prematurely overwhelmed with criticism too firmly based on practical experience.

Reference has already been made to the fact that the research staff are organized within five divisions and three departments. An important distinction here is that almost all the work of the divisions is reported to committees but roughly half of the department's work is not so scrutinized so that they are freer to explore new fields. In addition, the divisions themselves may spend up to ten per cent. of their resources on exploratory work which will not usually come before a committee unless it eventually forms the basis of a proposal for a new research project.

In this way the staff get plenty of valuable advice from the committees coupled with the freedom to ignore it on occasion. This ensures that the judgment and experience of both parties is utilized and that the relation between the two is one of partnership rather than supervision.

Another degree of freedom applying to the head of a division or department is the power to vary from time to time the allocation of his total resources between the projects in his research programme without previous reference to the committees. As new ideas arise and old ones are found to be unpromising, so resources are shifted from one project to another. At the end of each year a revised research programme is prepared for the following year and a written allocation of resources is made, which forms the basis of his annual vote. Each division and department is required to keep within the total vote made to it for the year although supplementary allocations can later be made in respect of particular projects or pieces of equipment. There is no costing in an accountancy sense of individual projects which would involve the filling-in of time sheets showing how the staff's time was apportioned to each project, and would render flexibility difficult. All that is required is costing on the basis of salaries and wages, materials and other resources used by the whole division or by sections of the division.

THE CHOICE OF PROJECTS

A research organization serving a large and varied industry has a formidable problem in avoiding the spreading of its resources over too many projects. Each member company or section of an industry attaches greater importance to certain projects or possible projects than do others. Furthermore, if the organization succeeds in attracting a fair proportion of men with ideas and in stimulating their creativity, one is liable to end up, particularly in applied research, with far more projects than can reasonably be carried. The projects actually in hand in BISRA number about 150 with some 50 potential projects on the waiting list. These numbers, however, are not very meaningful as the sizes of the projects range between an annual expenditure of £500 to £25,000.

To solve the problem of choosing the items for the research programme, BISRA employs the 'marginal approach'. An essential part of this approach is the use of the so-called '$(n \times p)$' formula and the whole procedure is roughly as follows:

(a) with the background of a continuous study made by the committees and the staff of the needs, opportunities and future investment plans of the industry, a member of the staff or sometimes an outside person puts forward an idea as to how a particular need can be met;

(b) the idea is developed in discussion, on paper and by preliminary experiments until it can classify as a potential project;

(c) each existing and potential research or development project is then assessed in priority, in terms of the *need n* of the industry and the *promise p* of the idea being successful in meeting the need. Only those having a high need *and* good promise qualify to go on the research programme, and, of these, those with a very high need or a very good promise have priority. Obviously there is an intermediate group with a high n and a very good p or vice versa;

(d) the research programme and the development of existing research staff is based on the assessments of $n \times p$;

(e) the marginal projects, that is those that only just got in or just failed to do so, are then re-examined in the light of a possible change up or down of the total of the existing research and development resources. The judgement (for judgement it is) to increase—or reduce—the resources is made as objective as possible, by means of wide consultation.

The Committee members play the larger part in assessing *need* and the staff in assessing *promise*. This is not only a matter of convenience, but a very practical method of smoothing the road to agreement. The staff assist the committees in attempting economic appraisals of the value of technical solutions to the industry. The Director and other members of the Centre have the special problem of bringing in to the factor p the availability of suitable staff and equipment, the needs for concentration of effort and various other factors. It should perhaps be added that, in practice, the building up of the research programme is not done quite as formally as might be implied from the above description.

THE APPLICATION OF RESEARCH RESULTS

The close links between the staff and the research committees again play an important part when the results of research come to be applied. Every innovation involves some expenditure and some risk and therefore has to be 'sold' before it can be realized. Members of committees who have usually followed the programme of an investigation from its start, are able to assess the risks fairly, to understand and appreciate the difficulties that are likely to be met and to know in what part of the industry a particular development stands the best chance of success.

Indeed much of the work, by its very nature, must be

carried out in works. The first stage is commonly a survey of a particular part of the steelmaking process. After an analysis and the formulation of a programme of trials, a company is selected and asked to arrange the trials or offer the facilities in collaboration with BISRA staff. The resultant agreement is generally a rather loose one with each partner paying his own costs; in some cases BISRA makes a repayment for local engineering and labour costs.

While the major responsibility for getting the results of research applied lies with the member companies, it is the responsibility of BISRA to ensure that each project is brought to a stage where it can be reasonably handed over. The problem of 'bridging the gap' between research and application is partly in the hands of the division whose staff are in close touch with industry through committees and other personal contacts. The wider dissemination of the Association's work is, however, entrusted to the Development and Information Services which come within the Secretary's Department. They are responsible for bringing to the notice of member companies reports issued by the research departments and for preparing shortened versions of these known as *BISRA Summaries*. Jointly with the research departments they organize conferences where free discussion of the industry's problems and the Association's work help to bring the two in even closer contact. They are also responsible for wider publicity and contacts with organizations, both domestic and foreign, outside the Association's membership.

EXAMPLES OF WORK

The field of BISRA's work is rather large, covering as it does all the stages of production from the ore in the ground to the finished article made from steel. Most of its effort is on the actual processes but the proportion of the work which is related to the steel product itself is on the increase. For example, a large amount of effort is going into a search for practical methods of making the ultra strong steels that have long been predicted as being theoretically possible. New techniques developed by the Association now make possible processes involving rapid heating and cooling cycles, sometimes involving deformation at a critical stage. As a particular 'avenue' of this work is opened up and its potentials assessed, the opportunity is given to steel manufacturers to develop improved commercial products.

A parallel example is to be found in the annealing of tinplate. The conventional, but quite modern method, is to do this continuously with the strip being fed through an enormous and costly set of ovens which heat it and of tanks which cool it, through the annealing temperature cycle. However, research into the cycle itself showed that the high temperature reactions occurred immeasurably fast and that it was only the lower temperature (about 200°C) part of the cycle which required time. Accordingly, a new and much simpler type of equipment has been designed which carries out the fast reactions continuously and very quickly. The strip is then coiled while at 200°C and kept in this state for about twenty minutes to allow the completion of the slow reaction.

The broad field of process control is common to most manufacturing industries and lends itself to co-operative research with an industry where a number of similar process units are employed. For example, the electric arc furnace has become a major steelmaking tool; its successful operation depends on the careful programming of every stage of the process from melting, through refining, to casting. Research carried out on BISRA's small-scale arc furnace and later with members on their own furnaces has led to the development of an automatic process controller which supplies the correct power input at each stage. With this equipment substantial saving in power costs, electrode consumption and furnace wear can be achieved. This incidentally is an interesting example of automation leading to savings in power and maintenance rather than in direct labour.

Organization of Research Establishments

BISRA has taken a lead in applying operational research to the iron and steel industry. A large part of the work of its Operational Research Department is done on a confidential basis for individual members. This work covers the field of development and investment, control of stocks, production planning, production control, transport problems, and maintenance. The value of such work can be gauged, not only by the steadily increasing amount of work individually paid for by members, but by the rapid initiation and growth of operational research departments in most of the leading steel companies. What was, fifteen years ago, something of a pioneering effort by the Association, is now on the way to becoming a regular part of steel works' management.

Co-operative work is done on more general operational research projects, including information systems, computer applications and human factor problems such as accident prevention and physical conditions of work.

Many other examples could be quoted, some successful and some unsuccessful. The Association's fundamental work on the process of sintering of iron ores has put the whole field on to a scientific basis and this has been of substantial assistance in the remarkable achievements in efficiency which have followed. On the other hand, a new process for the direct production of steel from powdered iron ore, which showed much promise in the laboratory stage, failed in the pilot plant despite a very intensive and costly effort to overcome technical obstacles. A balanced programme of an industrial research laboratory should contain a few rather speculative and somewhat revolutionary projects and it is among these that the casualty rate is rather high.

WIDER CONTACTS

The semi-national position of research associations gives them not only an opportunity but indeed a responsibility to build up and maintain contacts in many directions both at home and abroad. How does the research carried out by BISRA fit in, for example, with that carried out by the universities, other research organizations, and the laboratories of private industry?

A research association is concerned primarily with new techniques, equipment and improved products of common interest to the companies in its industry. It tends to support fundamental research in the universities rather than do such work in its own laboratories, unless, of course, there are special reasons to the contrary. Also it expects that the firms' own laboratories will in most cases carry technical development through to the production stage. The universities, the research associations, and the private firms, therefore, act more in series than in parallel.

This is perhaps best illustrated by Fig. 10, in which the abscissae represent the activities of scientists laid out in order, from science on the left to technology on the right.

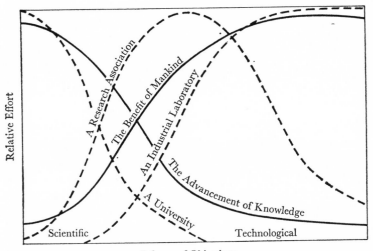

Balance of Objectives

Figure 10

The spectrum of research activities is defined by the relative weights of the two principal objectives of research, shown by full lines. The distribution of effort in some typical research organizations is shown by the broken lines, on the same spectrum scale.

Organization of Research Establishments

The definition of these groups is largely bound up with objectives. The principal objective of university laboratories is the 'advancement of knowledge', whereas the objective of research in industrial laboratories is ultimately the 'benefit of mankind'. It will be seen from this that there is no sharp line between the work of these organizations, but that the research associations provide a necessary link between the other two.

Research associations are not the only research organizations occupying this intermediate position, but they have a distinguishing feature in their ability to combine broad contacts with scientific and technological progress with an intimate knowledge of a particular industry. This is the basis of their strength and it explains in large measure the fact that nearly half a century after their inception, the research associations are more numerous and flourishing than they have ever been before.

11

BRITISH RAILWAYS RESEARCH
AND DEVELOPMENT

by C. C. INGLIS

INTRODUCTION

Unlike most industries, a railway can only sell a service—
the movement of people or goods from one point to another
—and with the growth in recent years of competitors such as
road transport, the aeroplane and more recently the hovercraft, there is a great impetus to the development of better
and cheaper services. The chief effort of research on railways
must therefore be aimed directly at quickly improving the
service it can offer, either by making it more attractive to
the customer, or technically more efficient so that rates and
fares can be kept at a competitive level. Owing to the
financial position there is room, during the next few years,
for only a small amount of long-term work which may pay
off in years to come.

British Railways are often the largest (and sometimes the
only) purchaser in Great Britain of some types of equipment,
for example the new large main line diesel locomotives, and
it might be asked 'Why do British Railways do any research?',
particularly as experience gained whilst supplying British
Railways strengthens a supplier in the export market and
often he sells products abroad largely because he can demonstrate their successful application on British Railways.

Although British Railways can rely to a considerable
extent on their suppliers for the research required in the
particular field in which each supplier is interested, there

remain problems that the supplier cannot tackle and on which research must be done from domestic resources. The supplier naturally concentrates on those projects which will increase his sales, in this country or abroad, and this policy will not always coincide with that of a large, specialized, user like a railway, whose main concern is to lower maintenance costs and to increase efficiency in use. Examples of the problems which a railway must deal with domestically include all forms of field testing, on vehicles and on the track; interaction of vehicles and track (which involves the riding of the vehicle, shocks which may occur in transit, wear, etc.); selection of materials to minimize corrosion; and maintenance and fatigue difficulties.

Manufacturers are continuously being stimulated to think about and make proposals for new designs, even if they do not come to fruition for some years, and financial assistance can be given where appropriate. It is therefore clear that British Railways must have a well equipped laboratory and testing service with technically equipped staff of the right calibre to discuss these matters with manufacturers.

It is important to draw a clear distinction between research and development in order to understand why all technical research on British Railways is brought together under the Chief of Research, whilst development remains the responsibility of the heads of the engineering departments.

During the development stage much of the detailed work involves dealing with *ad hoc* service troubles, which are essentially urgent and can only be dealt with speedily and economically by a department which already has a line-side organization throughout the railway, that is an engineering department. The practical application of new ideas, such as new type bogies, is essentially a matter for a department with considerable workshop facilities, such as are possessed by an engineering department, but which would not be economic for a research department. On the other hand, problems such as the application of disc brakes to trains involve basic considerations which are essentially of a research nature rather than development.

Since the responsibility for development is additional to the main task of the engineering departments, of producing and installing the new equipment in the modernization of British Railways, the closest liaison must be achieved between them and the Research Department. To help this, the Chief of Research is setting up Panels with representatives of the Research and Engineering Departments: representatives of the Research Department are also members of many railway engineering committees. In addition, members of the engineering departments frequently attend internal discussions of the Research Department and are members of some working parties within the department.

From these contacts it is possible to build up a research programme which, together with a development programme, is submitted each year to the Planning Committee for approval. In deciding the amount of effort to be put into the various research projects and evaluating them, the Chief of Research is assisted by a Director of Research Planning who may arrange systems-studies in association with other departments as required.

One of the greatest problems in a large organization is the dissemination of information throughout the system on British Railways. This is partly achieved by the distribution of a *Monthly Review of Technical Literature* which includes a section giving summaries of all reports from the Research Department and from the International Union of Railways Office of Research and Experiments (ORE) reports, which are available for loan from the Technical Library. Periodical accessions lists are also distributed whilst journals are circulated widely in all departments.

A further very successful method of making known the results of research, whether carried out within British

Railways or not, has been to hold conferences on selected subjects. Amongst the subjects dealt with have been 'Fatigue' attended by civil engineers; 'Marshalling Yards' attended by representatives of a wide range of departments concerned with the subject, and a second 'Fatigue' conference attended by mechanical engineers.

COSTS

The Research Department is financed through an annual budget of which the 'revenue', as distinct from 'capital' expenditure, is approximately £1 million. The Department and the programme are being replanned to cope with the major problems arising from the Re-shaping Plan for the Railways. A considerable expenditure, however, is still required to provide day-to-day facilities. This work has enabled records of performance of many materials to be built up over the years and forms a valuable source of reference.

The realistic and economic approach for a large service industry like railways, where big changes can only be introduced gradually, is to work out what is to be done and plan research accordingly. With the modern developments on British Railways, greatly intensified effort has been called for in both research and development; to meet this the engineering departments have set up development units and Research Department facilities have been expanded to meet the growing demand. In 1960 a new chemical laboratory was opened at Muswell Hill in which chemical research is being concentrated and a new engineering laboratory has just been opened at Derby.

The Research Department also arranges contacts with external Research Organizations, including those of other industrial undertakings, the D.S.I.R. and the Universities.

ORGANIZATION

The original organization of research to cover the needs of the whole of British Railways was set up in 1949, shortly after

184

nationalization, along lines recommended by a committee
of scientists led by Sir William Stanier, F.R.S. The present
organization is:

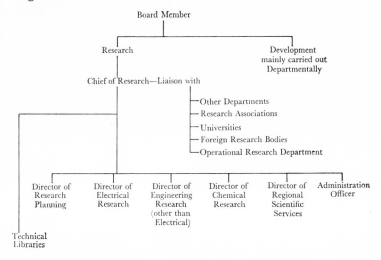

It provides for:

A Chief of Research, who is located at headquarters of
the British Railway Board and reports directly to a member
of the Board. His duties include the preparation of research
programmes and the annual budget of the Research Dept.
for presentation to the Board's Planning Committee. He is
also reponsible for the co-ordination of research work with
technical development and for contacts with research
associations and with universities. In addition he is a representative of British Railways on the Control Committee of
the 'Office of Research and Experiments' of the International Union of Railways, an association of most of the
railway administrations of Europe together with a few from
the Eastern Hemisphere, formed to undertake co-operative
research into railway problems and to pool the means of
carrying out research.

(a) A Technical Library which serves the whole of
British Railways, by the dissemination of information

185

throughout the organization. The Library has two branches, one in Derby which is more tuned to research and primarily serves the laboratories. The other branch is located at headquarters and serves all other departments in head-quarters and in the regions. The Library produces and, as previously noted, distributes a *Monthly Review of Technical Literature* which contains abstracts of articles of interest from a wide range of journals, both British and foreign, and provides a loan service for all officers on British Railways. It also provides abstracts of English language journals for the International Union of Railways and receives abstracts from most European railways of journals published in their own countries. A modest translation service is also available, as many of the articles of interest in railway research are only available in foreign languages.

(b) The Chief of Research keeps in touch with the facilities available for research in this country as a whole and contact is maintained at all levels with the Department of Scientific and Industrial Research, Defence and other Government establishments. In addition, the Board are members of many of the research associations, the results of whose work is also disseminated by means of the *Monthly Review of Technical Literature*.

RESEARCH FACILITIES

The Research Department covers four main fields: Engineering, Chemical Research, Regional Scientific Services and Electrical.

Engineering Division

Almost the whole work of this division is research as distinct from day-to-day service, though a proportion is devoted to *ad hoc* investigations. The Division is accommodated in a new laboratory, with greatly improved facilities, located in Derby. It is broadly divided between the fields of civil and mechanical engineering and shares a section concerned with field trials.

British Railways Research

Civil Engineering

Permanent Way. Expenditure on track renewals and relaying on British Railways costs approximately £23,000,000 per annum, and the interference with the running of trains due to such work is becoming of greater importance as train speeds increase. Much effort is therefore devoted to finding ways of extending the life of the track between renewals, including the development of concrete sleepers and long welded rails. New forms of motive power, particularly those with smaller wheels, have introduced previously unknown stresses in the rails. These stresses can now be measured accurately and the effect on rail life can be assessed. Work also continues on improving track components, wear and optimum rail section, with a view to reducing maintenance.

Soil Mechanics. Fundamental work is in progress on the properties of the formation under the track and the contribution the resilience of the track makes to good riding of the vehicles and to the comfort of passengers.

Structures. British Railways have the large problem of maintaining or renewing bridges and tunnels, many of which are over 100 years old and have been exposed to the corrosive action of smoke from steam locomotives for much of this time. The Engineering Division is taking part in co-operative research under the auspices of O R E, as mentioned earlier, in making field tests on particular classes of steel and concrete rail under-bridges. Field tests using strain-gauge techniques are being made to determine the pattern of stress and displacement in the bridges under normal traffic conditions with a view to improving methods of design and cheapening the cost of construction. The distribution of loadings determined during this testing will be used as the basis for loading in tests on full-scale bridges up to 40 feet in length to be made in the large test hall of the new Engineering Laboratory. Complementary work on small-scale models is also carried out within the laboratory.

Organization of Research Establishments

Mathematics. The group also contains a mathematical section, formed primarily to supply a computer service to the other members of the Engineering Division, but, with the growing appreciation amongst engineers of the possibilities of computer methods, it now assists the engineering departments of British Railways. It has a medium-sized digital computer and an analogue computer, and is staffed to tackle the mathematics of a problem in addition to writing the programmes and operating the machines. This has given the senior assistants a good insight into the practical problems which occur in such diverse fields as bridge design, shunting, and braking of trains. Perhaps one of the most useful functions of the Mathematics Unit has been the training of assistants from other groups of the Research Department and engineers from the main engineering departments in the setting up of problems with computers in mind. Several successful courses have been run on the computer and these courses are now an annual occasion.

Dynamics of Vehicles. The scientific background to the dynamics of railway vehicles running on rail tracks is still obscure and a long-term project is in hand assisted by a leading university. The problem of dealing with specific cases of vehicles known to ride badly or which have been the subject of a public complaint is dealt with as a development matter. The more fundamental measurements of accelerations and displacements required for a better understanding of the fundamentals of the problem are handled by the Research Department.

A series of projects in which the Research Department is participating concerns the modernization of the wagon fleet, including improvements to brakes, development of couplers and buffers, and studies of wagon marshalling and of shocks which occur in transit.

Mechanical Engineering

Strength of Materials. The present laboratory is equipped with a wide range of static and dynamic testing equipment ranging from a 100-ton Amsler Pulsator to small vibrating tables and Wohler machines. An important part of the new Engineering Laboratory will be devoted to an extension of these facilities up to maximum fluctuating loads of 800 tons. The main purpose of the equipment is to carry out fatigue tests on railway components ranging in size from large bridge units in steel or concrete, and full sized vehicles down to components of track or vehicles, with a view to improving designs of bridges and of vehicle components.

Statistical study has been made of rail failures over many years which have pinpointed the most prevalent rail defects and have guided the subsequent investigations into reducing rail failures. Portable ultrasonic and X-ray equipment which can be taken out on the track has assisted the Civil Engineer in this work on long welded rails.

Physics. Most of the work is devoted to the more fundamental physical problems and particularly into the thermal insulation of vehicles; the transport of perishables such as meat, fish, and ice cream; the reduction of noise, etc. A wide range of portable measuring equipment is used for most of the work which is carried out in the field.

Instrumentation

An essential feature of Research Department activity is to be able to measure or record the physical quantities involved in an investigation to the required accuracy. The Instrumentation Group was set up, as a team of specialists in measurement, to provide an instrumentation service to the remainder of the Engineering Division and occasionally to outside departments. Where possible commercial instruments are used, but, in a specialized field like railways, specially designed instruments are often required which can usually be made more cheaply than bought from outside suppliers.

It has been found economic to collect instrumentation into a single control as many instruments have applications to varying forms of engineering problems, for example strain gauge equipment is equally applicable to bridges and to coach bodies. It also ensures that specialized knowledge of the instruments is available within the department and simplifies organized inspection and repair.

Field Trials

Much railway research work must be done in the field. Attention has therefore had to be paid to designing portable instruments that will function reliably outside, sometimes for long periods. One solution has been the provision of mobile laboratories, three mounted in rail vehicles and one in a road vehicle. These are equipped with their own generator, dynamic and static strain-gauge equipment and dark room so as to be fully self-supporting when away from the main laboratory.

Chemical Research

Whilst most chemical research is carried out by industry, there are fields, particularly in application, where it is valuable for large consumers to carry out background research into their main purchases. On British Railways such work is carried out in the Chemical Research Laboratory, Muswell Hill, which keeps in touch with the production of new materials and investigates their properties from the point of view of railway applications. A typical example is the work on plastics which has led to their wide use in coaches.

One of the special groups of the Chemical Research Division is concerned with corrosion, a problem particularly important to railways as they have to use a good deal of bare steel on the track and on vehicles. This group works closely with a second group whose main concern is protection of all kinds of surfaces by paints and other kinds of films or treatment. One outcome of this work is the great reduction of the coats of paint applied to modern coaches and the mechanization of the processes, both factors giving considerable economies. Work is also in hand on the restoration of old brickwork and masonry, much of it damaged by exposure to locomotive smoke, and some interesting applications of hard setting plastic materials are under test. The growing use of concrete has raised a demand for basic work on its applications to railways and a concrete laboratory is included at Muswell Hill.

The economic maintenance of diesel engines is aided by the use of spectographs to analyse the oil in the crankcase. By this means contaminations arising from wear can be pinpointed in character and degree and a decision be made whether the engine is due for overhaul.

Train lighting (secondary cell) batteries offer a challenge to the railway chemist. Fundamental work is now in hand to improve the capacity weight ratio which could lead to either reduced weight for a given installed load or better lighting or heating if the same weight is retained.

Regional Scientific Services

Railways were amongst the earliest industries to appreciate the need for laboratories, and a railway laboratory was first opened at Crewe in 1863. Other railways were not slow to follow and British Railways now have Area Scientific Laboratories at the main railway centres. Originally they were intended to serve the local railway works but their functions have gradually spread until they now serve all departments. Their most important function is probably in connection with the control of purchasing of items costing some £30 million a year and for this purpose the chemist assists in preparing and standardizing purchasing specification for a wide range of commodities and subsequently, by acceptance tests, checks sample deliveries. Amongst the commodities so dealt with are steels and other metals, oils, rubbers, textiles, paints and timber.

Often, considerable basic work is involved in establishing the desirable properties of a commodity before the specification can be drawn up.

A Central Analytical Laboratory has been constructed

so that full economic advantage can be taken of modern automatic instrumentation.

The Area Laboratories also supply a general scientific service throughout the regions; they are the first point of enquiry of a local officer who has a problem and they can often give a quick answer. This day-to-day service is of value, particularly in dealing with claims by the public for items damaged in transit, or which have lost their label and need identification or which have been contaminated; such problems are referred to the Area Scientist for advice. As a result of this work a great fund of knowledge has been built up and is used by the Commercial Department, who are advised by a committee of chemists on conditions of carriage for dangerous goods, for example explosives, poisons, inflammable material and radioactive material. Also included in the general service of the Area Scientific Laboratories is the control of the purity of drinking water, forensic questions and assistance in the control of the local railway works.

Plastics

A specialist unit, for developing the application of plastics for railway purposes has been set up at Eastleigh and the Research Department supplies scientific services.

Amongst the prototype construction now undergoing tests is a container (a demountable van body) whose steel content is limited to skid plates only. The engineering advantages of such projects in plastics promise to be just as valuable as will be the replacement of steel or iron by a non-corrodible material.

Electrical Research

The Electrical Division is the most recently formed group in the Research Department and it has had to spend an appreciable time assisting with the problems that have arisen in regard to the new 25 kV electrification. It is at present housed in temporary accommodation and much of the work has had to be done in the field.

British Railways Research

An important function of the Electrical Division is to take full advantage of the potentialities of the 25 kV system of electrification for technical improvement. The advent of the power-controlled rectifier in semiconductor materials opens the way for considerable lowering of the capital cost and an increase in reliability by the use of simpler types of motor and this is being dealt with under a special panel. Industry is making a substantial contribution to this work.

Work is in hand on applications of solid state physics, particularly in the field of signalling, where the system must 'fail-safe' and where interlocking of signals and train detection offer interesting alternative and perhaps more economic systems to those used today. The use of magnetic methods is particularly promising.

The railways of the world are becoming increasingly aware of the possible application of cybernetics to railway practice and British Railways are well in the van of the work being done on this subject. The Electrical Research Division carries out basic studies, particularly in regard to the detection and identification of trains and the study of systems of control and communications. Long-term studies of this kind may well pay good dividends.

Among the problems raised by the 25 kV overhead electrified lines is that of pollution of the insulators, due to locomotive smoke and to industrial atmospheres, which might lead to flashovers. An exposure rack has been installed adjacent to the running lines and long-term studies of the problem are proceeding.

The Division is working in conjunction with a university on the problem of the application of the linear motor to railways. A small horse power motor has already been built and is undergoing proving trials which if successful may lead to the design of a motor of sufficient horse power to be of value to British Railways in specialized applications such as marshalling yards.

Operational Research

Operational Research does not now come within the control of the Technical Research Dept. but is the responsibility of a separate department. The following paragraphs may prove of interest. A lucrative investigation has been in the application of computer techniques to the control of wagons, whereby some twelve per cent. of the wagon mileage in the sample district was saved. The techniques are now being extended to a number of other districts and, if successful, the saving in wagon mileage could be reflected in a reduction in the wagon stock required by British Railways. It has now been shown that the timetables can be prepared by computers and the new timetable for one region has been drawn up this way, with a considerable reduction in the time-consuming work formerly involved and with the possibility of saving considerable expenditure.

Also in hand jointly with industry is a study of an automatic system of identification of wagons, the objective being increased detailed knowledge leading to more efficient use of the wagons. Systems studies are well under way regarding the best use of the information which will be available.

The system comprises code plates fitted to the wagon which are detected at focal points by lineside recorders. Some 75 wagons have been fitted with code plates and two recording points have been installed in a pilot scheme. Field trials on the equipment have shown satisfactory progress and wagons are regularly detected with 99 per cent. certainty and zero error in code reading.

No other system giving comparable facilities is known to have reached this stage of development. It is adaptable to other uses of a much less comprehensive nature, for example train reporting to supplement signalling, identification of the two ends of trains, and to give advance information to marshalling yards for wagon sorting.

Other activities

Contracts let for research or development to universities or to outside industry range from fundamental research, such as a study of cumulative damage in fatigue, to applied research, exemplified by systems tests carried out on the pilot scheme for the 25 kV overhead electrified lines. In the latter case all quantities likely to be of interest in future design were recorded on cards and the results can therefore be analysed on the Derby computer at any time in the future.

Other subjects contracted out to industry, involving only slight elements of research, include the development of disc brakes, buffers and couplings. The research required is largely testing of prototypes with investigations into weaknesses. Amongst the developments in the plastic field is the design of containers which would reduce maintenance costs and provide better equipment.

On the signalling side of British Railways, in addition to the signal interlocking already mentioned, contracts are let on a variety of subjects such as the development of a new system of checking that electric signal lamps are alight (to give improved proving of the signals) and vibration tests on miniature relays (which will save space and enable smaller signal boxes to be provided).

Future Programme

The Railway Board recently reviewed the programme of the Research Department and agreed in principle to the following primary aims:

(a) to extend the effort into the field of automatic control both for control of train movement and for the mechanization of manual tasks;

(b) to gain a more fundamental understanding of the dynamic problems of railway operations, for example fatigue, riding, longitudinal shocks, braking, passenger environment;

(c)   to reduce the cost of operating and maintenance procedures;

(d)   to increase reliability;

(e)   to rationalize and modernize laboratory testing and checking procedures;

(f)   to make the best use of developments elsewhere by continuing liaison with other railway administrations, through UIC and ORE, and with industry on an increasing scale.

The objective assessment which is made of all research programmes on the basis of these primary aims ensures the efficient and productive use of the research facilities of British Railways.

12

THE BELL TELEPHONE
LABORATORIES

by J. B. FISK

It is gratifying to us in an American industrial laboratory to be invited to participate in this collective presentation, under British auspices, on research and its management.

My predecessor, Dr M. J. Kelly, was privileged some years ago to present before the Royal Society a description of Bell Telephone Laboratories as an example of an institute of creative technology, in which research and exploration, the planning of systems, and final design of equipment for manufacture are associated under a single corporate management. For the purposes of the present volume, I shall discuss more specifically the conduct of research itself in this environment, a matter to which Dr Kelly himself had contributed with great wisdom and dedication. In so doing, I shall necessarily devote some discussion to the broader scope of our responsibilities which give our research its purpose.

Considering the diversity of fields covered by my fellow authors, there can scarcely be a problem in research planning and organization that has not, in some form, been dealt with in their institutions. Accordingly, I shall stress aspects of our work at Bell Laboratories that might be expected to give these problems, in our case, different magnitude or perspective.

I shall compress into three paragraphs a few facts about the Laboratories which, at least collectively, may suggest some uniqueness. Though there are other industrial laboratories that rank with or exceed ours in size, we are certainly among the largest in the western world. Scientific research in our company has had more than a half-century of orderly growth. The staff has always, in that period, included a good proportion of scientists of world repute. I scarcely need say that their prestige as individuals, and solicitude for a corporate reputation for scientific integrity, have over the years aided greatly in attracting new men of exceptional promise in the areas of science encompassed by our research. The subtlety of the end product, human communication, adds to the inherent challenge that these fields present to analytical minds.

We are the research and development unit for the Bell System, as the Western Electric Company is the manufacturing unit. The System is a very large enterprise—a privately owned enterprise engaged in providing communication services to the public. These services are highly complex and call for the most advanced technology. The enterprise itself is financially strong and its management has always recognized the need for good research to improve its services and advance the business. The nationwide communication system we have created, becoming daily more intricate and speedy, has been termed 'the world's largest computer'—a computer with more than 75 million separate points of access and charged with processing and transporting every variety of intelligence.

The role of Bell Laboratories in the conception and systematic growth of this gigantic yet sensitive mechanism begins at the forefront of research, extends across the entire breadth of creative technology through development and design for production, and concludes with engineering specifications to cover operation and maintenance by the various Operating Telephone Companies of the System. Accordingly, though we are sometimes thought to be primarily a research laboratory, only about twelve per cent. of the 4,200 professional scientific and engineering personnel of the Laboratories are actually enrolled in the research organization, in which our unprogrammed and unscheduled creative work is done. Finally, we have heavy obligations to the United States Government in the conception and development of both communication systems and weapon systems, and one-third of our people are engaged in such work for our Government.

The broad objective of the Bell System—to provide better and cheaper communication services—defines a channel for research activity of considerable breadth and scope, touching on many sciences, yet with sufficient unity of purpose to give a sense of mission to those engaged. This is felt to be essential to a successful long-range research programme. For without such a mission, an industrial research organization is at best only a community of scholars, capable, to be sure, of productive research for a period of time if wisely led, yet lacking the unifying influence of a university with its traditions and its educational responsibilities to give it long-term stability.

The responsibility of Bell Laboratories, however, is larger than that of research alone, as indicated in the preceding paragraphs, and includes importantly the development and systems engineering functions. I shall try to show that our association of research with development and engineering, far from impeding or diluting research, as is sometimes thought to be the influence of such an industrial setting, proves under careful management to furnish a free and stimulating atmosphere for research resulting in a prolific output of contributions to science.

Having used the terms 'unprogrammed' and 'unscheduled' with reference to research, I should admit that these are rather loosely employed. As compared with procedures necessary in the development areas, research is indeed unprogrammed and unscheduled. Actually, the President of the Laboratories and the Vice-President for Research give continuous thought to the total amount of research appropriate to meeting the responsibilities of the Laboratories' mission and to the division of this total amongst the various research disciplines so that a proper balance is maintained in the pursuit of new knowledge in these different areas. They, in collaboration with the directors of the individual research groups, try to outguess the future as to where the unexplored areas of science may yield discoveries of value to our industry. Where individuals of extraordinary insight or talent have a special interest to pursue, the broadest view is taken as to its applicability. 'Try as we may', wrote H. D. Arnold 37 years ago, 'to maintain an even and considered front in our attack on the boundaries of knowledge, there are always some salients which will yield only to siege or to extended flanking operations. So we find in the department men who are patiently and cunningly attacking old problems—problems which it might seem we had passed in our rapid progress, but which have still remained unconquered, and are frequently key positions of the greatest value. Compensating for these long established sieges are slender lines of adventure which have been thrust forward into the unknown far beyond any present hope of consolidation. In this virgin territory we find men, whose success must depend largely upon their own initiative and resourcefulness, striving for some point which may bring with its winning the conquest of new and broad regions.' Dr Arnold was the first Director of Research when the Engineering Department of the Western Electric Company was given its own corporate identity, in 1925, as Bell Telephone Laboratories under the presidency of Dr Frank B. Jewett. In the preceding two decades Dr Jewett had established a corps of trained scientists to work in the interests of telephony and had been, as had Dr Willis Whitney of the General Electric Company and a few others, a farsighted advocate of the introduction into industry of the same kind of scientific research—the unhampered quest of new knowledge—that had previously been almost an exclusive province of the universities.

One of our thoughtful research administrators of recent

years, Dr Ralph Bown, in reflecting on the latitudes necessary to a productive research organization, saw two freedoms
as requiring vigorous defence: the freedom to resist pressures
from the development departments to work on their specific
problems, and the freedom occasionally to carry ideas experi-
mentally into the applicational stage to a point where merit
can be demonstrated, when the researcher considers that
this merit has not been recognized or has been overshadowed
by development schedule pressures. The wise researcher will
know that these freedoms have to be merited and that they
impose obligations. The first freedom cannot ignore the
occasional emergency where all available skill must be en-
listed to solve a serious fundamental problem. The second
cannot extend to stubborn clinging to a favourite scheme
when wisdom would call for new approaches or a new
activity.

Dr Bown saw clearly, as had his predecessor in research
administration, Dr Kelly, that an indispensable requirement
for the protection of these two necessary research freedoms
was a *development* organization of the highest quality with full
competence and understanding in the fields charted by research. With such an organization able and eager to take
over research ideas at a well considered point, these ideas
can be quickly enlarged upon to supply the added basic
technology necessary for development and design of manu-
facturable components and assemblies for system use.

THE DEVELOPMENT ORGANIZATION

In Bell Laboratories the term 'development' is used to en-
compass the gamut of activities extending from the exploration of new ideas for new devices or new circuit arrangements
(in which the work is not readily distinguishable from
'applied research'), through the development and design of
components and systems to definite performance specifications and on a prescribed schedule, finally to co-operative
activity with manufacturing engineers. The objective of

development is to produce designs of equipment which can be manufactured economically which will serve useful purposes in the Bell System or in the nation's arsenal and which may draw on technology that is either new or old, most frequently both. Development occupies a large fraction of the Laboratories' technical manpower, as well as its budget—several times that of research. This is not because of an arbitrary management decision to place greater emphasis on applied technology than on fundamental science, but rather because it is apparently a law of nature that the exploitation of new ideas for practical applications requires more people and money than does the discovery of those ideas. At least that has been our experience at Bell Laboratories.

It is at once clear that personnel needed in development must be selected for aptitudes no less demanding on the scientific side than those of research people. Though their work has a large content of the technologic, and must reflect to a considerable degree economic considerations, it must still be done with an understanding of the principles of science and the scientific method we associate with the best research tradition. Compromise on this score would penalize development performance. It would also lead to deterioration of the intimate tie and mutual respect these people must maintain with their research colleagues. Development people would no longer be able to satisfy, without research help, pressing demands for improved devices or processes; nor would they have the competence or depth of understanding to pick up and carry on with the new discovery at an early stage leaving the researcher, thus freed, confident that his findings are in good hands.

The heads of our several research divisions so thoroughly appreciate the importance of the highly qualified development organization, not only toward meeting the overall mission of the Laboratories but also to the preservation of their own research freedom, that they have the strongest interest in its being staffed with competent people. They assist in the recruitment of personnel (often the distinction between a good research man and a good development man is not obvious). They are also alert to indications of growing interests in their own people towards problems of development, and, when appropriate, encourage such persons to transfer to the development organization. There are also occasions, though less frequent, for transfer of development people to research.

The development organization must maintain close ties not only with research, but equally importantly with the manufacturing unit of the Bell System, Western Electric Company. Here we encounter the problem of wide geographical separation. The Western Electric manufacturing plants are located in various cities of the United States spread more than a thousand miles apart. Such decentralization has obvious values to the operation of the Western Electric Company, but it poses a problem for the Laboratories. The solution to this problem has been to establish branch locations of the development organization in a number of the Western Electric plants. Thus the development work of the Laboratories and its design responsibility for the products Western Electric produces are carried out not only at the four headquarters locations in the New York–New Jersey area, but also at those branch laboratories, today nine in number. The effort is divided roughly 60 per cent. to 40 per cent. between headquarters and branch laboratories and is tending toward a 50–50 ratio.

In general, work in a branch laboratory tends to be more in the areas of the more matured arts, for example carrier transmission systems, crossbar switching systems, microwave radio and new telephone set design. In the headquarters laboratories the work tends to be more in the newer arts. However, there is much that is new and old in both areas and we try to keep matters that way.

Locating Bell Laboratories development engineers in the various Western Electric plants permits close working relationships between them and the manufacturing engineers. Conflicting problems of design for best performance and for most economical manufacture can be more readily resolved. Unforeseen problems in process controls, tolerance incompatibility, and the like, can be attacked with minimum delay. Finally, an understanding of and appreciation for the problems of his opposite number is most readily acquired by the development engineer of the Laboratories and by the manufacturing engineer of Western Electric as well.

The pattern or sequence wherein ideas move from research through development, and then into manufacture for use in systems, is one that continually repeats itself. Though less obvious, the feedback of ideas from development to research and from manufacture to development is also an important part of the whole process.

In recent times the invention of the transistor, and its revolutionary impact on the whole field of electronics, illustrates this pattern, in which Bell Laboratories has played a key role. Only a few months after our physicists, in their research on semi-conducting materials, had uncovered the possibility of amplification by the controlled flow of carriers in these materials, our development people, of comparable understanding but with keen interests in applications, set to work to establish the technology that has led to today's mass production of transistors, diodes, and related solid state devices. While the invention of the transistor and understanding of the control of carriers in solid materials is clearly attributable to our research organization, the technology making possible low cost, reliable, miniature, high performance transistors—all qualifications of vital importance in their practical application—came largely from the development organization. In turn, the techniques and equipment for large-scale, economical manufacture of these devices have been the work of Western Electric manufacturing engineers.

The Bell Telephone Laboratories

A third essential group involved in the progression of new ideas from conception to their use in our industry is the Laboratories' Systems Engineering organization, which is responsible for a clear statement of needs, performance and cost criteria to be met with respect to development projects to be undertaken. Our most recent organizational arrangements have placed telecommunications systems engineering and systems engineering for the Government under the same executive vice-president, while all development work for the Bell System and for the Government (including weapons development) is under another executive vice-president.

In the systems planning function, appraisals are made of the various technical paths that can be followed to employ the new knowledge obtained by research in the development and design of new systems and facilities. The most effective use of new knowledge may be in the creation of new services or defence systems, the improvement of the quality of existing services, the lowering of their cost, or some combination of these three. As the technology of communications and of weaponry has broadened and become more complex, the choice of the technical paths to be pursued in the utilization of the new technology has become increasingly difficult. It is this situation that has led to the evolution of systems engineering as a means of guidance.

Our systems engineers have intimate knowledge of the telephone plant and its operation; they maintain close contact with the engineers of the operating companies of the Bell System, with co-ordination by the headquarters engineering staff of the American Telephone and Telegraph Company. The teamwork of A. T. & T. Company engineers and our systems engineers makes available to the Laboratories in a most effective way the knowledge of the telephone system's needs and the opportunities for economy and improvement.

Systems Engineering also maintains close association with

Organization of Research Establishments

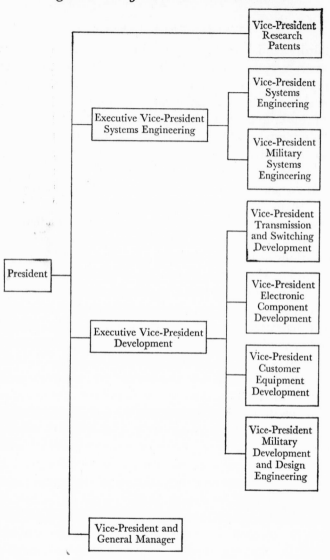

Figure 12

The three primary technical areas—research, systems engineering, and development—are illustrated by the current organization structure. Functions not directly associated with these are the responsibility of the Vice-President and General Manager. Systems engineering for both Bell System and Government are integrated under one head and development work for both Bell System and Government under another.

the work of our research organization and knows intimately the content of our new knowledge reservoir. It integrates the knowledge from operating experience, research and development, and with this as a background, makes sophisticated studies that appraise development projects for new systems and the apparatus required for these. Each study defines the objectives of the proposed development, describes the functional performance of equipment or systems which are needed, and often describes a particular embodiment of the system by way of example. Action can then be taken, with these studies as a guide, by our management or the government agencies in the selection of development projects. It is, of course, sometimes recommended in one of these studies that no development be undertaken at the time.

As the development organization proceeds with a project, systems engineers maintain close contact, continuously observe the technical difficulties encountered, the feasibility of more or better service, and amend the objectives and plans as required. In co-operation with telephone operating engineers or the interested government agency, systems engineers organize field trials often needed during the course of development, and are responsible for the tests and the evaluation of results. When a system is standardized and new equipment placed in manufacture, Systems Engineering, together with the development group, follows service performance of first installations and co-ordinates the 'growing pains' that accompany new systems as they enter service. It finally participates in the evaluation of the service and its economic or military worth.

Another important responsibility of Systems Engineering is to recommend the various technical standards that are important elements in determining the quality and reliability of telephone service. Typical standards pertain to frequency band width for voice and other transmission, noise and interference levels on circuits, distortion and cross-talk levels, and the range of energy levels of the signals. With advancing technology these various standards have gradually been tightened. This has been reflected in improvements in quality, speed, and reliability of service. There is a balance between service costs and the rigour of these standards, and it is the responsibility of Systems Engineering to co-ordinate with other organizations of the Bell System the factors involved in keeping standards and costs in balance, so that a well considered portion of the economies available through advances in technology will be used to raise quality and reliability and to increase the speed of service.

The staff members in the systems engineering organization must have a proper competence and background in each of the three areas with which they are in contact—research, development, and telephone company or defence operations. They are, therefore, largely men, drawn from those areas, who have exhibited special talents in analysis and the objectivity so essential to their appraisal responsibility. With respect to the contacts made with the research organization, it should be evident that such contacts made judiciously by and with the right individuals can provide for research people an atmosphere of encouragement and stimulation without annoying pressure or semblance of dictation.

THE RESEARCH ORGANIZATION

I have sketched above the relationship of the three major technical organizations, Research, Development, and Systems Engineering, primarily to give some sense of how the last two will draw on, sometimes relieve, and on occasion even inspire —but will not impede or divert—the first. I shall now return to the research organization itself and discuss briefly its philosophy and structure.

The inspired and productive research needed to support and promote our industry requires men of the same high quality as are needed for distinguished research in the university. The young men we have been selecting for research at Bell Laboratories are chosen mainly from the most

PLATE I

Murray Hill, New Jersey, is one of four major Bell laboratories locations and is the administrative headquarters. Here are accommodated most of the research activities and many of the development and systems engineering activities. Other major locations are in New York City (the original laboratory), Whippany, New Jersey (mostly for military development), and Holmdel, New Jersey, the newest development laboratory. Smaller laboratories are maintained at some of the Western Electric manufacturing plants and at a number of military installations as far separated as Kwajalein Island in the Pacific and Ascension Island in the South Atlantic.

able and promising of the doctorate and post-doctorate students in the graduate schools, and the environment we endeavour to provide is, like that of the university, stimulating to scholarship and a genuine desire to do serious research.

Publication of results of research is encouraged, and where invention is involved any necessary filing of patent applications is expedited to avoid or minimize delay in submission or in oral presentation. A policy savouring of trade secrecy would be inimical to the spirit of free research we consider it essential to foster. At the time of this writing (mid-1962) it is estimated that more than 1,100 Bell Laboratories' papers will have been published during 1962 in more than 150 different journals, including the bi-monthly *Bell System Technical Journal* and the monthly *Bell Laboratories Record*. Over the years, more than 60 books have been written by staff members of the Laboratories—of which many are classics in their fields. Liberal arrangements are made for travel to scientific meetings, including those held abroad, and a large number of foreign scientists are received as visitors to the Laboratories. Arrangements are also made from time to time for individual scientists to spend some months or a year at university laboratories of distinction in the United States or abroad, and for similar visits by others to our Laboratories.

It is essential, in order to keep up with the advancing forefront of scientific knowledge, to encourage these opportunities to exchange views with others. The research organization of an industrial laboratory cannot hope to provide by itself all or even a majority of the new ideas needed by its sponsors. A more realistic goal is the more modest one wherein the organization keeps in such intimate contact with the whole scientific world that it will know of new results promptly and, sensing their importance, can mobilize to take advantage of them. But only if our own people are themselves doing scientific work of the highest order, and are known and respected for their own contributions by professional society and university people of distinction, can they participate in and profit from these exchanges.

About half of the approximately 500 scientists and engineers in the research organization are in the Physical Sciences Division; the remainder are in two divisions more specifically oriented toward communications principles and systems in the sense of breaking new ground that might soon, or later, be of development interest. Each of these three divisions is under the general direction of an executive director who is responsible to the vice-president for research.

Until perhaps a dozen years ago it was sufficient to classify research in the physical sciences generally as either physical or chemical research. With the spectacular advances in understanding of materials and the remarkable and useful properties obtainable through precise control of their structure and composition, entirely new vistas in physical science have opened so that it is advantageous to classify the fields in a more detailed way without, however, in any sense restricting the freedom of the scientist to experiment or theorize or collaborate with others as his well considered broad objectives require.

Our present arrangement of research laboratories in physical sciences, each with its own director and several internal departments, is as follows, with primary activities briefly indicated.

Physical Research Laboratory. General and theoretical physics (especially the application of quantum mechanics and statistical mechanics to the understanding of the properties of matter); surface physics, plasma and atomic physics, magnetics and other solid state physics.

Semiconductor Research Laboratory. Physics and chemistry of semiconductors in particular.

Solid State Electronics Research Laboratory. Physical chemistry of devices, solid state spectroscopy, crystal electronics, optical electronics.

The Bell Telephone Laboratories

Metallurgical Laboratory. Physical metallurgy, chemistry of crystals, inorganic chemistry, metallurgical engineering.

Chemical Laboratory. Chemical physics, polymer research, organic chemistry, electrochemistry, analytical chemistry, plastics, resins, laminates and other materials.

I shall not lengthen this account with similar descriptions of the other research divisions, nor of the Laboratories' divisions in development or systems engineering. Briefly, however, with respect to the fields of activity in the two communications-orientated research divisions, these include forward-looking study and experiment in electronics, in microwave and guided wave radio transmission, and in the possibilities of light wave transmission; in possible future switching systems for communication (beyond a new electronic switching system for telephone central offices just undergoing completion of development); in visual and auditory research, including the study of physiological and psychological processes associated with sight and sound as well as improved methods of transmission. Their responsibilities include continued engagement with a fundamental problem peculiar to communication—the artful manipulation of relatively minute currents (infinitesimal compared with those of electric power transmission) to surmount electrical disturbances and provide faithful transport of intelligence.

These efforts have contributed outstandingly to modern communication theory and figure prominently in the sophisticated instrumentalities of recent space communication experiments.

Included in these two research divisions are a Mathematics and Mechanics Research Centre—a corps of specialists whose consulting aid is sought by all departments in the Laboratories in connexion with their projects—and a Computing and Analysis Research Centre with digital computing facilities and programming consultation likewise available to all Laboratories departments.

Organization of Research Establishments

In addition to these research fields, there is a modest but interesting research activity on interpersonal and intragroup relations which aims towards ways of improving human communication, learning, and effectiveness.

RECRUITMENT, SUPPORTING SERVICES, REWARDS

The men we engage for research are specially selected for interests, advanced training, and abilities as demonstrated in the university or elsewhere which qualify them to undertake productive research soon after they join the staff. The Bell Laboratories recruiting programme includes visits by our best engineers and scientists to more than a hundred universities and institutions of technology each year. Where the institution is a source of doctorate level men, we send a recruiter for engineering graduates with four or five years of university training and usually a different recruiter for those of doctorate training. I shall not go into the details of recruiting procedure but simply state that substantial effort and considerable expense are justified in trying to assure ourselves that a man can do creative work of a high order and will be stimulating to his fellows.

The Laboratories carry on, among numerous educational programmes, an advanced training programme for engineering graduates of four or five years' training. This is a company undertaking of considerable magnitude and not without direct and indirect benefits to the research organization. Each of these men (200 to 300 are engaged each year) spends half of his normal working time—at full pay—for two years in an intensive programme of graduate classroom training in the basic sciences. This is followed by a third year of study in the specific technology of communications. The programme is administered by New York University on our premises, except for branch laboratory engineers for whom arrangements are made with local universities. I mention this programme primarily to indicate the earnestness of our effort to ensure maximum capabilities in those men whose careers will be devoted to fashioning the communication systems of the future out of the tools and concepts furnished them by research.

These extensive recruitment and training programmes, though strongly supported by scientific and engineering personnel who are the beneficiaries, are organizationally the responsibility of the vice-president and general manager, as are the numerous other support activities and staff functions necessary in the operation of the Laboratories, so that departments having primarily technical responsibilities have a minimum of administrative burdens.

Much has been written, and there is general agreement, about the physical surroundings and working conditions appropriate to scientific and engineering work. In this respect an industrial laboratory must offer attractions comparable with those of university and government laboratories. All reasonable effort must be made to avoid unnecessary frustrations and impediments to good work. It could not be wise to invest heavily in people and be parsimonious about the physical things or technical or clerical assistance they need. Such things as square footage or equipment investment per scientist, or number of technical aides per scientist, vary over wide limits. Suffice it to say that when something appears reasonably justified and is wanted by highly competent people, it should be provided. Certainly a scientific library and library services of the highest grade are prime requisites. For our kind of work, computing, drafting, shopwork, glass working, tube making, metallurgical processing, and antenna testing are typical of the activities for which a prudently generous investment in facilities is well repaid.

A vital organization must provide opportunity for adequate financial rewards to the individual scientist and engineer. Our performance appraisal system is comprehensive and thorough. A large amount of executive time is devoted to administering the plan. The policies associated with merit appraisal and with salary level are described in a booklet which is available for reading by all professional staff members. Since it is basic in our salary policy to pay for talent and productiveness rather than organizational rank, a scientist does not have to assume management responsibility to receive substantial financial rewards. Those who do become 'managers' must have displayed and must continue to provide technical leadership as well as administrative direction.

THE OUTLOOK FOR RESEARCH IN
BELL LABORATORIES

At no time has the prospective importance of research in our industry appeared greater than at present. The almost explosive growth in electrical communication—auditory, visual, printed record, command and control, and other forms—over long and short distances, by wire, cable, radio beams, now satellites, and prospectively by way of light beams—will generate increasing demands for new techniques, instrumentalities and systems for which new ideas from the Research Laboratory will be eagerly sought. New materials —semiconductive, superconductive, ferromagnetic, piezo-electric and other, with refined methods of fabrication to achieve new properties—will be needed in increasing variety.

It is certain that great achievements, and accompanying satisfactions, await those rare individuals who have the gift of uninhibited insight essential to creative research. It is the task of our research management to attract and retain such men and see that in their probings they are not insensitive to the practical needs of our industry. It is the task of overall management to understand the potency of uninhibited research thus sensitized, to supply its needs, and to see that its discoveries are converted to usefulness promptly and effectively.

13

THE RUTHERFORD HIGH ENERGY PHYSICS LABORATORY

by T. G. PICKAVANCE, PH.D.

ORIGIN AND PURPOSE OF THE LABORATORY

The Rutherford High Energy Physics Laboratory was started in 1957, on a site adjacent to the AERE, Harwell, as the first project of the National Institute for Research in Nuclear Science. A second laboratory is being built in Daresbury, Cheshire. The principal purpose of both laboratories is to provide and operate, for use by universities and other bodies, equipment for research in nuclear and high energy physics.

It is generally recognized that teaching at university level is inseparable from research, and that research prospers when associated with advanced teaching, but in some important fields of fundamental research the cost of the essential apparatus prohibits its widespread distribution to universities. Moreover, the problems of administration and management of the largest projects are on a scale so far tackled in the United Kingdom only in Government establishments; a large capital investment in one field of research in a particular university, if accompanied by a need for large numbers of specialist supporting staff, may be an undesirable impediment to flexibility in the future programme of the university.

High energy physics was the first field to suffer from these difficulties. Although it is one of the most important subjects of research, because its unsolved problems are at the root of the structure of matter, it has no foreseeable direct applications and, therefore, must look to Government funds for support. In Britain, much accelerator development and some pure research was done from 1946 onwards by the AERE, Harwell, and shortly afterwards several universities were equipped with high energy accelerators with the help of grants from the Department of Scientific and Industrial Research. As the subject grew in scope and in its appetite for resources, its full support could not be justified as a part of a programme to develop nuclear energy, and its demands became out of balance with the universities' resources and their needs in other fields.

The remarkably successful CERN Laboratory, started in 1952, enables research workers in Western Europe to enjoy facilities for high energy research comparable with those in the U.S.A. and the U.S.S.R., so long as there are active laboratories within the larger member states. A plan becomes possible whereby the biggest laboratories can be international, backed up by complementary national laboratories to fulfil regional needs and to be integrated with universities much more closely than is possible with an international centre. A third feature, just as important, is that there must be active schools in the universities, using their own equipment to study those parts of the field, and closely related fields, which can use smaller and less expensive apparatus. A closely related and very important field, which does not need such massive support as high energy physics, is nuclear structure physics. The overall organizational problem is to determine and achieve the right distribution of national funds and effort between these three lines of activity, in the presence of competing needs of other important branches of research. But this is outside the scope of this article.

NIRNS ORGANIZATION

The NIRNS was formed with an independent Chairman (Lord Bridges) and fifteen other members, broadly representative of the various interests involved: seven from universities, three from the United Kingdom Atomic Energy

Authority, two from the University Grants Committee, two from the Department of Scientific and Industrial Research, and one from the Royal Society. They derive their authority from a Royal Charter, granted in 1958 and giving broad powers to create facilities for and to engage in research in nuclear science, and for training in this field, in collaboration with universities and other bodies. The use of the facilities of the NIRNS is provided free of charge to the universities.

There are no full time or executive members of the Governing Board, except that, of course, the chairman has executive powers, and the policy is carried out by the staff of the Institute. The directors of the laboratories are responsible directly and individually to the Board, and attend all meetings. They therefore have the maximum possible freedom and autonomy in pursuing the Institute's chosen policies, and the Board have the closest possible contact with and control over them. There can only be one secretary of the Institute, since there can ultimately be only one channel of official communication between the Institute and other bodies. Executive control was first vested in the directors by the device of a 'double-hatted' appointment for the secretary of the NIRNS, who was on the staff of the Director of the Rutherford Laboratory in the capacity of secretary of that laboratory.

The physical effort to back the Institute's programmes was initially provided by staff of the Atomic Energy Authority, who still provide many important services, and the Institute is funded on a sub-head of the Authority's Parliamentary Vote. Thus, although the programme and policy are in the hands of the Institute, who make their own requests for funds, the Authority exercises overall financial supervision on behalf of the Office of the Minister for Science* and the Treasury. This is a transitional arrangement which has been most helpful to the Institute; the final system has not yet been decided.†

---

* Now the Department of Education and Science.

† The Science and Technology Bill, 1964, proposed the creation of a Science Research Council which would take responsibility for the work of the NIRNS.

Organization of Research Establishments

The Board seek the advice when necessary of a Physics Committee, for example on major new schemes for scientific equipment, and the Physics Committee makes use of *ad hoc* specialist working parties in appropriate cases. Financial control is delegated to a General Purposes Committee, and a Personnel Committee approves senior appointments and deals with rates of pay and conditions of service. There are special committees to deal with the use of nuclear reactors for research and the management of the Institute's Atlas computer. The Rutherford Laboratory has a Visiting Committee, chaired by a member of the Board and meeting in the Laboratory twice a year; it is advisory to the Director, and not to the Board, who, however, receive the minutes together with those of all the other NIRNS committees.*

DUTIES OF THE DIRECTOR

The Director is responsible for the operation of the Laboratory and for its internal organization, and has authority to make appointments within the approved staff complement. He has financial authority to approve commitment of Institute funds up to reasonable limits, beyond which he makes submissions to the General Purposes Committee. The limits have been set after experience, to give the G.P.C. proper control while avoiding tedious delays and excessive paper work. They vary from about £5,000 for new capital expenditure on one item to higher sums for items within an approved estimate for a major capital scheme already adopted, and higher still for non-capital expenditure such as provisioning stores and materials within approved estimates. All action is reported to the G.P.C., whether prior approval is required or not. The Director attends Board and G.P.C. meetings, to report on the Laboratory's plans and progress and to assist

* *Note added in proof:* In 1963 an Executive Committee of the Board was formed, to replace the General Purposes and Personnel Committees and to expedite Institute business in the operating phase of the Laboratories. The NIRNS Chairman chaired this Committee, which was composed of several Board members, the Directors, an Administrative member, and a Financial member representing the Accounting Officer.

the Board in their discussions. He is a member in his own right of all the Committees except the G.P.C. which is not advisory but acts on behalf of the Board, and the Visiting Committee which exists to advise him.

NUCLEAR AND HIGH ENERGY PHYSICS
PROGRAMME

The broad outlines of the Rutherford Laboratory programme were determined at the outset by a decision, taken in 1957 in consultation with high energy physicists, to design and construct the 7 GeV proton synchrotron Nimrod. The requirement was to produce a source of elementary particles on which universities could base their high energy research for some time, and which would be complementary to the big accelerator then under construction by CERN in Geneva. The decision to site the Laboratory adjacent to the Atomic Energy Research Establishment at Harwell, outside the security fence, enabled the Authority to offer to the NIRNS a partly built 50 MeV proton linear accelerator. This machine has been completed by the Institute and has been used for nuclear research since 1960. The main research programme is therefore based on the exploitation of these two accelerators by the universities. The bigger machine did not come into operation until late 1963.

The machines must also be used by research staff of the Laboratory. Only in this way can a good service be given to the university teams, and a balanced scientific community be built up in the Laboratory. Nevertheless the purposes of the Institute will not be achieved unless the university staff use the majority of the running time, and do so in such a way as to be genuinely pursuing their own programmes as full members of their own universities, accompanied by their own research students. This is the central organizational problem.

The smaller machine, which is a very powerful research tool in a relatively neglected but important field, has been valuable in giving the Institute and the universities early experience of this problem on a readily manageable scale. The results are encouraging. About 60 post-graduate specialists in nuclear research have been regularly using the machine; nearly 50 are university staff, fellows, and research students from eight university departments. The others are from the AERE, who continue to be interested in this field of research, and the research staff of the Laboratory.

The whole programme of experiments is derived from regular seminars attended by the visiting and resident research workers, and occasional conferences on selected topics with larger attendance. The first proposal of a particular experiment usually takes the form of a talk at one of the seminars, either by the research worker, resident or visiting, who wishes to do it or by someone else who puts it forward as a suggestion. The next step, if the proposal is well received as a competitor for machine time, is an approximate assessment of the machine time, auxiliary equipment and technical support required to achieve significant results, and then there is more discussion and often exploratory runs. The survivors of processes of this kind form the experimental programme; decisions are taken collectively by the participants in the programme, aided by advice from theorists and from the NIRNS staff experienced in the techniques of the accelerator and its auxiliaries. A NIRNS physicist has charge of the machine and is the chairman of the discussions, but does not act as the director of research. His NIRNS team conduct experiments of their own, but also help the university teams in a variety of ways. Life around a big accelerator is difficult; the experimental apparatus is usually very complicated and has to be co-ordinated with the machine to give the best performance of the complete experiment. The resident research staff become expert in making the best use of the machine, and it is part of their job to pass this expertise to the visiting teams.

The visiting teams vary in size and experience. Some, from universities with strong nuclear physics schools based on their own machines, can soon fend for themselves and of course prefer to do so. Others, including occasional isolated individuals, are knowledgeable in nuclear physics but have, initially, little or no experience in the use of big machines. It is found desirable to have mixed teams, containing staff of the NIRNS and one or more universities, brought together by interest in the same series of experiments and by a desire to pool resources and experience. The pattern continually changes as interests develop and change, and with the ebb and flow of pressure on machine time.

Every university has the right to use the Laboratory, but no attempt is made to ration accelerator time on the basis of equal shares for each. The time is allocated so far as possible on the scientific merits and the needs of the experiments proposed, with spare time for the inevitable speculative ventures which should certainly not be discouraged and with an eye to general justice. People who are turned down, because their proposals are judged impracticable or of insufficient interest to be put on a long waiting list for running time, do not have to go away and think again unless they wish to do so. They can join forces with another group with an experiment in preparation. With three-shift operation of the machine no 'good' proposal has yet been turned down, although the waiting time has sometimes been uncomfortably long. Judgement has to be exercised, also at the seminars, as to when an experiment can be said to be finished. It is normal in this type of research, except in the simplest experiments, for several running periods to be allocated with intervals for the team to assess their results and develop their methods, and the end is reached when it is judged that sufficient accuracy has been achieved; competition with other experiments is obviously a factor to be considered. This is all quite normal in research with accelerators but the NIRNS has a special position with respect to the universities. Diplomacy and tact are high on the list of qualities which must be displayed by the NIRNS staff concerned. The Visiting

Committee can be used as a forum for complaints of unfair treatment which have not been settled on the spot; fortunately this has not yet been necessary.

The machine is scheduled at regular down-to-earth meetings conducted by a senior NIRNS physicist and attended by the leaders of the teams with experiments in preparation; at this stage there is an approved programme, and scheduling is a practical problem concerned mainly with logistics.

Nearly all the experiments on the accelerators need quite elaborate auxiliary equipment which is beyond the capacity of universities, financially or technically, to provide for themselves. Some of the equipment is, or becomes, standard, adaptable to many needs, and stocks of these items, determined by experience, are held in Laboratory stores and are issued as required. Other equipment has to be specially developed. This is paid for by the Institute and capital items remain their property but are, of course, available for use by universities. The development effort is provided by the Institute or by the university, or both, as available and required; by common consent the universities help themselves in this respect as much as possible, not only to minimize the load on and the size of the Laboratory staff but also to enable the universities to play as full a part as possible in their own research.

When preparatory or analytical work is done at the university, essential financial support is provided by the Institute through agreements with the university. These experimental agreements, which are supervised financially by the Laboratory, cover all expenses except the payment of salaries to academically qualified staff.

During the performance of experiments at the Laboratory, the services of NIRNS technical staff to help the visiting research workers have been found to be necessary, and are provided.

The Rutherford Laboratory

The basic task of the Laboratory staff is to operate the accelerators, to adapt them to the changing needs of the research programme, to initiate and to exploit new developments in accelerator science and technology, and to join the universities in nuclear and high energy research. There are other items on the programme, notably services to universities and others in developing and designing equipment for their domestic programmes. Two accelerators are currently under design by the Laboratory, a cyclotron for the Atomic Energy Authority and an electrostatic generator for Oxford University. A different project, outside the Institute's normal field because its use will not be restricted to nuclear science, is the installation of a Ferranti Atlas computer for use by universities, the Atomic Energy Authority, Government Departments and the Institute. The Atlas Laboratory will be administratively a part of the Rutherford Laboratory, but its operation will be generally supervised by a special committee appointed by the Board. Other work is associated with aid to universities in the use of nuclear reactors for research, including the provision of radiochemical facilities.

The total staff at present engaged in this work is about 950, and is expected to grow to about 1,200, of all grades including industrial employees. In addition, supporting services are provided by the UKAEA on repayment by NIRNS for water, gas, and electricity supplies, building construction, purchasing through the Authority's Contracts Branch, use of the AERE main library and such matters as home-to-work transport, management of the Institute's guest house for visitors, staff hostels and so on.

As is usual in large research laboratories, we have decentralized the organization to the limits possible without wasteful duplication of staff or facilities, and have delegated responsibility to make the basic unit a group small enough for the group leader to be an active working member.

A simplified distribution of staff into Divisions and groups is given in Table 6.

The proton linear accelerator directly occupies 100 physicists, engineers and supporters, excluding the 50 visiting research workers. The senior physicist in charge of the work is assisted by the leaders of the three groups listed in Table 6. The accelerator physicists and their associated engineers operate the machine, but also have a research and development outlet because the accelerator is itself a piece of research equipment and requires improvement and development, and possible replacement in the future by something better. A past example was the development of a polarized ion source, which has greatly extended the range of research possible with the machine. An example of a current piece of research is the study of superconducting materials as applied to linear accelerators. The PLA draws on various central Laboratory services. Some services obviously demand or are well-suited to centralization, but the PLA is virtually self-sufficient for its day-to-day needs in engineering and workshop effort for the nuclear and applied physics work and has local administrative support.

Nimrod is a much bigger project, and it has just undergone the transition from construction to operation. It would not be useful to give here the history of the construction project; it has had its problems, interesting as well as difficult, but is only a preliminary to the real job of running a research laboratory. To discuss in detail the present plans for operation and research use of the machine would give a false impression of finality and certainty. But the problems can be outlined, together with a general indication of the lines on which solutions are being sought.

The machine itself now occupies only 15 per cent of the scientific staff of the Laboratory, and many of its builders are now engaged in the development of apparatus and of techniques for high energy research. There are several different lines of development of experimental and ancillary

PLATE II

The 7 GeV proton synchrotron Nimrod, under construction at the
Rutherford High Energy Laboratory.

*Table 6.   Distribution by Divisions and Groups
of Rutherford Laboratory Staff (October 1964)*

	Scientific	Engineering	Executive, Clerical, etc.	Industrial
Director	1			
Assistant Director	1			
Division Heads ..	5	1		
Nimrod Division				
Machine Physics ..	44	2		3
Beams Physics ..	24	1		2
General Physics ..	12			1
Machine Engineering ..	7	84		65
H.E.P. Engineering ..		42		14
High Energy Physics Division				
Counter Group (resident team) ..	12			
Counter Group (with visiting teams) ..	14			
Bubble Chamber Research	6			
Electronics Group ..	13	3		1
Applied Physics Division				
Bubble Chamber Technology ..	24	25		6
Cyclotron Group ..	21			
High Magnetic Fields ..	5			
Computing and Theory	30			
PLA Division				
Nuclear Physics ..	16	1		1
Machine Physics ..	25	1		1
Engineering ..		36		25
Engineering Division				
Central Engineering ..	6	86		94
Cyclotron ..		5		
Safety ..		5		
Administration Division				
Scientific ..	6	1	1	
Finance and Accounts ..			25	
Personnel ..			14	
General Administration*			71	40
Non-Divisional				
Electrostatic Generator	12	2		1
Radiological Protection	9	1		
Totals ..	293	296	111	254

* General Administration includes local administrative support to Divisions, secretaries of senior staff, etc.

apparatus, associated with electronic and visual detection of elementary particle phenomena, mechanized reduction of experimental data, and extraction of particle beams from the accelerators and their transport and separation into the different types. In addition, most of the theoretical physics, and computing based on the Orion computer at the Laboratory, is concerned with Nimrod. High energy physicists who join in the research use of the machine have to collaborate in all these developments, and initiate many of them. Already over 100 research workers are using Nimrod.

The physics groups concerned with the various aspects of this work are already quite numerous. Some are fully manned, but others will need to grow considerably. They need to interact closely, and to work to a coherent plan, but must be able to generate new ideas and adapt themselves to new scientific and technological situations which can arise very quickly. Their supervision and co-ordination is a job for more than one man, but all are concerned with the same end-product of published results in high energy research, based on one machine but carried out by visitors from many laboratories. The arrangements for nuclear research by universities on the PLA have worked well enough to justify their extension as a basis for the more complicated high energy research on Nimrod. A small panel of distinguished physicists join the Director and the Head of the H.E.P. Division in making the final selection of experiments to be mounted on Nimrod, and detailed written proposals are submitted to this panel after a process of colloquia and seminars analagous to that used at the PLA. The HEP Division has been made numerically quite small and has been freed so far as possible from managerial and technological responsibility. The Nimrod Division operates, maintains and develops the accelerator, and is responsible for beam separation and transport and for engineering assistance to the high energy physicists. The Applied Physics Division is responsible for computing, for data reduction techniques in the more elaborate particle detection systems, and for the development and operation of bubble chambers.

The physicists, engineers and supporters of the Nimrod operation and development groups include all the plant supervisors and operators, specialist 'trouble shooters' and accelerator development staff, with specialized design and workshop effort. The high energy physicists are joined by engineers and technicians in planning, deploying and operating research equipment in the experimental areas, again with specialized close support. But both route to Central Engineering those longer-term jobs which can be done, and often can be done best, in a rather more detached atmosphere.

Central Engineering provides maintenance services for the whole Laboratory, has a team of design and development engineers and operates central development-type electrical, electronics and mechanical workshops. The senior engineer in charge is responsible to the Chief Engineer, who is also responsible for 'non-radiological' safety and for building works. The Engineering Division includes estimating engineers, who are an essential part of the financial control system, and engineers responsible for an important outside manufacture service. It is the policy of the Laboratory to pass to industry as much engineering and manufacturing work as possible. Very often the equipment is so specialized that we have to design it ourselves, but even then we prefer not to make it. Detailed drawings, when we have to produce them, are often made on contract; we employ relatively few draughtsmen. Most of the laboratory apparatus, as opposed to major plant which always goes to industry, is made on running contracts by relatively small firms who are tested by competition at intervals. This proves to be economical and enables us to minimize the size of our own workshops which are kept mainly for jobs requiring special expertise, for extremely urgent items, and for work which has to be done on fixed equipment.

Fig. 13 illustrates the formal lines of responsibility in the Laboratory at the upper level.

The usual attempt has been made to build the organizational structure around the people available rather than to start with a theoretically perfect structure and to fit the people into the 'boxes' afterwards.

Of course some of the managerial matters are functionally obvious from the start, but in research and development it is easy to organize the life out of the establishment.

The Director and Division Heads are the Management Committee of the Laboratory and meet formally in this capacity once a fortnight for about two hours. Although there is always a specific agenda, committee papers are usually limited to rough notes to aid discussion and brief minutes recording important decisions. These senior staff and the most senior Group Leaders, together with the Head of the Atlas Computer Laboratory, are the members of the Senior Staff Forum who meet once every four weeks, also for about two hours. The present membership is sixteen. This Committee is not merely a useful mechanism for disseminating Management Committee views and decisions, and for helping the Director to sense the feelings of his staff; it is also an effective arm of management. The members are senior people who together represent and work in every aspect of the Laboratory's activities. There are no formal terms of reference, and no specific powers of approval, but anything from the internal scientific programme to minor but contentious administrative matters may be put for decision by the Director or the Management Committee, or raised by a member.

Priorities in the internal programme and, therefore, Divisional staff complements and budgets, are finally determined by the Management Committee but are based on discussion at the Senior Staff Forum as well as on scientific discussions at various levels.

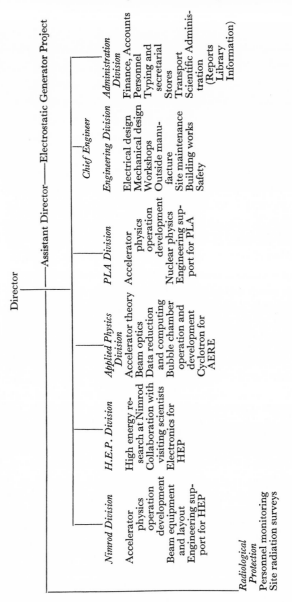

Figure 13
Rutherford Laboratory internal organization.

PROJECT MANAGEMENT

High energy research needs a continuous supply of capital equipment for particle detection, beam handling, data reduction, and adaptation of the accelerator, and often several major capital schemes are current simultaneously. The practice in the Rutherford Laboratory is to have a management committee for every capital project costing £100,000 or more. The approved estimate for each is kept separate from the rest of the Laboratory finance, and detailed financial control is delegated to the appropriate management committee by the Director, who, nevertheless, signs all demands over £2,000. The chairman of each committee is a senior member of the Laboratory staff personally concerned with the project, and he is assisted by the finance and estimating staff. It is important to note that these committees do not decide what projects shall be started; their function is to ensure businesslike organization and proper financial control of projects already adopted, and each is wound up as its project is completed. Most major projects require the services of several groups in the Laboratory and in one or more university departments, but there is always a project leader. Smaller projects are handled by individual group leaders or senior staff, and here the Director signs all demands over £1,000.

Although an exception has to be made when the Laboratory undertakes a major project on behalf of an outside body, we resist the creation of a new group unless its function as an essentially self-contained unit can be seen to be consistent with the long-term programme, and with the retention of a research outlet for those existing groups which have service functions depending upon research-minded staff (for example the Nimrod Accelerator Physics Group). The object is to avoid frequent dissolution of groups as projects are completed, but of course groups sometimes have to be wound up. Thus we disbanded our separate Accelerator Research Group some time ago when we took on a new project, and for the time being left our important interests in this field to the PLA Accelerator Physics Group and the Nimrod Accelerator Physics Group, and several interested individuals who work in other groups. Similarly a strong team of high vacuum specialists, an essential part of the Nimrod design and construction team, was not perpetuated as a Vacuum Group after the completion of the machine, in spite of our continued interest in high vacua.

STAFF STRUCTURE

A third of the Laboratory staff came by voluntary transfer from the Atomic Energy Authority in 1960, and the others have been recruited directly by the Laboratory. The staff structure is at present essentially the same as that of the Authority, and is, therefore, similar to that of the Scientific Civil Service. Table 7 gives the present distribution of the staff in this structure. The Institute have recognized as negotiating bodies the same staff associations and trade unions who represent Authority staff, and have their own Whitley Council and Joint Industrial Council on the pattern established in the Civil Service.

We employ a proportion of our research staff on fixed term appointments of several years' duration. In the nuclear and high energy physics groups the majority of the honours graduates (equivalent to the Scientific Officer class in the Civil Service) are on fixed term appointments of up to five years. We recruit for these groups at early post-doctoral level, and the posts are similar to Fellowships but are not so called because they can carry organizational duties. Salaries, increments, and promotion prospects are the same as for corresponding members of the permanent staff.

There are similar fixed term posts in the applied physics research groups, but here the majority of the staff are permanent. All the operations, technical, and supporting staff are permanent.

Table 7. Total Rutherford Laboratory Staff (October 1964)

Scientific

Scientific Officer Class (incl. 28 Fixed Term)	107
Experimental Officer Class	120
Scientific Assistant Class	66

Engineering

Engineer Class	76
Assistant Design Engineers	25
Draughtsmen	16
Technical Class	152
Non-Technical Class	27

Administrative

Photoprinter Class	5
Stores Class	5
Executive Class	25
Clerical Class	44
Secretarial and Typing grades ..	32

Industrial

Skilled Craftsmen	148
Others	106
Total ..	954

There are important advantages in having a proportion of fixed term appointments. They attract young research workers who wish to remain mobile, help to exploit the potential of the Laboratory for advanced training, give some flexibility for future changes of programme and some movement in the inevitable periods of severe complement restrictions, and strengthen the bonds between the Laboratory and the universities since many holders of these posts will take university appointments. They are also a ready-made mechanism for accepting research workers from overseas; about 20 per cent. of the fixed term posts have been held by scientists from foreign or Commonwealth countries.

BUDGET

Budgeting follows the normal practice in Government-financed organizations. Estimates are submitted annually to

The Rutherford Laboratory

the Government by the Institute, together with planning forecasts for five years. The drafts are prepared in the Laboratory on the basis of committed and anticipated programmes of work, and are finalized by the General Purposes Committee and the Board. The NIRNS grant is finally determined by the Office of the Minister for Science and the Treasury and is a 'cash spend' budget for a single year; it does not, for example, fix the final cost of any particular project. Major projects are separately approved and financially controlled by the Treasury, but are funded from the normal budget. There is, therefore, an elaborate system of financial control in the Laboratory, of which the project management committees already mentioned form an important part. The individual budgets of the Divisions for research and development work and for recurrent expenditure are determined by the Laboratory Management Committee, and a system of project numbers is used for recording commitments and expenditure for the guidance of Group Leaders. In the research and development field the Group Leaders operate on commitment budgets because the expertise of the Finance Officer and his staff, aided by the estimating engineers and the Contracts Branch, are needed to translate commitments into cash payments within a particular financial year.

A substantial part of the total expenditure has been on capital items; in the financial year 1964/65 capital expenditure is approximately £1·7 million out of a total expenditure of £6·2 million. The proportion of capital expenditure is now decreasing slowly. Experience elsewhere has shown that total expenditure rises steadily shortly after the completion of a very large accelerator. Comparison with the Rutherford Laboratory is difficult because we started to spend on experimental equipment much earlier than has been usual in similar laboratories, and there has, therefore, been an overlap with machine construction. Future expenditure will of course be a matter of balancing the needs of research and availability of funds.

233

CONCLUSION

There are both unusual problems and unusual opportunities in a laboratory such as this. A creative scientific atmosphere has to be developed in a community where only one man in ten is a graduate research physicist, after several years during which most of the people have been struggling with the construction of a very complicated machine in a directed and tightly-organized team. It is hard for many to see the machine as a beginning, and not an end in itself. On the other hand, the linear accelerator brought the purpose of the Laboratory to realization on a minor scale three years ahead of the operation of the big machine, and became the focus of physicists from many universities. This has repeated on a national scale the earlier experience of CERN, who also started with a relatively small machine.

The inherited staff structure and various traditional professional attitudes tend initially to hinder the creation of a unity of purpose centred on pure research. But the unusual concentration on one main line of research helps greatly—particularly as everyone can see that he is working in a really exciting field, and that he has colleagues all over the world with whom there is interchange of people and complete and open exchange of information and results. It is difficult to achieve the essential co-operation of large numbers of people in the complictaed Nimrod research programme, without suffocating in a pyramid of direction or a morass of powerful or over-democratic committees. The chosen solution, which shows promise, is to rely on the compact groups led by carefully chosen people, general supervision by three or four senior staff with authority to give direction when they feel this is necessary, committees or working parties which appear excessive in number but seem to work well, and frequent colloquia with occasional minor conferences. We attempt to confine rigidity in organization and practice to overall financial control, industrial safety and a number of other duties of good management, not always with complete success.

A rare and valuable privilege is the extremely close association with the university staff and research students who use the facilities of the Laboratory and join our own staff in development projects. They already come in large numbers, not only to do experiments on the linear accelerator and Nimrod, but to discuss problems with Laboratory staff, to attend the inevitable committees, to give and attend lectures and colloquia, and sometimes just to meet each other. This association, the Laboratory's reason for existence, is also our greatest help in trying to build a scientific community and not just a factory for producing proton beams.

It is a pleasure to acknowledge the generous help at many levels which we have received from the United Kingdom Atomic Energy Authority, and especially the co-operation which we enjoy with our distinguished neighbours at the AERE, Harwell. We have profited greatly from close collaboration with many laboratories working in the same field in four or five countries, especially CERN, the Lawrence Radiation Laboratory at Berkeley, California, and the Brookhaven National Laboratory, New York.

14

CERN: THE EUROPEAN ORGANIZATION FOR NUCLEAR RESEARCH

by Dr J. B. Adams, C.M.G., F.R.S.

THE FORMULATIVE YEARS, 1950–1954

The idea of setting up an international laboratory for nuclear physics research jointly owned by the European States, and the foundation and rapid growth of this laboratory at Meyrin, Geneva, all derive from the quite different interests and ambitions of two professional groups, statesmen and scientists. The success of the laboratory and its continuing prosperity have come about because both groups have found it essential to maintain their interests in the organization.

Up to the outbreak of the Second World War, nuclear physics was one of the most active and rewarding fields of fundamental research in Europe, but after the war, physicists returning to the front line of this subject, high energy nuclear physics, found the European laboratories very poorly equipped for this research. To a certain extent a lack of modern research tools acted as a stimulant and ingenious experimental programmes were devised that did not need expensive nuclear particle accelerators and elaborate electronic measuring instruments. One of the many elegant examples of such programmes was the nuclear emulsion experiments of C. F. Powell at Bristol University, using cosmic rays as the source of high energy particles, small photographic plates and optical microscopes as the measuring instruments, and the wives of research physicists as scanning machines. Many of the post-war discoveries of new nuclear particles were made with these techniques. There comes a time, however, when sheer ingenuity cannot compensate for the lack of essential apparatus and the growth of this field of research depended upon nuclear particle accelerators which would give intense beams of specified particles of known energies in place of the capricious cosmic rays. The university laboratories, where this research was carried out, did not have budgets that could afford such apparatus, and there seemed no way of finding the large sums of money necessary.

However, the European countries struggling back to civilization after the war became seriously interested in the peaceful applications of some of the wartime developments. New national laboratories were being planned, particularly in Britain and in France, to exploit nuclear fission as a source of energy, and the physicists involved in setting up these laboratories were in many cases those who had taken a prominent part in high energy physics research before the war. It is not surprising to find that high energy nuclear physics appeared as part of the programme of these new laboratories. The first major post-war nuclear particle accelerator built in Europe, a 180 MeV synchrocyclotron, was completed at the Atomic Energy Research Establishment at Harwell in 1949, and later the Commissariat d'Energie Atomique built a 2.5 GeV proton synchrotron at their laboratory at Saclay. High energy nuclear physics was thus able to acquire some of the necessary experimental facilities under the umbrella of atomic energy development, but these were still rudimentary compared with those existing and being planned in the United States, and they were not freely available to all university physicists due to security restrictions.

Young physicists graduating in the years around 1950 and inspired to research in fundamental particle physics by professors who themselves had taken an important part in the golden age of this subject in Europe could either choose to struggle with inadequate equipment in the European laboratories, or to emigrate to the United States where modern apparatus and vastly greater opportunities for their research were offered to them. Emigration was made doubly attractive by the high salaries available in the United States, which gave the European physicists and their families a standard of living very much higher than the one they had learned to expect in Europe. Many of the brightest physicists left Europe during these post-war years and they began an exodus to the United States that has not yet been arrested.

By about 1950 it became apparent that no single country in Europe was prepared to pay the price of equipping its laboratories to take part in the front line of high energy nuclear physics research, and the subject might well have declined irretrievably had it not been that several European statesmen were becoming interested in the concept of European unity and were seeking ways of making this unity manifest. It was the bringing together of these interests with the aspirations of the scientists that opened up new possibilities for high energy physics research in Europe.

The first public linking of these two interests occurred in December 1949, at the European Cultural Conference held in Lausanne. M. R. Dautry, at that time the Chief Administrator of the Commissariat d'Energie Atomique, and one of the leaders of the European movement, read a message from Louis de Broglie in which a proposal was made to create an international research institution in Europe which would be financed on a scale transcending the individual possibilities of the member states. Dautry pointed out in his speech that nuclear physics would be an appropriate subject for such an institution, since by general consent it fell outside any security classification. Later on, in June 1950, I. Rabi, in his official statement to the General Conference of UNESCO in Florence, gave further public expression to the idea of regional international laboratories and moreover indicated the general American sympathy towards European scientific co-operation. The resolutions passed at the Florence Conference enabled the Director of Natural Sciences of UNESCO, P. Auger, to take action in two respects. First he set up a special office in UNESCO and appointed J. Mussard as its secretary, and secondly, together with E. Amaldi, he proceeded to get together a number of physicists to help him with the planning of a new European laboratory. At the first meeting of this Board of Consultants, it was suggested that two projects should be studied simultaneously, first a large particle accelerator second to none in the world in energy, and secondly a smaller accelerator, which could be constructed quickly, so that experiments could be started as soon as possible on a European basis. In December 1951 UNESCO called a meeting in Paris, to which all European governments were invited to send delegates, and at a second meeting in Geneva, soon afterwards, eleven governments signed an agreement establishing a provisional organization. The United Kingdom was not amongst these eleven, but remained an uncommitted 'observer' during the whole life of the provisional CERN. The Council of this newly created organization, meeting for the first time in Paris in May 1952, set up four study groups, the Synchrocyclotron Group under C. J. Bakker, the Proton Synchrotron Group under O. Dahl, the Laboratory Group under L. Kowarski, and the Theoretical Group under Niels Bohr. E. Amaldi was appointed to the top post of Secretary-General, and from time to time members of these Groups, who worked on a part-time basis in their own laboratories, met to bring together the results of their studies. At the third meeting of the Council in Amsterdam, it was decided to locate the new laboratory in Geneva, and at the fourth meeting in January 1953, the United Kingdom had become so interested in the organization that Sir Ben Lockspeiser, head of the DSIR, attended the meeting and took a leading part in the drafting of the convention of the permanent organization. The provisional

CERN came to an end at the sixth meeting of the Council in Paris in June 1953, when a Convention was signed by delegates of twelve member states setting up an Interim CERN with an Interim Finance Committee and a Nominations Committee to select senior staff for the permanent organization. The permanent organization came into force on 24 September 1954 when seven of the signatory governments had ratified the Agreement, although it was not until 24 February 1955 that all twelve governments ratified.

During the period between the signing of the Convention on 1 July 1953 and its ratification on 24 September 1954, the organization had no legal existence and all work should have stopped, since in the event of insufficient signatories it would all have been a waste of time and money. In fact, the Interim Council and the Study Groups continued to plan the laboratory and to design its apparatus. The credit for this unorthodox action, which resulted in an enormous saving of time, must go to the many highly placed diplomats and administrators who risked their reputations on the eventual success of the venture, and to the young scientists and engineers who left secure positions in established laboratories in their own countries to lead a pioneer existence with their families in a foreign country, with no more than a 'moral commitment' to fall back on if it all failed. About twenty physicists and engineers of the Proton Synchrotron Group moved their families to Geneva in the months following October 1953 and established laboratories in the Institute of Physics of the University of Geneva, and the Laboratory Group and an administrative nucleus were set up in the Villa Cointrin near the airport of Geneva in January 1954. The members of these groups, who were by now full-time staff members of CERN, came from all over Western Europe, many from countries which had recently been at war with each other, and they laid the foundations of the CERN laboratories. For them, CERN was not only a scientific laboratory; it was an expression of their faith in Europe as a

PLATE III

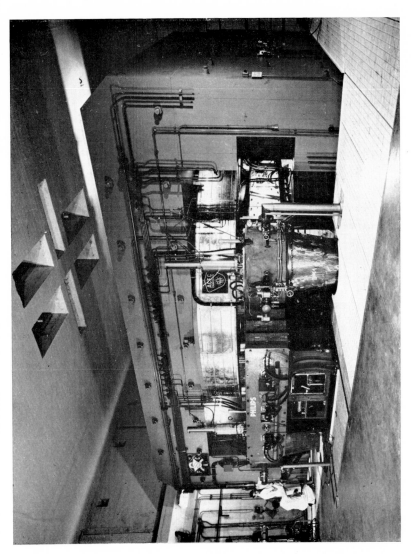

CERN Proton Synchrocyclotron. Maximum proton energy 600 MeV

PLATE IV

CERN Proton Synchrotron. Maximum proton energy 28 GeV. View inside the underground ring-shaped building showing a section of the accelerator. The diameter of the machine is 200 metres.

cultural entity, fully able to contribute to the main cultural activity of our epoch—scientific research—on an equal footing with the United States of America and with the U.S.S.R.

The Interim Council had to face many financial problems during this period. An initial endowment of 1 million Swiss francs was soon exhausted, but by means of gifts and additional contributions, 3.7 million Swiss francs were spent by the organization by September 1954, when ratification of the Convention took place. This was a very large sum of money for governments to spend on an organization which had no legal existence, and great credit is due to the members of the Interim Council of CERN, who made it their business to find the money for the scientific pioneers working in Geneva. R. Valeur of France, the chairman of the Council during the whole of the interim period, and Sir Ben Lockspeiser of the United Kingdom, chairman of the Finance Committee during the same period, both used their considerable authority to guide the young organization during this difficult period, and to create around them an atmosphere of confidence in the new venture.

THE BUILDING OF THE CERN LABORATORY,
1955–1960

Due to the combined efforts of the hundred or so CERN staff and the Interim Council during the formulative years, the permanent organization started with well-developed plans for its laboratory and its apparatus, a nucleus of staff already integrated into effective teams, a site in Geneva and above all a morale and sense of purpose that has rarely been seen in Europe in peacetime. At the first meeting of the permanent Council of CERN on 7 October 1954, the pattern of external government of the laboratory and its internal management were established, and this pattern did not change in any important way until the completion of the building phase of the laboratory.

R   241

Organization of Research Establishments

The Convention laid down the membership of CERN and the procedure to be adopted at meetings of the Council. Each Member State was entitled to send two delegates to the meetings, and most States sent one eminent scientist and one senior member of the government department which handled the contribution to CERN. Thus Sir John Cockcroft and Sir Ben Lockspeiser, the head of the Department of Scientific and Industrial Research, were the two delegates from the United Kingdom. The Council therefore consisted of some of the most eminent scientists in Europe and some of its most able administrators, and fortunately for the stability of the organization, the great majority of these delegates stayed on the Council until after the building period was over. Many of them had also taken an active part in the formulative stages of CERN, and had been members of the Interim Council, and thus there was no break in the continuity.

Sir Ben Lockspeiser was appointed President of the Council at its first meeting and three advisory committees were set up; a Committee of Council to deal quickly with urgent business, a Finance Committee to deal with construction contracts, staff contracts and other financial matters, and a Scientific Policy Committee to advise the Council on the programme of the laboratory. The first Director-General of CERN, and its chief executive, was Felix Bloch, a Swiss theoretical physicist who had moved to Stanford University, but he resigned after a year in office and C. J. Bakker, a Dutch experimental physicist, was appointed in his place.

The period 1955–60 was not only the construction phase of the laboratory but also was the time when many of the fundamental principles underlying the organization of the laboratory were settled, and it is appropriate at this juncture to mention some of the solutions that were adopted.

The pattern of organization of research laboratories in the different countries of Europe has evolved from the local conditions and historical practices of these countries. University research laboratories are governed according to

242

Organization for Nuclear Research

patterns established for an essentially classical education, and are strongly reminiscent of the monastic systems from which many are derived. State-owned research laboratories such as AERE, Harwell, and CEA, Saclay, are moulded on the Civil Service patterns of Britain and France. Neither of these systems is particularly suitable for large research laboratories, and many people were afraid that an international laboratory would find itself burdened with even more inappropriate systems of organization. However, at the time CERN was set up, Europe did not exist as one single state with a commonly agreed organizational pattern, and advantage was taken of this situation to design a system for CERN specifically suited to the needs of a research laboratory. Future European laboratories will no doubt be modelled on the system that CERN evolved during these years, and depending on its ultimate efficacy, be either blessed or saddled with it. Many of the CERN rules and regulations have simply been taken over from the better national practices. For example, contracts for experimental apparatus or the buildings are awarded on a competitive basis. There must be at least three tenders and the contract goes to the lowest bidder who can, in the opinion of CERN, carry out the work satisfactorily from a technical point of view. The staff are selected by the laboratory from all over Europe by advertisement and competition. In both these cases the danger for CERN lay in the Member States wanting to obtain a share of the contracts and a share of the staff posts in rough proportion to their contributions to the organization. This danger was fortunately avoided by the wisdom of the Council and the foresight of the founders of CERN.

It is perhaps more interesting to mention some of the differences from national practices. One that never fails to excite alarm is that the meetings of the Council are held in public, and within the capacity of the council chamber, the staff of CERN, the press and even the general public can attend the meetings. As a result, the staff of the laboratory have got to know the members of the Governing Board and there is a free exchange of views between them at all times. Furthermore, CERN enjoys one of the best press relationships of any of the international organizations in Europe. This general principle of no secrecy also led to the rejection of the notion of patenting ideas and inventions made at CERN. It was argued that fundamental research is a cultural activity which should not be made to pay in the commercial sense, and that governments and combinations of governments must decide whether or not they can afford this activity, without the lure of financial gain.

The early critics of international laboratories emphasized the difficulties of building up a high quality staff on an international basis. They argued that CERN would never attract first rate physicists, engineers and administrators away from secure posts in their own countries, and that after the first wave of enthusiastic pioneers, CERN would only secure second class expatriates who would be more interested in the affluence of the organization than in the work of the laboratory. Furthermore, they foresaw difficulties arising with the many languages used in Europe.

CERN attempted to meet these problems in the following ways. The staff salaries were fixed at a level somewhere between the average university and industrial salaries in Europe and it was made quite plain that CERN was a European organization which did not pay American or international salaries. At first the level was fixed too low and the early staff suffered some hardships, but by trial and error a level was soon reached that gave the staff a standard of living in Geneva comparable to that which they had at home. Without the lure of high salaries, CERN had to ensure a scientific reputation and a respectability that would attract the right staff, since it was not sufficient merely to discourage the gold diggers. The presence of so many eminent scientists on the Council, men such as Niels Bohr, Heisenberg, Cockcroft and Perrin, and their personal efforts to encourage good physicists to join CERN, soon established a high reputation for the laboratory. Also, with so many highly placed diplomats and administrators on the Council, its respectability could hardly be questioned. Above all, the programme of CERN was so exciting and attractive to young physicists and engineers, that anything available to them in their own countries was insignificant in comparison. Thus it turned out during these years that CERN had no serious recruiting problems but managed to recruit some of the best of the European physicists and engineers, and it never lacked technicians and administrators. Nowadays, with many other interesting international scientific adventures on the horizon, it would probably be more difficult to get together such a powerful staff.

The language problem resolved itself quite simply. It was soon discovered that an inability to express oneself forcibly in another language lowered the tensions normally experienced in a research laboratory. In any case the real difficulty lies not in understanding what somebody else is saying but in forgiving him for saying it, and this has little to do with language difference.

Some of the staff problems, common to all research laboratories, were perhaps faced more resolutely by CERN. Many centre around the difficulty of creating the right atmosphere for research work in an organization where over 80 per cent. of the staff are not research workers, but are people carrying out other essential jobs in the laboratory. It is not always easy for an administrator with a fine record in a civil service type of organization to adapt himself to the conditions in a research laboratory, and an excellent industrial engineer can find engineering in such an environment frustrating and confusing. The method generally adopted by CERN, therefore, was to recruit only those people who were seriously interested in working in a research laboratory, and to promote those that succeeded in carrying out their jobs in this environment.

There was only one promotion board that dealt with physicists, engineers, administrators and technicians together, and this board claimed no absolute judgement of the capabilities of the staff in their separate professions. The criterion for promotion was the ability of the staff member to carry out his job better than his other professional colleagues in the CERN laboratory. The administrators, engineers, physicists and technicians were encouraged to think of themselves, not as members of separate professions each with a career to follow independent of the laboratory, but as members of CERN with a professional job to do inside the laboratory. In a staff with so many complicated and interwoven loyalties, it was desirable to emphasize in a material way an overriding loyalty to CERN. It should be remarked in passing that trade unions are as yet in an embryonic state in Switzerland.

The staff contracts at CERN are initially for a fixed term period of three years, but one renewal for a further period of three years can be made, after which time the person must either leave the organization or be given an indefinite contract. These rules apply to all staff whatever their profession, and the percentage of indefinite contracts was planned not to exceed about 20 per cent. of the total staff. The indefinite contracts are not permanent in the ordinary civil service or university professorial sense, but can be broken by the staff member or by the organization. However, CERN can only break an indefinite contract if there is no suitable job for the staff member to do in the laboratory, and the organization in this case must pay indemnities which can be as high as four years' salary, depending on the age of the man and his length of service with the organization. It was accepted by the staff that the laboratory must be free to re-arrange its staff from time to time, but if it happens that the organization is obliged to dispense with the services of a staff member who has been encouraged by the award of an indefinite contract to plan a career in the laboratory, then the organization must compensate him for giving the creative years of his life to the laboratory.

These conditions for the staff contracts were drawn up with two points in mind: firstly the fear that CERN might become a laboratory with a permanent staff isolated from the European community that supported it, and separated from the university scientists for whom the facilities had primarily been built, and secondly the hope that these conditions would help towards solving the problem of maintaining the creative power of a research laboratory. The second point, which is a relatively new one, has arisen with the post-war growth of large research laboratories not directly part of universities. In universities there is a natural flow of young graduates into and out of research laboratories which maintains their vitality. It is a fact that creative ability decreases with the age of a scientist, and while some compensation comes from increasing experience, it is unfortunately not a sufficient substitute in a research laboratory. Thus, in those laboratories which are not teaching institutions, some flow of physicists must be encouraged, and for many years there was strong opposition in CERN to the idea of giving indefinite contracts to the physicists. Although this has been relaxed to some extent nowadays, very few physicists are on the indefinite staff of the laboratory. It was soon realized, however, that until the national and university laboratories could offer the physicists leaving CERN a chance of continuing their research work at home, these physicists were more likely to end up in the American laboratories than in the European laboratories, and instead of CERN attenuating the drift of physicists to America, the net result would only be to increase the experience of those leaving Europe. This problem will be taken up later on in this article.

At the end of 1959 the CERN proton synchrotron came into operation and a wave of jubilation mingled with relief spread over the whole organization. Europe was now equipped with facilities for high energy research as good as existed anywhere else in the world and parity had been reached with the great American and Russian laboratories for the first time since long before the war. For over six months CERN had by far the highest energy machine in the world, since its sister machine at Brookhaven did not come into operation until mid-1960—a fact which did a great deal of good to European morale. By this time Sir Ben Lockspeiser had retired from the DSIR and from the Presidency of the CERN Council, and it fell to M. de Rose, his successor and himself one of the earliest begetters of CERN, to preside over the official opening ceremony of the big machine of CERN early in 1960. Most people at this time thought that the building period was safely over.

THE RESEARCH PERIOD—1960 ONWARDS

Experimental high energy physics research at CERN began, of course, when the synchrocyclotron came into operation, and even before that time, since many of the CERN physicists had been sent to work on the Liverpool University machine. Furthermore, theoretical physics research had been going on since the beginning, first at Copenhagen and later on at CERN itself, when a theoretical group was established in Geneva in 1956. Many notable results of work done with the synchrocyclotron were published long before the proton synchrotron came into use. However, it is convenient to call the period after the building period the research period, because it was only then that CERN came up against the real problems of using large accelerators for research work.

Although the experiments using the synchrocyclotron had been very successful, the way of using this accelerator was not very different from current experimental practice in many European laboratories where similar machines were already in use, and many people were convinced that re-search with a bigger machine would be similar in character and differ only in scale. It turned out that the experience with the synchrocyclotron was very deceptive in this respect and CERN in 1960 found itself with the largest machine in the world and not very clear ideas about its exploitation. Also it was soon apparent that the amount of apparatus built for the experimental programme was insufficient, partly due to the machine operating a year before its target date. These errors of planning and hesitations were due primarily to inexperience, and indeed the lack of modern accelerating machines in Europe for so many years had made it impossible for anybody to get experience of experimenting at such high energies. While the American physicists had been steadily proceeding up the energy scale with machines such as the 3 GeV Cosmotron at Brookhaven and the 6 GeV Bevatron at Berkeley, gathering experience and making fundamental discoveries at each stage, the European physicists had had to be content with cosmic rays and very modest equipment. Also the organization essential for experiments with these very large accelerators was foreign, and even distasteful to . many physicists in Europe, and a great deal of time was wasted in discussions about the broader philosophy of physics at this time. In all it was a rather humiliating experience, following as it did the wild jubilation at the early functioning of the big machine.

In the middle of sorting out the experimental programme, CERN suffered a tragic loss when its Director-General, C. J. Bakker, was killed in an aircraft accident in New York in April 1960 while on his way to a conference. Thus 1960, which should have been the brightest year for CERN, became one of the most difficult in its history. The Director-General appointed to succeed Bakker, J. B. Adams, who had up to this time directed the work on the proton synchrotron, was faced with the task of re-organizing the laboratory to meet the needs of the research phase. A Directorate of five people was formed to guide the main functions of the laboratory, physics research, applied physics (that is experimental apparatus development) and administration. Professors G. Bernardini and V. Weisskopf were appointed Directorate

Members for Research and Dr M. G. N. Hine and Mr S. A. ff. Dakin were appointed Directorate Members for Applied Physics and Administration, respectively. The six original divisions of CERN which had been set up to build the laboratory were re-arranged to suit the experimental programme and the senior staff available to lead them. It is interesting to note that one of the debates during the year preceding the operation of the big machine had been whether it was advisable to perpetuate the Proton Synchrotron Division after the machine came into operation. This Division, which had successfully designed and built the machine, had become one of the biggest in CERN, and it was felt that adding experimental physics teams to this Division in order that it could both operate the machine and carry out the research programmes would so inflate its numbers that it would be difficult to control. Some people argued that research work and machine operation were quite separate jobs and should not be mixed together, and from this came the idea that one division should operate the two CERN machines and one division should be responsible for all the experimental programmes. However, by 1960 the experimental teams building and using track chambers had grown so large that one division containing these teams, and the others using different experimental techniques, would itself have been too large. As a compromise, therefore, two experimental divisions were created, one for track chamber experiments and one for experiments using counter-techniques of different types, and a further two divisions were created for operating the two accelerating machines. This arrangement could hardly have worked efficiently had it not been for the presence of the Directorate and for the co-ordinating committees for the experimental programmes which had to be set up for quite different reasons.

The founders of CERN had conceived the laboratory as a place where the most modern facilities for high energy research would be built for the physicists of Europe to use.

However, it was never very clear to whom these physicists should belong. Some people argued that they should belong to the universities and should visit CERN from time to time to use the experimental facilities of the laboratory. From this idea came the concept of 'truck teams'—groups of physicists and technicians coming to CERN with their apparatus to use the beams of particles from the accelerators. Other people, realising the problem of experimenting with large machines, admitted the need for some resident physicists on the CERN staff who would provide a background of experience and local knowledge of the CERN facilities. The fear of all people, as has already been mentioned, was that so many physicists would join the staff of CERN that the 'outsiders' at the European universities would never get time to do their experiments with the machines. The 'truck team' idea was tried out with the synchrocyclotron with moderate success, but when the time came to use the big machine, it was realized that the visiting teams would be impotent unless integrated with CERN staff, who themselves knew something of the problems of experimenting with giant accelerators. Thus the truck teams evolved into 'mixed teams' of visiting physicists and CERN physicists. In the early part of 1960, however, many physicists in Europe felt that CERN was not welcoming visiting physicists as much as it should, and of course the early difficulties with the experimental programme of the proton synchrotron did not allay these fears. Therefore, in addition to the reorganization of the divisions of CERN and the setting up of a Directorate, it was necessary to overhaul the arrangements by which external physicists could use the CERN facilities and influence the experimental programmes. There seemed no way out of this problem but to set up committees composed of physicists from both inside and outside CERN and to let them determine the programmes. A Nuclear Physics Committee chaired by one of the research members of the Directorate was set up, and three sub-committees, one for each of the experimental techniques; track chamber experiments, photographic emulsion experiments and counter experiments. The chairmen of the sub-committees who were all senior physicists from outside the laboratory brought the agreed programmes of their committees to the Nuclear Physics Committee and, together with the CERN senior staff, argued out the final programmes for the two machines. From these programmes, the running schedule of the machines was worked out, usually for six months ahead, and time allocated to the different experiments.

Much as one dislikes committees, and cumbersome as these appear on paper, the system worked remarkably well, and it is still in use with only minor modifications. These committees also brought together the two experimental divisions of CERN, since their experiments were examined by the committees, together with those proposed from outside, and it enabled the divisions responsible for operating the machines to have an authoritative programme on which to schedule the machine operations.

By the end of 1960 the reorganization of the laboratory was completed. The committee system for determining the experimental programmes had just started, and the Directorate was beginning to get a grip on the problems of research with the big machine. More important still, the experimental staff of the laboratory were rapidly learning how to use the big machine, and although it is dramatically convenient to write of 1960 as a bleak year because of the depressing events that happened, it must be remembered that research with the synchrocyclotron had been going ahead even more successfully than in the past, and many of the experiments with the big machine during that year gave interesting and very useful results.

How well CERN learned its lessons and gained in experience can be seen from the contributions it made to the International Conference on High Energy Physics held at CERN in June, 1962.

Organization for Nuclear Research

For the next few years, the programme of the CERN laboratory is clear enough—both accelerators must be used to the full as research tools, and the necessary resources must be found by the Member States to push ahead with the research programmes using the existing facilities. However, a few years ago, neither the Council nor the laboratory quite realized the implications of fully exploiting the CERN facilities. There had always been a comfortable belief in the Council that the budgets of the laboratory would rise during the building period, reach a maximum towards the end of this period and thereafter drop to a modest level which would remain constant with the years. The European governments had signed the Convention on the understanding that the initial outlay on the laboratory would be between 120–130 million Swiss francs but by the end of the building period the total bill amounted to 240 million Swiss francs. Considering that the original estimate had been made with little idea of what such a laboratory entailed, and remembering that the proton synchrotron was not even designed at that time, it was not perhaps a bad estimate, and Sir Ben Lockspeiser, from his extensive experience of these matters, predicted as early as the first meeting of the Council that the laboratory would cost twice the original estimate. Many governments felt that after 1959 some more rigid financial control was needed to level off the annual expenditure, especially since it was apparent by then that the old idea of a falling annual expenditure after the building period was unrealistic. At the end of 1959, therefore, the Council insisted that a fixed sum should be accepted by the laboratory for the next three years, allowing effectively the same expenditure in each of the years 1960, 1961 and 1962. As subsequent events showed, this decision had very unfortunate effects, but at the time, with the notion that the construction of the laboratory was finally finished and the fact that the cost was twice the original estimate, it was perhaps excusable. The result was to limit the building of experimental apparatus for the proton synchrotron and to limit its future exploitation just when it was coming into experimental use, and these limitations contributed a great deal to the general unpreparedness during 1960. In fact, the budgets for these three years were not kept down to a fixed level—pressure of events raised them to 70 million and 80 million Swiss francs respectively in 1961 and 1962 (see Fig. 14). Even so, the effects of trying to level

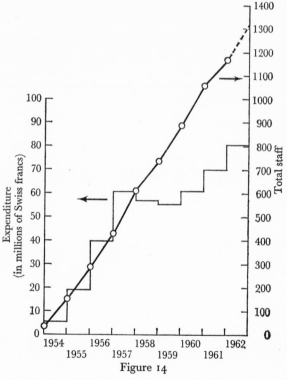

Figure 14

off the annual expenditure during these critical years, before the laboratory had reached a state of equilibrium, stunted its growth. For example, the proton synchrotron in 1962 is only just coming into full operation, there is still a serious lack of some experimental equipment, and experimental areas for further exploiting the possibilities of the machine will only be completed in 1964. However, it should not be imagined that the European governments were in any way displeased with CERN at that time—on the contrary CERN was considered a great success and an excellent example of European co-operation. By the end of 1961, however, the lessons had gone home and the idea of levelling off the expenditure of the laboratory was replaced by a more realistic plan of limiting the rate of expansion in the next few years until the final equilibrium size for the laboratory is reached.

In parallel with using the existing facilities, attention must be given to new major facilities for the CERN laboratory. These could well be a new accelerator of perhaps 300 GeV energy, costing far more than the present proton synchrotron and taking longer to build. If the research work needs such a machine in say ten years' time, a start must be made soon, and therefore the problems of what is needed from the physics point of view and how it should be supported are even now urgent ones. It has been suggested that the next machine, because of its immense size and cost, might become a world machine and be built as a joint project by Europe, the U.S.S.R. and U.S.A. together. The addition of a pair of storage rings to the present 25 GeV proton synchrotron to make available a centre of mass energies of 50 GeV may provide an attractive extension to the physics programme. Whatever the outcome, Europe must be prepared to go forward with this research or once again face relegation to second place in this research field.

The relationship of CERN to the laboratories in the Member States has already been mentioned above in connexion with staff problems, and there are other important links. Nowadays no laboratory is an isolated unit, alone in its field of research, and CERN is but the peak of a pyramid of laboratories whose wide base is the many university laboratories in Europe. The well-being and nourishment of all levels of this pyramid is as important to the success of

CERN as the availability of funds for its own laboratory, for it is from the universities that well-trained research physicists come to use the facilities of CERN, and it is back to universities or to national laboratories that they should go after working in the CERN laboratory.

At the very beginning of the CERN idea, there were those people in university laboratories who saw CERN as a threat to their own existence. CERN, they thought, would become the darling of the governments of Europe, something to lavish funds upon; in short, the affluent international laboratory, and as CERN absorbed the moneys of Europe the laboratories of the Member States would wither away from neglect. In fact just the opposite happened; CERN acted like a catalyst to release more resources for the national laboratories, not so much for those in the universities, but for new regional laboratories set up in the different countries and used by the local universities. The National Institute for Research in Nuclear Science in the United Kingdom, the CNEN Laboratory at Frascati, near Rome, the Saturn accelerator at the CEA Laboratory at Saclay, the DESY project at Hamburg and the electron accelerator at Bonn all started after CERN came into existence. A wave of accelerator building passed through Europe and new facilities were built up in the different countries to supplement those at CERN. In some countries more money was invested in the national laboratories than these countries contributed to CERN. For example, in the United Kingdom the National Institute for Research in Nuclear Science has an annual budget of some £6 million, while the United Kingdom contribution to CERN is about £1·7 million per annum.

All this has changed the role of universities in this research work and has created problems that, as yet, are by no means solved. Two important things have happened. Firstly the larger facilities for this research are no longer in the university laboratories but in national or international laboratories, and secondly, because the new laboratories are not teaching institutions, the teaching of physics and research in physics is developing in different localities. The links between research and teaching, which are so important to the health of the whole subject, now depend to an increasing extent upon the flow of physicists between the three types of institution, the universities, the national laboratories and CERN, and on the material prosperity of all three. If these links are broken, as could very easily happen if, for example, national and international laboratories took over the teaching functions of the universities, or if one of the three types of institution is starved of resources, then the whole pyramid will crumble.

Considering the three types of research institute at the present time, one has the impression that the university physics faculties receive the weakest support of the three, although their relative strength varies in the different European countries. In Italy, for example, there is a well-planned national attempt to make it possible for university physicists to use CERN and to integrate the university programmes with those of CERN. In the United Kingdom, on the other hand, the cutting down of funds for extra university posts, the difficulties of getting money for university-based apparatus, and a certain reluctance by the universities to change their way of life to a system in which the physicist must combine teaching at the university with research elsewhere, have all contributed to a slow start in making use of the new facilities. For it is clear that unless there are sufficient posts at the universities, physicists cannot be away from the university for a year or more at CERN if the teaching programme is to go on. Also, not all the experimental apparatus is located at CERN. A large fraction of the analysis of experiments carried out at CERN must and should be done at the universities, and this needs expensive equipment. Furthermore, it is desirable that the education of a research physicist should include a first research degree at the university before he embarks on the difficult and complicated task of research work with the big accelerating machines at CERN. Although the national research laboratories provide some of the facilities for this doctoral degree work, they cannot provide all of them, and the equipment in many university laboratories in Europe for this research is very primitive. The experience with CERN has shown that it is not sufficient to build a well-equipped international laboratory unless it is arranged that university physicists can make good use of it. Some countries have speedily reacted to this challenge. Italy and France are good examples, others have not even the means to discuss it, but must resort to *ad hoc* committees as a temporary substitute for a well-planned permanent system. For one reason and another, therefore, not all the Member States of CERN have found the way or the means to benefit as much as they could from the facilities of CERN. Yugoslavia, a founder-member of CERN, has recently withdrawn from the organization because it found there was too great a disparity between the resources available for physics research on a national scale and the size of its international contribution to CERN. This withdrawal, which was accepted with great reluctance by the other Member States and which they tried by all helpful and friendly means to prevent, demonstrates that unless a country has a healthy and well-nourished national and university programme in high energy physics it cannot for long justify the cost of contributing to an international laboratory such as CERN. This is not to say that CERN is only for the larger or more wealthy states, since the contributions to CERN allow for relative wealth and size, as can be seen in Table 8. The larger states have also found themselves facing the same problem, and this has led to considerable discussion about the financial control of laboratories, to which Member States are bound by international agreement. The budget of CERN for the year following the current one is decided, according to the Convention, by a simple majority vote in which each Member State has one vote. Thus it is possible for, say, seven small Member States to get Council approval for a budget for

Organization for Nuclear Research

Table 8. List of Member States and percentage contributions
to the budget for 1961

Member State	Contributions (%)
Austria	1.87
Belgium	4.02
Denmark	1.93
Federal Republic of Germany	18.92
France	20.57
Greece	1.12
Italy	9.78
Netherlands	3.73
Norway	1.56
Spain	4.16
Sweden	4.10
Switzerland	3.19
United Kingdom	24.40
Yugoslavia	0.65

which the other six larger ones pay the vast majority of the
financial contributions, although in practice an 'understanding' prevents this happening. What can happen,
however, and what has indeed happened, is that a major
contributor, finding perhaps that the funds for its national
programme have fallen out of balance with its CERN contribution, wishes to slow down the growth of CERN but is
unable to convince the Council of CERN that this is either
necessary or wise. In this case the Member State, if outvoted
on the Council, is bound by the Convention to pay its
contribution or to withdraw from the organization. Whereas
inside one Member State the Government, through its
Treasury and other bodies, can exercise absolute control on
the development of science in that country, at least during
the term of office of the government, it has only one voice
amongst many in determining the development of science
on an international basis. The situation can therefore arise
that an individual state is driven to expand its own scientific

research effort in a particular field, perhaps against its own judgement, in order to keep its national and international programmes in balance. The alternative of withdrawing from the international organization is generally not attractive for a large Member State, since it implies some cultural or economic deficiency at home. This levelling out of national attitudes towards scientific research in which the more enlightened states (or the more headstrong, if one is on the other side) can influence the policy of the others may mean that individual states must come more quickly and more positively to a conclusion as to whether they want to continue with a particular field of research or to drop it completely. A lingering death for a research subject in which the cost of the equipment has led to international action is no longer so easy.

In conclusion it might be useful to bring together some of the main reasons for the success of CERN. Right from the beginning the aims of the organization were sharply defined, and the objectives were sufficiently ambitious and attractive for both the scientists and the statesmen of Europe to be fired with a sustained enthusiasm for the programme. There was never any question that CERN's programme could be carried out by a single Member State. The whole operation was a joint venture in which both statesmen and scientists played their parts without giving the impression that the other was in some way an inferior partner. As a consequence, great risks were taken during the formulative years by both partners, since there existed a mutual confidence between them. For the scientists, CERN offered the only available way to create experimental facilities for high energy physics in Europe on a scale comparable to that of the United States of America and the U.S.S.R. For the statesmen, it was an experiment in European scientific co-operation, and part of the concept of the unity of Europe. Outside Europe CERN has played an important part in world scientific collaboration. By means of a generous grant from the Ford Foundation, it has been possible to invite many senior scientists from

Organization for Nuclear Research

America to CERN for periods of a year or more. It was through CERN that some of the earliest contacts were made with the Soviet scientists working on high energy physics research, and one of the first international conferences on this subject attended by American, Soviet and European physicists was held in Geneva in 1956. These conferences, which have become a regular feature of the life of this subject, now take place every two years successively at Rochester University, U.S.A., at a laboratory in the U.S.S.R. and at CERN in Geneva. Nowadays, by means of staff exchange arrangements, CERN has some of its staff working in the Soviet laboratories and Soviet scientists working at CERN.

Undoubtedly mistakes have been made in the short life of CERN, but these have been mainly due to lack of experience of either the scientists or the statesmen, and both have learned a lot in the adventure. Of course this is only one person's account of the early years of a young laboratory which has yet to face the problems of middle age, and the interpretations of events and simplifications of motives inevitable in a short account of this nature cannot expect universal approval. The sheer vitality of CERN has certainly led the organization into some self-dramatization from time to time which, because the author was himself involved in the events of these years, has probably leaked through into this article. The author would like to acknowledge the use he has made in writing this article of an authoritative report by L. Kowarski entitled *An Account of the Origin and Beginnings of CERN* (CERN Report No. 61/10). Also it should be noted that this brief history covers the period up to the end of 1961, at which time Professor Weisskopf succeeded the author as Director-General of CERN. It has fallen to Professor Weisskopf to make the Directorate and Committee System into an efficient and successful working arrangement and to expand the research phase of CERN's activities so that it now ranks as one of the best of the large high energy physics research laboratories in the world.

15

WHAT MAKES A GOOD RESEARCH ESTABLISHMENT?

by SIR EDWARD BULLARD, F.R.S.

Each chapter of this book describes a particular research establishment set up to meet some need or to study some field of knowledge. Each describes the nature of the work and the organization needed to do it. As might be expected, the accounts of the smaller organizations concentrate mostly on the work done and say little about the organizational problems of getting people to do it; their attitude may be summarized as 'we leave our people alone to get on with their jobs'. In the large organizations, employing several thousand people, the organizational problems loom much larger and become one of the main concerns of the management. The present chapter will be devoted to a more general consideration of how to keep scientists happy and productive, which is the central problem of the management of a large research establishment.

Fifty years ago there were no large research establishments and it was only during the last war that most scientists became conscious of the problems of operating them efficiently. The difficulties arise in large part from the inevitable differences between a research establishment and the traditional university research laboratory in which a scientist first learns his trade. We all have, at the back of our minds, a memory of some laboratory, such as Rutherford's Cavendish, dominated by a revered father figure and containing the brightest young men of their generation (or at any rate what seemed so to us) working on problems of profound significance and each writing a paper or two a year for the *Proceedings of the Royal Society*, describing work done with apparatus assembled from brass sheet, bits of glass tube and sealing wax. Alas, few of the laboratories described in this book are like this, and obviously most never can be. Physics and engineering have changed and biology is going the same way; there are irresistible pressures leading to larger establishments where the workers do not know all their colleagues and to a loss of independence where the unit is at best a small group and where each individual and group is dependent on the work of others.

A research establishment is not, however, just another large organization employing several thousand people; it is not like a factory or a railway or a regiment or a warship. Its purposes are less clearly defined and its effectiveness much harder to assess.

Although it may be difficult to assess the achievement of a laboratory in terms of the worthwhileness of its contribution in relation to the money and resources it uses, it is not difficult to get an impression of whether it is a 'good' laboratory or a mediocre one. It is possible to walk round a laboratory, talk to the men working in it and come away with a rather definite impression of the quality of the work. One can often do this even if one knows very little of the subject under investigation or of the past achievements of the laboratory. Such judgements are based, I believe, on a recognition of an attitude of mind of the staff to the work and to the establishment. This suggests that the first consideration in the organization of a research establishment is the fostering of the right climate of opinion. This consideration is, perhaps, more important even than the intellectual quality of the staff. Everyone knows men of the highest attainments who have achieved very little because they found themselves for a long period of years in an organization where they felt frustrated and unappreciated. On the other hand, the last war showed many examples of outstanding achievements by groups of very modest attainments working with improvised facilities. Some men, of whom Rutherford was the outstanding example, can make those who work with them not merely appear outstanding but actually produce outstanding results; that much of this ability often departed when the assistants were no longer working with Rutherford was unfortunate, but only emphasizes the importance of the atmosphere that such a man can create.

At a rather lower level, the problem of keeping the staff satisfied plays a larger part in a research organization than it does in a factory. The work of a factory can be planned and measured and reasonable performance enforced without a very delicate consideration of the wishes of the staff. In a laboratory, if the staff are actively dissatisfied, or even if they do not identify their own wishes and ambitions with the work, the establishment will quietly and imperceptibly lapse into mediocrity. There will be no very conspicuous signs that anything is wrong, the cost per worker will not change, the bulk of published work and of unpublished reports may stay about the same; all that will happen will be the departure of a few bright young men, some difficulty in recruiting and an uneasy feeling among visitors that perhaps the establishment is not as interesting as it used to be and that perhaps the staff complain about the management more than they should.

One of the main difficulties in running a research establishment lies in combining in one organization people with very different attitudes to their work. It is necessary to insist on fairly strict time-keeping for industrial and clerical staff, but how can you do this if you also employ a mathematician who claims that he can only work effectively in the middle of the night? There is no simple answer, but an explanation of the nature of the difficulty may help.

Any establishment has to hire and keep its staff in competition with other employers. If it is to get a sufficient share of the best people it must provide what they feel to be as good

A Good Research Establishment

a life as that offered by other potential employers. The things that conduce to the contentedness of most research workers are easy to state, but not always easy to provide. Most people like working on problems of their own choosing, with adequate facilities, in a pleasant place, with colleagues of similar tastes, in a society that values their kind of work and is willing to pay a competitive price for it.

The easiest to provide of these needs is reasonably pleasant working conditions. One may not be able to provide a view comparable with that over the Cam seen from the windows of the Master of Clare College, but one can avoid the creation of a research and development slum such as that until recently occupied by the Fuel Research Laboratory of DSIR or by the pre-war Bell Telephone Laboratories on 6th Avenue in New York. The maintenance of a satisfactory environment requires a continuous conscious effort. Arguments of economy and expediency frequently lead to overcrowding, the conversion of corridors into offices, the building of huts, the cutting down of trees and the erection of blank walls opposite windows. To avoid these things costs money; so also does the provision of a pleasant canteen, a lecture hall with comfortable seats and a library with books covering not only what is strictly relevant to the work in hand, but also some related fields. If these things are to exist someone must decide that they are more important than some fairly urgent technical need and be willing to put them near the top of the priority list in the face of the complaints of those genuinely needing buildings and equipment for the work of the establishment.

At first sight the preference of most scientists for working on what they wish to work on poses an insoluble problem. A large establishment has a purpose and its main effort must be directed to that purpose. In practice the problem usually arises only in establishments that are otherwise unsatisfactory. Most people's interests are not as firmly fixed as they believe. A young man starting his first job will often say that he wishes to go on working at the things about which he has written his Ph.D. dissertation. This is natural enough; these are the things he understands and which he has come to think of great importance and interest. Often it is necessary for the director of the establishment to tell him that, at the moment, there are other things that just have to be done and to which he can make an important contribution. If all goes well, the man's interest will quickly be transferred to the new field and it will become the field he would choose to work in. If this is to happen it is important to take a little time talking around the subject and showing its ramifications and connexions. A corner of a subject taken in isolation may appear dull unless it is explained in relation to the whole investigation of which it forms a part. If you tell a man to study the best methods of cleaning a stainless steel tube in which a vacuum is to be produced, he may not be enthusiastic, but if you explain that the release of gas from the walls is one of the main things that prevents the development of a thermonuclear reactor and the production of unlimited power for ever, it looks rather different.

The transfer of interest to the new subject depends greatly on the attitude of the rest of the staff concerned with it. If the man finds an enthusiastic group getting results or struggling with a difficult problem which they regard as important, it is easy for him to join them. On the other hand, if he finds a disgruntled group who are unsuccessful and are blaming their lack of success on lack of facilities or the faults of the management, the new recruit will usually not settle down satisfactorily and will not be as useful as he would otherwise be. Of course there will always be misfits, such as the man in the Admiralty's operational research section whose real interest was in the deceleration of the earth's rotation; but they are not, in my experience, very numerous, and under present conditions, it should not be difficult to find suitable jobs for them elsewhere.

In practice it is usually more difficult to persuade a man

to stop working on a project that is no longer important than it is to induce a new recruit to take an interest in something he has never met before. After a few year's work, a man acquires a vested interest in his problem. He is the expert in it, perhaps the first expert in the country. He is a member of international committees for discussing it. He knows all the other experts. His emotions and feelings as well as his intellect are wrapped up in it. There is not much that can be done in an extreme case, but remedial measures are possible in the earlier stages. It does not much matter if a man of 55 becomes a monomaniac on a subject of considerable but decreasing importance. It will last him out. It is very different with a man of 30, and it is essential to avoid too narrow and exclusive a specialization for too long in the earlier stages of a man's career. A man should become an expert in something in his twenties. But if he is a good scientist, his interests will develop and change with the subject. If they do not, and he appears to be settling into a rut, it may be necessary to persuade or coerce him to change his line of work, otherwise when he is forty-five he may have become a narrow specialist in something that is no longer of much interest.

The problem of stopping work that has become unfruitful is part of the problem of revising the research programme of a laboratory. This is the most important function of the senior members of the staff and its nature is often misunderstood. It is only in the extremest emergencies that one can say, 'Let us write down what has to be done, estimate the staff required, engage them and get on with the job'. Nearly always one has to say, 'For the next year at any rate I have such and such staff; what are the most useful things for them to do'. One may then go on to say, 'Clearly we cannot do all that should be done; we must get some more money and staff', but for one reason or another this can practically never be done at once. In month to month planning the work must be adapted to the staff and not the other way round. A great deal of emotional energy can be wasted and frustration produced if this is not appreciated. However important your work, you can't have what is unobtainable and you have no moral claim on what doesn't exist. On the other hand, no one can be expected to do the things for which sufficient resources do not exist. If staff and facilities are limited, as they always are, so must the programme be. It is necessary to be exceedingly firm in resisting commitments that go beyond resources. At any time there will always be important problems that cannot be dealt with. The feeling of being expected to produce quarts from pint pots is an important source of dissatisfaction and the only solution lies in a deliberate policy of leaving much desirable work undone. In deciding what to leave undone it must be remembered that the value of a project depends on the chance of achieving useful results as well as on the importance of the results if achieved, 'das schönste Glück des denkenden Menschen ist, das Erforschliche erforscht zu haben und das Unerforschliche ruhig zu verehren'.*

Probably the importance of a line of work is more difficult to judge than its practicability. Some things, for example the thermal conductivity of bricks, are obviously of practical importance and are interesting because of this importance. There is little risk of such things being missed or neglected, but there are also things that are important because they are interesting, things that one feels lie at the root of an industry and will somehow, somewhere, sometime pay off. The study of semiconductors was such a topic in 1945; here was a class of solids with odd and ill-understood properties, more complex than the metals or the electrical insulators, but about which one could see the glimmerings of a theory. Looking back, it seems very natural that the understanding of a new field of this kind should lead to new substances, new devices and new industries. It is easy to see this now but, in fact, very few organizations were willing to risk the money and effort needed to reap the rewards. The difficulty is that

* Goethe, W. V. *Aphorismen über die Natur.*

there are so many interesting things that one might investigate; how does one pick those that are about to become practically important? In part it is a question of timing; leave it too late and everyone is in the field and the cream has been skimmed off; start too early and there may be no applications for a century. Some narrowing down is easy; no institute of applied research would put a major effort into the study of fundamental particles or cosmology (unless, of course, it had a government contract to do so); but ask whether an oil company should try to understand the genesis of petroleum or to develop new methods for dating rocks and the answer is not so easy. Essentially the difficult thing is to make the right choices; anyone can draw up an exhaustive research programme covering a field, the problem is to choose which parts of it should receive 80 per cent. of the effort.

The importance of the choices that must be made increases as research becomes more expensive and facilities more elaborate. A few years ago E. S. Hiscocks* estimated that the annual cost of maintaining one graduate scientist in a British laboratory was £2,000 to £5,000 and did not vary greatly over a wide range of subjects. I have the impression that this figure has at least doubled since Hiscocks wrote. The increase is partly due to the increased scale of operation which has made it profitable to make and sell sophisticated and expensive instruments which did not exist and were not worth making ten years ago. Everyone now needs a computer to analyse his observations and, naturally, if the observations are to go into a computer he needs digitizing equipment and tape decks to record the data. There is an element of fashion in these things, but they are not imaginary needs; if one is to compete effectively with other well-equipped laboratories one must have them. The great English scientific tradition of 'string and sealing wax' is not an unmixed blessing; it can lead to expensive and ineffective pottering in which highly

* Hiscocks, E. S. *Laboratory Administration* (Macmillan, 1956), Appendix XV.

qualified staff spend their time designing and constructing ingenious devices which do indifferently what could be done well by proper equipment bought ready made.

The decisions on the main lines of work of a laboratory are necessarily taken by one man or by a small group and it is primarily for this reason that it is so important that the director and section heads be sensible, knowledgeable and articulate. They have to make the basic decisions on what is important and what is practicable and to obtain the support and agreement both of those who provide the funds and of the staff of the laboratory.

Once these decisions have been made a great degree of decentralization is desirable. The more a small group can feel that it is its own master, the better; it should feel responsible for its own progress and should get the credit for its successes. Nothing is so inimical to a good spirit in a laboratory as a feeling of interference from above by what are thought of as ill-informed but irresistible authorities.

Sir Lawrence Bragg has pointed out that one man can really deal continuously and intimately with only a few others, and that this alone requires some kind of decentralized tree of authority if decisions are to be made with an appreciation of the issues involved. In practice this means that a large establishment must be divided into nearly autonomous divisions, and that within these divisions there must be groups, small enough to know each other well, and responsible for particular pieces of work. It should never be forgotten that the chain of increasing responsibility is usually that of decreasing detailed knowledge. The man doing a job usually knows more about it than the superintendent of his division, or the director of the laboratory. He may need encouragement, interest, advice, and occasionally adverse comment; but he does not need frequent interference. You cannot do a man's job for him; if he can't do it himself he should be encouraged to undertake something within his powers. It is inefficient to 'keep a dog and bark oneself'.

A Good Research Establishment

In practice there are many ways in which the autonomy of the groups within a laboratory must be restricted. In a large establishment things like pay, accounts, recruitment and promotion must be rigidly centralized. Others like workshops, computing facilities and analytical services must be at any rate partially centralized. These things are inevitably the cause of a good deal of friction. Every group would like to control the tools of its trade, and as far as possible it should do so. The limit is set by expense. A jig borer may cost £40,000 and ten groups may need to use it once a month. Clearly it would be wasteful to buy ten of them, and the proper thing to do is to have one with a skilled operator in a central workshop. An Avometer costs £20; if two men in next door rooms each use it once a day it is worth getting one for each. Some middle course must be taken, but the guiding principle should be that, on the whole, people know their own business best, and that it should only be taken out of their hands when there is a clear and important gain by centralization.

It would, I think, be generally admitted that the best laboatrories are usually newly formed ones or ones that are expanding. The atmosphere of improvisation, impermanence and change seems conducive to creative work in a way that a large settled organization with an established hierarchy is not. In the expansionist atmosphere of the last twenty years this problem has not been very conspicuous, but it is clear that the doubling of scientific activity every five or ten years which we have come to regard as normal cannot continue much longer. We shall be forced to discover means of maintaining the efficiency of establishments, the size and expenditure of which does not increase rapidly. How this is to be done is not clear. The trouble is partially due to the rather slow turnover of staff which is usual in government and university laboratories in this country. If a man feels he is fixed in a job for life he is less likely to remain bright and original than if he has the expectation that success and outside reputation will

271

lead to a better job somewhere else. Perhaps the enthusiasm with which, over the last twenty years, politicians and academics in this country have pursued egalitarian ideals has not had an altogether favourable effect. Why should it be regarded as almost morally wrong for an organization to obtain a man it wants by offering him more pay, or other benefits, than he is getting in his present job? I have the impression that the intense competition to engage able men, which is such a striking feature of the American scientific scene, has a most beneficial effect. We can hardly hope, and perhaps would not wish, to emulate the manoeuvres of the richer American universities and weapons contractors, but we can surely admit that all men are not equal and find some way of loosening the present rather rigid arrangements about pay and pensions so as to encourage or allow a little 'poaching' of staff and some approximation to a freely competitive market for talent. If we do not, the pull of the U.S.A. for many of the brightest of our young scientists will become irresistible.

Perhaps the key to the successful organization of a research establishment is to run it so that the staff know that they can easily leave for a better job, but find it so rewarding a place to work in that most of them stay.

INDEX

Abbreviations:

AERE Atomic Energy Research Establishment

BISRA British Iron and Steel Research Association

BRRD British Railways Research Department

BTL Bell Telephone Laboratories

CERN European Organization for Nuclear Research

ECGC Empire Cotton Growing Corporation

GRO Glaxo Research Organization

IAP Institute for Animal Physiology

NIMR National Institute for Medical Research

NIRNS National Institute for Research in Nuclear Science

NPL National Physical Laboratory

RAE Royal Aircraft Establishment

RHEPL Rutherford High Energy Physics Laboratory

SPRU Social Psychiatry Research Unit

UKAEA United Kingdom Atomic Energy Authority

abstract service (BRRD), 186

administration,
see organization, structure of

Aeronautical Research Council, 47

age distribution of staff (AERE), 72-3

Agricultural Research Council, 113-14, 115

America, migration of scientists to, 73, 238, 247, 272

analytical services, 150, 191, 271

animals, supply of, 79, 119-20, 149, 150

armed services, and NPL, 14; and RAE, 29-30, 45; and AERE, 63; and NIMR, 88

automation, 177, 194

autonomy, of groups, 32, 271; of senior individuals, 109

aviation, civil and military, interaction of, 48

buildings, of NPL, 22, 24-5; of AERE, 69-70; of NIMR, 78-80; of IAP, 116; of ECGC, 141; of GRO, 151-2; of CERN, 243

centralization, activities requiring, 21, 271

colloquia, *see* discussions

committees, in organization, of AERE, 3; of NPL, 15; of RAE, 41; of UKAEA, 69; of BISRA, 172; of CERN, 250, 251-2

computers, 269, 271; at NPL, 11, 16-17, 18, 19, 26; of BRRD, 188, 194; of BTL, 211; of RHEPL, 223, 228, 238

consultants, university staff as, at AERE, 75

continuity, importance of, 109-10, 130, 131, 146

contracts, for staff of CERN, 246-7

control, of biological therapeutic substances, by NIMR, 90

cost accounting, 4-5, 33, 50, 173-4

creativity, 1-2; age of scientists and, 4, 247; support of, by ancillary staff, 43, 214

cybernetics, 193

decentralization, in organization, 270

design, at RAE, 28-9; at AERE, 55, 77

development, relations between research and, 149, 182, 199, 201-4

development contracts, 26, 195

Director of a research establishment, 3-4, 5, 270; of NPL, 20; of RAE, 37, 40; of AERE, 55, 58, 64; of NIMR, 92, 94; of SPRU, 99, 106-7; of IAP, 120; of ECGC, 130, 132; of GRO, 150; of BISRA, 170; of BRRD, 182-3, 185; of BTL, 200; of RHEPL, 218-19; of CERN, 242, 249

Directors, deputy, at RAE, 33, 35, 40

discussions, on policy, at NPL, 21, at AERE, 58, at IAP, 120; scientific, at Cavendish Laboratory, 2, at AERE, 68, at NIMR, 95, at SPRU, 106, at IAP, 120, at RHEPL, 234

divisions (departments), of NPL, 8; of RAE, 29-30, 34, [fig.2]; of AERE, 56-7, 65; of NIMR, 81, 93; of IAP, 117; of GRO, 152; of BRRD, 186; of BTL, 210-11; of RHEPL, 225-9; of CERN, 250

Department of Scientific and Industrial Research (DSIR), and NPL, 7, 13; and research associations, 168, 169; and BISRA, 171

Index